AGREED
SYLLABUS OF
RELIGIOUS EDUCATION

LANCASHIRE EDUCATION COMMITTEE

Printed by
T. Snape & Co. Ltd., Preston

CONTENTS

CONTENTS

CONTENTS

CONTENTS

Appendices

PREFACE

In recent years, new developments in religious education have made necessary the revision of the Committee's Agreed Syllabus.

In accordance with the Education Act 1944 a Conference was convened in 1964 to prepare a new Syllabus and two Drafting Committees were appointed. The Chairman of the Primary Drafting Committee was Mr. J. Haworth and Mr. K. D. Exley was the Chairman of the Secondary Drafting Committee. Mr. J. B. Rapp served as secretary to the Drafting Committees. Both Committees have met jointly and separately on very many occasions to prepare and discuss fully the content of the new Syllabus. The understanding, commitment, and wide knowledge which members contributed to these meetings are evident in the Syllabus set out in the following pages. I should like to express the appreciation of the Education Committee to the members of the Drafting Committees and their Secretary for the generous way in which they have given so much of their time over a long period to the preparation of the Syllabus.

J. R. HULL, Chairman

PREFACE TO THE
REVISED FIRST EDITION

In July, 1971, the Standing Conference agreed to the reprinting of the Agreed Syllabus and set up a Working Party to re-edit the First Edition. Under the Chairmanship of Mr. K. D. Exley, Mrs. E. H. Church, Canon C. W. D. Carroll and Messrs. J. Haworth and E. J. B. Todd have, after a careful review of the First Edition, re-arranged certain paragraphs and amended certain headings. They have indicated by an asterisk those publications which are no longer obtainable and have revised the list of contents.

The Standing Conference have recommended to the Education Committee that the new C.E.M. Bibliography should be purchased for Lancashire Schools as an Addendum to the Bibliography contained in the Syllabus. The Education Committee have accepted this recommendation and a pocket has been provided on the inside back cover of the Revised First Edition for the retention of the C.E.M. Bibliography which will be issued to Schools when it is available.

The content of the First Edition remains unchanged.

M. W. INGOE
Chairman of the Standing Conference

THE CONFERENCE

The following persons served on the Conference convened to prepare a new Agreed Syllabus of Religious Education to be adopted by the Lancashire Education Committee.

Chairman

Mr. J. R. Hull *(Chairman of the Lancashire Education Committee)*

Representatives appointed by the Lancashire Education Committee

Sir Fred Longworth, Mr. P. R. Marsh, Mr. H. Nevin.

Representatives appointed by the Church of England

The Rev. Canon W. J. Bucks *(Carlisle Diocese)*, the Rev. Canon C. W. D. Carroll *(Blackburn Diocese)*, the Rev. Canon L. F. Hopkins *(Liverpool Diocese)*, the Rev. Canon C. P. Sherwood *(Manchester Diocese)*.

Representatives appointed by the Nonconformist Churches

The Rev. Dr. K. H. Crosby and the Rev. A. Reid *(Methodist Church)*, the Rev. Professor J. H. E. Hull *(the Congregational Church)*, Mr. D. D. Pringle *(the Baptist Churches)*.

Representatives appointed by the Teachers' Associations

Mr. J. E. Calderbank, Mrs. E. H. Church, Mr. K. D. Exley, Mr. P. S. Gedge, Mr. J. Haworth, Mr. W. Higham, Miss K. M. Jagger, Miss P. Roberts, Mr. E. J. B. Todd, Mr. J. A. F. Waller.

PERCY LORD,
Chief Education Officer

FOREWORD

In a changing society the religious education of children and young people presents parents and teachers with a challenge. It follows that those who are responsible for the making of an Agreed Syllabus are faced with a complex situation not because the denominations find it difficult to agree but because the changes in society as well as in education have to be considered. Indeed the main-stream denominations have little difficulty in agreeing, within wide limits, on the bases of the Christian faith. On the other hand the schools will, to a great extent, reflect the trends in the society which they serve. Few would deny that the secularisation of our culture is increasing. Not all theologians regard this as an unfavourable movement and point out that we must look for Christian evidence in many forms of activity outside as well as inside the Churches. In school, everyday experiences, including the teaching of many subjects not specifically religious, often raise issues which can lead to a new insight into aspects of religious truth.

For too long the field of religious education has been to some degree isolated from the critical re-assessment to which other aspects of the school curriculum have been subjected. It is now recognised that we have to consider the stages in the development of children and their capacity to understand the language and imagery of the Bible. It was, therefore, decided at the commencement of our work, to invite the schools to submit their views on the aims of religious education as well as the means of presenting the material used in teaching the subject. Every county and voluntary controlled school maintained by the Lancashire County Education Committee was asked to submit views on the aims of religious education, to mention the difficulties in teaching the subject, and to offer suggestions about the content. As a result of this enquiry, twenty-one schools were asked to submit further details of their work and several schools were visited in order to make personal contact with teachers and pupils.

Material for this Agreed Syllabus was taken from many sources. Grateful acknowledgment is made to the West Riding Education Committee's 'Suggestions for Religious Education' with regard to books and for some passages in the text, to Dr. Ronald J. Goldman for his advice and practical help, to the Rev. Brian Brown for his work in the preparation of the Alternative Secondary Syllabus and to the Rev. Peter J. Hardman for his reading of the Sixth Form Section. To them and to other officers of the Christian Education Movement we owe our thanks for the work done over a period of years in connection with the early leavers in secondary schools. Not least we are indebted to Mr. K. M. Edge and to many other teachers who gave material help by submitting their schemes for consideration.

In conclusion I should like to place on record my appreciation of the courtesy and willing help given to us by the Officers and Staff of the Education Committee in preparing the many drafts which had to be considered by the members of the Drafting Sub-Committees.

J. B. RAPP,
Drafting Secretary

ACKNOWLEDGEMENTS

Acknowledgements are made to the following holders of Copyright for permission to quote from a number of books and other material.

A Report from the Central Advisory Council for Education (England) 'Half Our Future' pub. by Her Majesty's Stationery Office, Crown Copyright, 1963

The New English Bible – Oxford and Cambridge University Presses

The Revised Standard Version of the Bible – Thomas Nelson & Sons Ltd.

Theology of Culture – Paul Tillich – Centre for Religious Leadership U.S.A.

Prayers of Life – Michel Quoist – M. H. Gill & Son Ltd., Dublin

Encounter with Modern Society – E. R. Wickham – Lutterworth Press

Experiential Approach to Christian Education – Douglas Hubery – N.C.E.C.

The English Bible – F. F. Bruce – Lutterworth

RELIGION AND LIFE

The Place of Religious Education in Schools

This Agreed Syllabus gives to teachers the opportunity to experiment and develop their own methods while keeping within the scope of an arrangement of material suitable for the age and ability of the pupils for whom it is intended. Changes in educational thinking, together with a new insight into the way in which the religious ideas of children grow, have had to be considered. In the forefront of our thinking has also been the need to present the Christian message in a way that is relevant to the age into which these children are born. It is also realised that all schools have their particular problems and that it is the teachers who are mainly concerned with the way in which the material will be used and presented to the children. It remains the responsibility of each individual school to formulate a suitable scheme of work based on the Agreed Syllabus.

It cannot be assumed that the children attending our schools will be brought up in a home where religion has a place. Nor can it be assumed that they will move into a society which is concerned with Christian values. Perhaps, to a majority of parents, religious language is difficult to understand: to others, a minority, a devotion to a family tradition of church or chapel makes it almost impossible to span the gulf which separates those who are outside the experience of organised religion and those within; there is a wide gulf between the two.

For children growing up in a rapidly changing society there is a search for certainties and security in a world of shifting values. All of them are faced at some time with the questions, 'What am I?', 'Why am I here?', 'To what end was I created?'. Not all of them can be articulate, but it is unrealistic to assume that they can travel far along the road to maturity without seeking for reasonable answers. It is for the most part in the schools of this country where they will look for guidance and where they may expect to receive the help they need in coming to terms with life. In a country whose culture and traditions have received the deep impress of Christianity it is an inescapable duty to help them to find out what has been and is the Christian answer.

In this situation what is the teacher called upon to do? Many of the difficulties about which teachers complain are based upon a misunderstanding of what is expected of them. A great many are uncertain about the intentions of the Agreed Syllabus, its aims, and purposes. All teachers would shrink from the idea of the deliberate indoctrination of children within the system of our maintained schools and, for some, the teaching of even an agreed presentation of the Christian faith would appear to be just this. It must be said that there is also the indirect form of indoctrination. To deny children an informed view of an area of knowledge so closely related to the history and underlying principles of our way of life is to indoctrinate by default: to leave unanswered the insistent questionings of young people and, in particular, those most closely related both to their personal development and to their social development as members of society, is to admit either that we have nothing to say, or that their questionings are not relevant. The valid claim for religious teaching in schools must always be that there is a truly religious interpretation to life

1

in the widest sense, and this transcends the narrower view of indoctrination into a set pattern of belief. If this is so, religious teaching is concerned with the whole of the school's activities; all subjects or fields of study have something to offer and in this many members of staff with different points of view can contribute. There is no teaching situation, in fact, where we do not impress our views in some way, either by what we say and do, or by the way in which we carry out our duties. There is no way of escape from this dilemma. On the other hand it is clear that a sense of commitment to a way of life is always, in the end, a matter of personal conviction. Having received the answer to his question, the Rich Young Ruler went away sorrowing. He was left to think things out for himself. What we are most concerned to do is to offer to the children in our care religious knowledge which is up-to-date and in sufficient depth to enable them to think. The final answer does not, nor has it ever rested with us.

'The question implied . . . is not: What is the Christian message? Rather it is: How shall the message (which is pre-supposed) be focused for the people of our time? In other words, we are concerned here with the question: How can the Gospel be communicated? We are asking: How do we make the message heard and seen, and then either rejected or accepted? The question cannot be: How do we communicate the Gospel so that others will accept it? For there is no method. To communicate the Gospel means putting it before the people so that they are able to decide for it or against it. It is to be accepted or rejected. All that we who communicate this Gospel can do is to make possible a genuine decision. Such a decision is based on understanding and on partial participation.' (1)

The Growth of Religious Ideas

There is no reason to assume that religious education should be free from the kind of critical reassessment to which all other aspects of educational thinking have been subjected in recent years. In the past the conveying, or purveying of information was regarded as one of the main functions of teaching. While this is still a matter of paramount importance, the emphasis has shifted to a consideration of how children learn, the principles of motivation, and the stage of development in a child's life. Children, it is realised, learn mainly by experience. It is through experience, in the widest sense of that term, that children can be led to discover the meaning behind the facts presented to them. Their capacity to grasp and understand religious ideas and concepts is made possible by their growing experience of life.

In the nursery and infant school it would appear that much direct or formal presentation of material is unsuitable. The Bible contains many stories which, while appearing simple, contain very difficult religious ideas. To present them at too early an age may do harm rather than good. At this stage, activity and experience have a far more valuable part to play. The theme of God the Creator, God the Father, may best be understood if the child is helped to see the wonders of creation in his 'nature table' or 'adventure corner'. Here he will be brought to appreciate the beauty of

---

(1) Tillich, Paul   Theology of Culture,   O.U.P.
Ch. 25

created things. So too in the friendly atmosphere of the school he will be encouraged to share, to give as well as to receive, to help and to serve. Stories which support these experiences can be told to the child but no story which destroys the child's image of God as a loving father should be used. For this reason many stories in the Old Testament, however thrilling they may be, should be avoided.

In the next phase of development, which is roughly from seven to nine years, we are faced with similar difficulties in the choice of our material. Too often the telling of stories from the Bible has been the main vehicle of instruction. At this stage children take literally that which is told to them with the authority of an adult, and they are not able to understand that the story may be symbolic and, too, symbolic of an age which had beliefs which are now rejected by Christian teaching. Again, the idea of historical development which is involved in this is beyond the grasp of young children. It is important to remember that for most of the period when children are in the primary stage of education, the question 'Is it true?' is asked in the context of meaning, 'Were these real people?' and, 'Could we have seen all this happening?' They are concerned with things in concrete terms: the deeper religious ideas are beyond them in a classroom situation in which we are mainly concerned with the formation of concepts by an intellectual process. We are, therefore, quite justified in spending time on interesting activities which are not primarily religious but which will make the understanding of religious concepts possible at a later stage. There is a close parallel here between the experiential stage of teaching in mathematics and the concepts needed at a later stage in the study of abstract mathematical relationships. Thus material which helps the child to understand the background to the Bible narrative, whether it is in the form of geographical information given visually, or a simple introduction to some of the more startling confirmations made by biblical archeology of the realities behind the Bible stories, is not out of place. Without this knowledge it may well be impossible to grasp the deeper religious interpretation later on.

To this extent the teaching at this stage is a preparation for a deeper knowledge when the child is ready for it. Perhaps the most important part of the teaching will be to present an image of our Lord which is strong and vital. Too often an impression is left of the 'Jesus mild and gentle'. Although gentleness and tenderness are Christian virtues very much in evidence in the portrayal of the life and teaching, it is too often overlooked that Jesus did not shrink from accepting the rigours of periods in the wilderness, climbing mountains, and even physical danger when facing hostile crowds.

The next period, although in practice it is divided by the transfer to secondary schools at eleven years of age, covers the age group from nine to thirteen. Although mental abilities vary considerably, for the majority, the first year in a secondary school is, in terms of development, a continuation of the primary phase. There is a demand for realism when the human Jesus described in an historical setting has most meaning. Boys and girls are passing through what is perhaps the most stable period emotionally. (2)

---

(2)Ross, J.   Groundwork of Educational   Harrap
                     Psychology — pp. 144
                     and 146

It is at this stage that some introduction to the origin and nature of the Bible is appropriate. It will be necessary to prepare the way for the change from a literal interpretation to the deeper levels of thinking made possible by the development which occurs in a child's capacity for thought. Unless this is done the majority of young adolescents find religion childish or, for the sake of security tend to accept quite uncritically the most literal interpretation of biblical stories.

Between the ages of 11 to 13, when there is a 'break through' in most subjects, childish modes of thought are left behind and a more intellectual quality emerges. An acceptance of the literalist view of the Bible may persist yet there is a move towards a 'non-literal' interpretation accompanied with a discontent with much religious teaching. There is a desire on the part of adolescents to think for themselves and this is made more insistent by the impact of more systematic science teaching and an increasing awareness of the agnosticism of the age. What is needed is something to think about and to think with. This calls for a much more positive approach to the question of what Christianity really stands for. Part of the expression of adolescence is seen in the desire to appear cynical and unconcerned, but beneath this is a real need for altruism.

Adolescents are faced with a far more difficult situation than was the case in former times. We have to take into account the challenge of other faiths, many scientific discoveries and that technological advance is made to satisfy some of the desire for adventure and the opening up of new areas of knowledge. There is a need to relate belief and the Bible to their experience in such a way that their understanding of the truths of Christianity may grow. We must help them to see what the truth is. This is nowhere put more clearly than in the Report of the Central Advisory Council for Education (England).

'There is a straightforward teaching job to be done here. Just what do Christians believe about God and man, life and death? Many fourteen year olds will not know unless they are taught – but it is often assumed that they know this already. An information service is important, and they ask for it. In their last years at school there is a need also to help them to see the difference that being a Christian makes, or should make, to the answers that have to be given to problems of living. Some of these problems are personal and immediate; some are collective and social – relations with parents and with friends of the opposite sex; problems of conflicting loyalties to friends and to moral standards; nuclear weapons and the colour bar; the care of the old, and the thalidomide babies.' (3)

What do Christians believe?

Language, the primary means by which we communicate with one another in normal circumstances, can also be the means of creating barriers between people. In no case is this so obvious as in the attempts to define our beliefs.

This is not to suggest that the efforts to do this in verbal forms are valueless; that in so doing we are striving to define the indefinable. If it were so all poetry and much literature dealing with human situations

---

(3) Half our Future, A Report of the Central Advisory   H.M.S.O.
     Council for Education (England) p. 168

would be meaningless, for the springs of behaviour are complex. Nevertheless we are called upon to make the attempt to express the beliefs upon which we base our actions in meeting the challenge of life. We plan each day ahead, or accept events fatalistically on the assumption that there will be a continuing series of days, each having a beginning and an end, and following in regular pattern: we adjust our reactions according to the time of year and the vagaries of the climate. We live on the basic, but often unacknowledged assumption, that these are certainties on which we can rely, even though weather and climate may be gloriously uncertain.

This search for a belief by which we may live is as old as man and has been expressed in many ways but all the assumptions on which we base our actions are derived from experience. Religious truth is, in the words of Professor Jeffreys, '. . . normal experience understood at full depth'. (4) To clarify this experience we express these assumptions in words, often crystallised in the form of symbols. In all the great civilisations these symbols have been developed in art forms (music, drama or the visual arts), but in their most didactic form beliefs have been expressed in the written language. It is because words can become a prison house for ideas as well as a means of enlightenment that most of the difficulties arising from the communication of the Christian faith have arisen. This applies to doctrinal statements which were not in the first instance the deliberate decisions of men meeting together to discover a basis for agreement, but decisions to determine how their experience should affect such statements of belief and how these might be expressed.

The main difficulties in making religious statements

In our endeavour to express our religious convictions we have to use words in a symbolic way. No other vocabulary exists. Unfortunately, such terms or phrases have been accepted quite literally and taken as true in a physical or material sense and so misunderstood. Many of the ideas expressed in the Old Testament are metaphorical statements. For example, the idea of immortality expressed in the story of Elijah where he is carried up to heaven in a chariot of fire (II Kings 2 v. 11) conveyed the prevailing belief that Elijah would return to continue his prophetic work in person (St. John 1 v. 21) and so his body could not experience corruption. In New Testament times the ending of Our Lord's appearances to his disciples after his death and resurrection was expressed in the phrase 'ascended into heaven' (Acts 1 vv. 9–11). The disciples, and all who believed in a flat-earth, expressed their experience in this way; the physical ascent from earth to heaven was, to them, the obvious way of expressing this truth. No other form of expression was possible and they expressed religious truth in terms of the current knowledge of the material universe (in the age into which they were born). Another example of the way in which the contemporary knowledge about physical conditions determines the way in which incidents are recorded in the New Testament is to be found in the accounts in which demoniac spirits are mentioned. To those living in Palestine in the first century A.D. various forms of epilepsy or mental disturbance were regarded as originating in the possession by the sufferer of 'demoniac spirits'; with advancing medical knowledge in the seventeenth century such phenomena were regarded as due to an

---

(4) Jeffreys, M. V. C.   Glaucon, p. 118   Pitman

'unequal proportion of the humours'. In the present state of medical knowledge, in the context of the twentieth century, they could be classified as diseases of 'para-diabetic' origin.

Again the meaning of words changes even in comparatively recent times. The word 'prevent' is one of the more obvious examples. In the context of the seventeenth century (as used in the Book of Common Prayer 1662) it meant 'to go before'; in our own time it has come to mean 'to avoid'. The words 'substance' and 'person' had a different meaning when they were first used. The word 'substance' in the phrase 'of one substance with the Father' means having the same essential nature as the Father (God) being perfect in the sense that God is perfect. In the attempt to express the teaching about the Trinity the word 'person' was used to show that God has clearly defined ways of revealing Himself. The Trinity does not mean that God is three individuals joined together in some mysterious way.

In our search for Christian truth we have to look behind the actual words to the spiritual experience they were intended to express. Ways of expressing these truths change but the spiritual experience the words were intended to convey remains. Our task is to interpret these experiences in a way the modern generation can understand in the light of their knowledge and experience; this does not mean watering down the challenge of the Christian faith. It means doing for our generation precisely what St. Paul and St. John did for theirs.

What can we believe about God ?

There are many things which are incapable of formal proof and require methods of investigation quite different from the mathematical approach. This applies equally to all art forms, poetry, music, and other forms of art including drama: even though the form may be analysed, the nature of beauty goes far beyond what can be assessed in any quantitative sense. It is, for the same reason, impossible to define God since God has no boundaries; there can be no limit to what is by its nature limitless. So too, we have no spiritual language with a special meaning for spiritual things (although the spiritual is no less a reality): we can only use metaphors. It is the particular claim of the Christian that he sees in the Incarnation, the life and teaching of Jesus Christ, the historic event in which all that God should mean to us is so revealed. One problem that is troublesome to many, especially in the light of all that science has to say, is however, the reconciling of God as Creator with the God of Love as revealed in Jesus Christ.

The picture of nature 'red in tooth and claw', is often quoted as a direct challenge to the conception of the Creator as a God of Love; but the complex of natural forces which go to the making and sustaining of our universe could only be supported by a principle of self-sacrifice. Most forms of organism depend for their existence on this higher principle that for the continuance and development of the life-form, life, in its initial stages, must be protected; and in its highest forms guided and taught, at some sacrifice to the parent. This reaches out inevitably to the self-sacrifice which is Christian love.

The apparent conflict of science with religion is much more than a conflict of fact. With our growing knowledge of the physical universe it may be difficult to sustain the view of man as central to creation. Nevertheless, the Christian view of man is that without freedom of choice there could be no values of a worthwhile kind to choose from. Mankind is dependent, as all creatures (i.e. created things) must be on a Creator, and is supported and guided by Providence.

The belief in an ultimate Spirit or Force as the basis of all creation has been held by most people, and this is the way in which we use the word Creator as applied to God. It is not necessary to suppose that God created the world and set it going once and for all time at some definite moment. Rather it would be reasonable to conceive of God as a great Artist continuously creating and using the world for His purposes. He chose and created the material upon which He works but He is also dependent on the nature of the material as to how He works: in this sense the word 'Almighty' does not mean able to do anything but rather 'all sovereign', that is, upholding all things. There are obviously things which God could not do and remain God. The fact that we believe that there is a purpose behind the universe is an acceptance of a form of self-limitation because it rules out whatever runs counter to this purpose.

From whence did the early Christians draw their belief? How did the Apostolic Fathers go about assessing its soundness? It is generally agreed that in order to understand the message of the Scriptures we have to go back to the documents of the early church and the circumstances in which they were written. The followers of Christ soon formed what became a tradition: this was 'following God and the teaching derived from Him', which in the final resort went back to Christ Himself. 'But' they would argue, 'if He was the Supreme Teacher, the immediately accessible authorities, both for the facts about His Person and for His message were (a) the prophets who had foreseen His ministry and (b) the Apostles who had worked with Him and whom He had commissioned'. (5) It is unlikely that Christian teachers, in the early days, had only the books which now form our New Testament in mind when they spoke of the testimony of the Apostles; still less that they thought of the life of Christ as the sole basis of their belief. It is much more likely that they were thinking of the common body of facts and teaching which were being used in the day-by-day services of the church. This would include most of the Old Testament as we know it and, by the beginning of the second century, most, if not all, of our New Testament. They were concerned to proclaim the 'Kerygma', the 'Good News', which is the Gospel. That is why in Stage One of the Agreed Syllabus care has been taken to provide the basis on which a deeper knowledge of the Gospel may be based in terms of an understanding of the origin and nature of the Bible as a whole.

The relation between Science and Religion

The difficulties in making religious statements to which reference has already been made have a parallel in the field of science. Just as it is necessary in the search for Christian truth to look behind the actual words to the spiritual experience they seek to express, so too it is necessary to have an understanding of what is significant and what is not in the language of science, and to appreciate the limits of interpretation which

---

(5) Kelly, J. N. D.   Early Christian Doctrines   A. and C. Black
p. 31

are built into any scientific statement. Much confusion and misunderstanding can arise from trying to evaluate the meaning of a statement in everyday terms without regard for the scientific context in which it was originally made. The invasion of our mid-twentieth century society by so much pseudo-science is just as fruitful a source of error in our understanding of what science is really saying as is a thoroughly unintelligent and unduly literalistic approach to religious statements. An adequate understanding of the relationship between science and religion demands an appreciation of both kinds of statement, and without this appreciation it is impossible for any satisfactory synthesis of belief to be achieved. Regrettably the conservatism of some theologians and the arrogance of some scientists (particularly since the middle of the nineteenth century), led to a situation where it was commonly assumed that theology had nothing to say to science and science nothing to theology: each discipline claimed to be the only one competent to deal with 'reality', whereas in fact there is only *one* reality, and both science and religion have their parts to play in describing different, but related, aspects of it. At a deeper level still there is a much stronger link between scientific discovery and theological revelation than the great majority of people suspect, and as a link between the two disciplines, human personality has an absolutely fundamental and quite indispensible role.

It is true, however, that for many years there appeared to be good evidence for a conflict between the teachings of science and religion. To find the origins of this it is necessary to go back in time to the beginnings of modern science, to the time when the Bible was the sole authority in spiritual matters and Aristotle was the authority in scientific affairs. At first, the conflict was not between science and religion at all but between the old, essentially deductive Aristotelean science, and the new science which sought truth not through a static, unchanging universe, but by the appeal to experiment. By the Middle Ages, Thomas Aquinas had Christianised Aristotelean beliefs. In so doing he had also planted the seeds of conflict, for the eventual overthrow of Aristotelean truth also implied the overthrow of Christian belief. Nevertheless, from the start the new science was regarded as a religious activity. Its protagonists from Galileo to Newton, from Ray to Boyle, from Descartes to Pascal, all saw it as a means of bringing man nearer to God and as a way of understanding God's world. The break between science and religion began to come with the atomisation of knowledge, and when the enormous power of science and its influence on men's way of thinking began to affect people's lives appreciably. Even now it is not always appreciated what a tremendous event the scientific revolution was. As Professor Butterfield says in 'The Origins of Modern Science': (6)

> 'The scientific revolution of the sixteenth and seventeenth centuries outshines anything since the rise of Christianity, and reduces the Renaissance and Reformation to the rank of mere episodes, mere internal displacements within the system of medieval Christendom.'

It is equally important to note that the new science arose and prospered in the one civilisation in the world which had a strong belief in the rationality of nature and its Creator. It was faith in the regularity of nature springing from an antecedent faith in the rationality of God that made modern science possible.

---

(6) Butterfield, H.   The Origins of Modern   pub. G. Bell
                         Science A.D. 1300–1800

The spectacular success of the Newtonian synthesis in the late seventeenth century led to a mechanistic view of the universe which ruled supreme until the turn of the nineteenth century. The method of science was supremely vindicated in the field of astronomy, mechanics and heat, and the discoveries of science were the starting points from which the industrial revolution (with all its social and political implications) was able to grow. The Victorian idea of progress and the greatly increased prospects of man controlling his environment gave to science an authority and a position which accentuated the controversy between science and religion. Further the application of the methods of science in the fields of biology and geology led to a questioning of the Biblical view of the origin of not only the earth but also man, and at the same time planted in the minds of the uninformed seeds of doubt about other theological issues. The fruits of this conflict are still present, despite the fact that a fundamental change has come over the understanding of science and the fact that there has been a revolution in man's historical and theological thinking.

What then, are the grounds for the statement that a synthesis is now possible between science and religion? What changes have taken place which have enabled men to see them as complementary disciplines, both contributing to our understanding of reality, and both necessary for a proper appreciation of the world in which we live, our lives and our experience.

In the first place the old deterministic view of the universe has gone, destroyed in the end by the methods of science itself. It became clear in the first twenty years of this century that the Newtonian view of the universe was not adequate, and that it was necessary to think in terms of probability and chance: only in the limiting situations of Newtonian science could they be accepted as practical certainties.

Secondly, the boundaries of science have expanded at a phenomenal rate and continue to do so. One of the results of this has been to underline the facts that the findings of science are never final and that its importance and power lies not so much in concrete discoveries as in its unique method. This has led in turn to a much better appreciation of its limitations, and a somewhat different view about the possibilities of progress.

Above all, it began to be seen that whereas science itself may be amoral, those concerned in making scientific discoveries and those who sought to apply those discoveries can find themselves facing a terrible moral dilemma. Science is no longer thought of as an academic discipline from which the practitioner can stand completely detached. Indeed it has become appreciated that the picture of the detached observer, calmly working in a disinterested manner and without personal involvement has always been completely false. The true process of making scientific discoveries has in it a considerable subjective element which is indispensible, and indeed, even at an elementary level, the scientist is called upon to use powers of judgement, which in themselves have no scientific basis.

To sum up the matter as far as science is concerned there has emerged in the last fifty years a new concept, much more humble in its scope, much more cautious in its nature, and in its roots much nearer to theology than was ever dreamed of a hundred years ago. For man seeks to make sense not only of the expanding picture of the universe which science rolls out before him but also is himself a part of this picture and is seeking to find his place in it.

The traditional Christian answers to the questions that men ask have sometimes been lost in the conflict which was supposed to exist between science and religion. The new thinking in theology and a better appreciation of what science is and what its limitations are, have opened the way for a helpful, honest but by no means final synthesis between the two.

The importance of an experience of community life

Christianity owes its origin to the historical experience of God, choosing to reveal His nature to man through the experiences of life. It follows that the unique insight of Christian theology is that the God of the Bible is met, served and experienced in the challenges of everyday living. For the growing child this means that he is constantly facing questions of ultimate significance and ultimate concern in his normal experiences as he matures. Probing the depth of these experiences he asks, whether consciously or not, who am I? what am I doing here? what is my relationship to the created world? what are my responsibilities to other people? where is my place in society? what is the meaning of it all? But these fundamental questions are never answered in vacuo. They find meaning only within a living community. They are ultimately summed up in the basic theological question: 'What does it mean to live in community?'.

The theological issues facing the growing child weigh heaviest upon him in three spheres – in his personal relationships with parents, friends and adults in the community; in his adjustment to the demands of the adult community represented most sharply and radically in adolescence in the transition from school to work; and in his gropings towards independence and intellectual and moral freedom. In an affluent industrialised society the moral and spiritual demands of the Christian faith, emphasising personal concern for the well-being of others, the priority of persons over things and possessions, the importance of people over machines and stressing partnership instead of prejudice, are met and judged in the real experience of the young person.

This means that in the choices he makes, the attitudes he adopts and in his reaction to the pressures of living in relationship with others in the community he faces ultimate choice. In the transition from youth to maturity he is, whether consciously or unconsciously, both reflecting and judging the ethical and moral standards of adult society.

Contemporary society, however, has experienced a breakdown in the sense and practice of community as previously understood. Since the industrial revolution with the collapse of community units such as the parish and the village and the growth of vast industrial conglomerations, society has been atomised, families uprooted, population become mobile. Leisure pursuits and family health, formerly the sole personal concern of the family, have shifted in the new mass society to the more impersonal responsibility of the community. That which was formerly 'our' responsibility has become 'their' responsibility as society has divided into the anonymous 'Them' and 'Us'. The peculiar self-interest this divesting of responsibility has produced (to which the social workers' increasing case load bears witness), accentuated by the loneliness and isolation of the mass housing estate or soulless suburbia has resulted in a preoccupation with one's own material comforts and standards. Provided 'they' will look after others why is there need to expend energy in looking after anyone but oneself? This attitude of mind seems to justify lack of concern for the aged, deprived, lonely and handicapped. The fragmentation and self interest of adult society is complicated for the adolescent by the divisive impact of a popular culture, which is aimed at emphasising the distinctiveness of adolescence and separatedness of the teenager from adult society in order to exploit the affluent teenage market.

It is no wonder that in such a society Tillich can talk of contemporary man's estrangement from his environment and his sense of loneliness and intense dissatisfaction. For the biblical doctrine of man poetically expressed by the writer of Genesis is that 'it is not good that man should live alone' but rather that man was meant for partnership with God and his fellow men in a community. Man is only man in relationship with others. The Bible nowhere knows man alone. It is assumed that man is corporate with the same inter-relatedness and inter-communion as the parts of the body – all of us are the parts of one body.

The Jews were a community, the Early Church was a community and until the onset of mass and industrial society; Christian society was conceived as corporate and communal. Man was felt to 'belong'. There is a sense in which Christian thinking and teaching is still geared to a pre-industrial society. If Christianity is to communicate to modern man in his need, it must stress the need to find community within the mass. If the young person is to find himself and discover some answer to his loneliness and sense of isolation, he must see his place in an interrelated, interdependent community in which he has much to give and much to receive. In discovering this sense of belonging and partnership in his own experience where he is facing all the particular concerns of adolescence the young adult will find an answer to the ultimate question: 'What is man that Thou are mindful of him?' – who am I?

The Newsom Report stresses that children growing up in a welfare state need to know how the welfare state works and what their place in it really is. One of the functions of the school is to assist parents and the rest of society in preparing pupils for their place in adult society. Community care and responsibility raise not only theological issues but sociological, historical and other issues as well. The study of man's community in depth involves not only religious education. It concerns social studies, community studies: history, English, geography – conceivably even mathematics. It concerns every teacher and activity of school life. For the school is a community in itself in which community life is experienced by child and adult. Every aspect of school community life has a theological and an educational role to play in the nurturing of the child.

The discovery and exploration of community is incomplete without service to the community, because it is in self-giving in the service of others that man has come to discover himself and his God. Service to others is characteristic of a society which is Christian. It is important that pupils growing up in contemporary society should understand the ethic which underlies it. As we serve others we serve God. All service is of God. As we give ourselves in service to others we co-operate with God. As we serve we worship Him. But as all service is impossible without community within which and through which to serve, so true worship is not possible outside a community. It is as a community in which service is experienced that the school comes together in worship each day. The validity of the worship may well depend on the reality of the sense of community and service the school has engendered.

Some Conclusions: The principles that have guided the compilers of the Agreed Syllabus

Much of what has been written might be regarded as theory unrelated to the problem of how to deal with religious education. The answer has been well expressed in the words of Douglas Hubery:

> 'A concern for an experiential approach to Christian education does not arise, however, merely from theory. It arises much more from an awareness that it is precisely in this experiential way that God Himself has chosen to communicate to the world of men. And the implications of this have not always been appreciated nor explored sufficiently by biblical scholars and Christian theologians. One owes them too great a debt to offer carping criticism. Yet it remains true that the more successful have been their efforts to synthesise, the greater has been the likelihood of their concern to pass on to others their syntheses and nothing else. Christian education is not only concerned with aspects of God's truth; it is also concerned with the communication of that truth. And behind such truth there needs to be studied the means whereby the truth has become known. The Bible, and the consequent unfolding of the history of the Christian Church, are not text-book repositories of Christian truth. They are records, inspired records, of the means adopted by God to reveal the truth. And God has chosen to communicate to men through experience, through life situations.' (7)

This brings us face-to-face with one of the most perplexing problems which all those concerned with religious education have to resolve.

There are, and there will continue to be, differences in interpretation of what is the nature of revelation and in a document of this kind the greatest measure of agreement will not be acceptable to everyone. At some points we may have to agree to disagree while accepting a wide measure of common ground. To stress the need for bringing what is revealed into a close relationship with the needs and experience of the growing children is not to invalidate the Word of God as revealed in Scripture: it is to create a bridge whereby that which is revealed can be given a measure of reality to the child of today.

If we distinguish between inspiration and revelation, does it mean that writers were inspired to speak a word to their generation but that this word is not of necessity a revelation to us? To which it could be answered that if one allows that God speaks through individuals we can distinguish

---

(7) Hubery, S. D.   The Experiential Approach   N.C.E.C.
                       to Christian Education

between the content of revelation and the mode of expression (by which is usually meant inspiration). Men have always used words (whether in an oracular sense or in writing makes no difference), to express their deepest experiences but the words have been charged with meaning at a level of the cultural development of the age in which they were spoken or written. It is by experience at all stages and levels of development that the truths have been verified.

It has been truly said that the function of religious education is to bring children and adults into an encounter with God. This encounter is only one of its functions and today we have to recognise that this has to be done within the context of our modern industrial technological society.

'We need understanding and imagination to see how interdependent and interwoven are the human and technical factors. And with the great advance in new techniques, we should make supreme efforts to understand the complexities of the human and social needs, and resolve to meet them. We must not believe that this is beyond our capacity. It will mean good social philosophy, and will require a spiritual sensitivity in the handling of secular things. It could give great purpose to our Western society desperately in need of more adequate social goals – namely the creation of a humane, mature, technological society.' (8)

Worship in School

A characteristic of Christianity should be joy: joy in the fact of life, and joy in the knowledge that Our Lord came that we might have life more abundantly. Even when we remember the sorrows of Christ we see light breaking into the darkness in the triumph of Easter. Thanksgiving and praise are perhaps the natural modes of worship especially for the young to whom Christianity must be presented as life-fulfilling, not life-denying.

In worship in a school we are concerned far more with the 'feeling' aspect of religious education while in the classroom we are dealing mainly with intellectual development. This may be an over-simplification but it is sufficiently true to guide us in the often difficult process of devising the pattern of a service for the children in which we can employ hymns and music, poetry, choral verse speaking, literature including what is appropriate from the Bible, and prayers. There is also a place for dramatic activities, a device frequently employed in the school broadcasts of the B.B.C. in their service for schools. The main requirement is that the worship should be sincerely offered.

Most head teachers will be concerned with the corporate act of worship as laid down by law. Apart from the fact that it should not be distinctive of any denomination the opportunities for creating the right atmosphere are many and varied. It may be difficult where the hall is used for other purposes at other times to create the atmosphere of worship which is so desirable; nevertheless, many schools succeed in doing this. As in the case of classroom activities the corporate act of worship must be suitable for the age and ability of the children for whom it is intended. This may sometimes be the cause of difficulties where there is a wide age range and a considerable difference in the ability of the children. In this situation, most frequently occurring in combined junior, mixed, and

---

(8) Wickham, E. R.   Encounter with Modern   Lutterworth Press
Society

infants' schools it is always possible to hold a short corporate assembly, shortened for the younger ones by their withdrawal during the singing of a hymn. Where there are special difficulties of accommodation the Local Education Authority may agree to a modification of the arrangements for assembly.

In any assembly the first essential is to create the right atmosphere. A quiet entry of the classes to the hall is desirable although this does not mean, necessarily, marching into, or standing in lines. The purpose of the quiet period is to evoke expectancy rather than an attitude of unnatural piety; many schools find it helpful to play carefully chosen music either by means of recordings on a tape, gramophone records, the piano, or other instruments. It may be helpful to have some feature such as a well-arranged vase of flowers, a suitable picture, or a simple cross as a centre of interest. At each stage of education there will be variations on a basic theme which is to commend the new day to God, and to ask his blessing as a recognition of His concern and love for us and all created things.

Infant Schools

The whole infant school curriculum centres on the wonders of the world, and school worship can help the child's intuitive understanding of God as Creator and Father of us all. To do this the subject must be realistic, within the child's experience and often inspired by the day-to-day events with which he is familiar. In this the individual teacher's collection of hymns and prayers is most valuable.

The length and pattern of school worship should be varied although the demands made on the children's power of attention and their physical stamina should never be excessive. A prolonged period of standing and unsatisfactory ventilation are always to be avoided.

The use of silence should never be overlooked although a too long period may lead to thought wandering; 'thinking quietly' can nevertheless be understood by young children. The introduction of suitably worded petitions will clearly link with much of the teaching; a simple act of worship may sometimes arise spontaneously after a lesson in the class-room.

Junior Schools

As in all acts of worship the first essential is to create the right atmosphere and the main considerations must be sincerity and appropriateness in terms of the children's age and ability. Although the pattern of worship is bound to vary from school to school there are certain features which will nearly always be included:

(1) The service will have a theme or central idea around which the individual items will be arranged.

(2) These can include an opening sentence or sentences, perhaps from the Bible or suitable non-biblical material which introduces the theme.

(3) Although the order of occurrence will vary the service would usually include a hymn or hymns, prayers and a reading from the Bible or other suitable material.

Variety and interest is given if other members of the staff, individual children, or a whole class occasionally plan and take the service. In any case the children should take an active part in the worship, and it should be borne in mind that nothing but the best is good enough to offer to God.

Occasionally the service can be the focal point of a school project and serve to bring together what has been taught or discussed in the classroom. Such occasions call for a special effort; due regard should be had to the main point of an appeal, or topic, on which the whole school has worked for some weeks. On these, as on all other occasions, the words used in the hymns, the version of the Bible from which a reading is made should be clear and meaningful; modern translations of the Bible can be a help although many would agree that the Authorised Version remains unchallenged for the beauty of its language.

Secondary Schools

At this stage, the theological ideas contained in the service should be sound, and the devotional element in keeping with the age and ability of the pupils. There is a place for petition, adoration, confession, thanksgiving and intercession; all these aspects of worship are natural to older children and may be introduced in some form of liturgical service so long as the responses called for are simple and direct. Within this framework prayers which, because of the sheer beauty of their language, have been used by worshipping communities of all denominations can be introduced. The use of a school choir, or orchestra, can add greatly to the musical quality of the occasion.

Memorisation

There are three principles which may guide those who wish to include memorisation in their scheme of work. They are:—

1. The first would be concerned with what it is considered desirable for children to know by heart in order that they may the more effectively join in acts of worship. This would apply particularly to the daily act of worship taken at the school assembly.
2. The second would be concerned with what is considered to be desirable to encourage children to commit to memory for its own sake. Such would include passages of scripture which have a link with a lesson and arise in consequence of this. Certainly they should be meaningful to the child, not overlong and within the capacity of the child in terms of his ability to learn.
3. The third would determine those passages which a child may choose to learn for personal reasons. It is sometimes useful to preserve these in the form of an anthology to be made and kept by each child as an individual collection. This may provide an opportunity for work in art and craft.

Suggestions for Passages and Prayers

It is not possible to stipulate the age at which any passage may be learned as so much depends on the ability of the pupils. The following are suggestions only:—

The Lord's Prayer (it is suggested that the version Matthew 6 vv. 9–13, New English Bible be taught).

The Ten Commandments. These may be presented in a simplified form.

The two-fold Law of Christ.
'Hear O Israel, The Lord our God is one Lord; and thou shalt love the Lord thy God with all thy heart, and with all thy soul, and with all thy mind, and with all thy strength. This is the first commandment. And the second is like, namely this: Thou shalt love thy neighbour as thyself. There is none other commandment greater than these. On these two commandments hang all the Law and the Prophets'.

See also N.E.B., Mark 12 vv. 29/31.

Hymn Books

It is not possible to recommend one hymn book as entirely satisfactory for Schools. Some hymn books contain too few hymns, while others include hymns which are unsuitable. A good basic hymn book should be supplemented by specially selected collections if possible involving instrumental activity, no matter how simple this may be. A hymn practice should be made as enjoyable as possible, the addition of records, chimes, percussion, etc., helping towards this atmosphere of pleasure and purpose.

Since musical publications are constantly appearing and also going out of print, the music section of the Agreed Syllabus, which is included for use over a considerable period, should be concerned more with establishing principles rather than providing lists of currently available material.

The Use of Music in Assembly

Recorded music should be part of the assembly and should not be a background to marching in and out. The music should be chosen carefully to give support to the particular story or theme of the assembly concerned. The best guide to the use of music in this way may well be the British Broadcasting Corporation, whose well-organised Religious Broadcasts demonstrate this point most clearly.

Usually, however, music of a calm and dignified nature is always acceptable: music which does not draw clear pictures or tell obvious stories or conjure the more excitable moods. Such a list is virtually endless, and depends so much on taste and availability, but it might well include the following:

Mendelssohn	Italian Symphony (slow movement)	ACL 4
	Violin Concerto (2nd movement)	ACL 4
Barber	Adagio for Strings	} Xep 9000
	Essay for Orchestra	
Bach	Brandenburg Concertos (Nos. 3 and 6)	} OL 50160
	2-Violin Concerto (2nd movement)	
	Sheep May Safely Graze	abe 10206
	Air (Suite 3)	} cep 736
	Air (Cantata 208)	
Grieg	Holberg Suite	7 er 5172
Vaughan Williams	Tallis Fantasia/Greensleeves	} ACL 144
Delius	Walk to the Paradise Garden	
Elgar	Enigma Variations (selected movements)	ACL 55
Handel	Fireworks/Water Music (selected movements)	GL 5758
Handel	"Berenice" Minuet	} 7 P 269
Clarke	Trumpet Voluntary	
Strauss (R.)	Metamorphosen for 23 Instruments	} PL 9400
	4 Last Songes (orchestral passages)	
Mozart	Slow Movements from most of the Symphonies	
Poulenc	Harpsichord Concerto (2nd movement)	ALP 1967
Schubert	Symphonies 5–8 (2nd movements)	RB 16263

The music should be heard sufficiently often to become familiar. If five excerpts are selected, one for each day of the week, and used for a half-term period, the music can become familiar without becoming tedious. In such a case as this, care would be taken to select works by different composers to give as much variety of style as possible. The above list provides between 40 and 50 satisfactory examples. It will be noted that the majority of these examples are instrumental pieces. Choral music is not generally satisfactory for this purpose.

Specially chosen music for seasonal festivals is again dependent on the record stocks and individual needs : schools cannot, on the whole, be expected to purchase records which may be used very infrequently. (Most of the above records are 7-inch "extended play" or popular, less expensive 12-inch recordings.) However, the following are worth consideration :—

Lent

St. Matthew Passion (excerpts) (Bach)	ALP 1572
Sinfonia Da Requiem (3rd movement particularly) and indeed most of the "general" range (Britten)	LXT 6175

Easter

Easter Oratorio (Bach)	PL 8620
Sonata pian'e forte (Gabrielli)	GGC 4072
Brandenburg Concerto 2 (Bach) 1st and 3rd movements	cep 635
Closing Section (Alleluia) (Walton) "Belshazzar's Feast"	33 CX 1679
Prelude and Fugue in G (Bach)	7 eg 8814

Christmas

Ahmahl and the Night Visitors (Menotti)	RB 16083
St. Nicolas (Britten)	LXT 5060
Christmas Story (Schutz)	OL 50020
Christmas Oratoria (Bach excerpts)	RG 190
King's College Carols (several collections available)	
The Childhood of Christ (Berlioz)	OL 50201–2

Complete Religious Works

Whole scripture lessons could occasionally feature an entire musical work. Satisfactory works depend on the age of the children, but one or two which might be used are :

Belshazzar's Feast (Walton)	33 CX 1679
Noye's Fludde (Britten)	NF 1
Cantata Misericordia (Britten) (The Prodigal Son story in Latin text)	LXT 6175
Ahmahl and the Night Visitors (Menotti)	RB 16083

In addition there are suitable passages to be found in almost every major work, but it it not perhaps practical to suggest that a school purchases a Brahms or Bruckner symphony to isolate a small part of one movement.

Note also the Olivier records of Bible Reading with Music accompaniment.

SUGGESTED LIST OF BOOKS AND MUSIC

Basic Hymn Books

Songs of Praise	O.U.P.
English Hymnal	O.U.P.
Westminster Hymnal (for Roman Catholic Worship)	
Ancient & Modern (Revised)	Clowes
Hymns for Church and School	Novello
The English School Hymn Book	U.L.P.
100 Hymns for Schools	O.U.P.
Songs of Praise for Boys and Girls	O.U.P.
Christian Praise	Tyndale Press
The English Hymnal Service Book	O.U.P.
Kingsway Hymn Book	Evans
Hymns for Use in Schools (S. of P.)	O.U.P.
Hymns of the Kingdom	O.U.P.

Collections for different Age-Groups

(a) *Infant*

First Hymns (McMahon)	O.U.P. *
Children Praising (Wiseman)	O.U.P.
Infant Praise (Kitson/Foote)	O.U.P.
Hear Us Heavenly Father	O.U.P.
Prayers and Hymns for Little Children	O.U.P.

(b) *Junior*

Sixty Hymns for Juniors	Schofield & Sims
The Morning Cockerel Hymnbook	Rupert Hart-Davis
Prayers & Hymns for Junior Schools	O.U.P.
With Cheerful Voice	A. &. C. Black
The Junior Hymn Book	Hamish Hamilton

(c) *Advanced*

Easy Anthem Book	O.U.P.

Additional Collections

(a) *Modern Hymns*

Five Hymns in the Popular Style (John Gardner)	O.U.P.
Versions of The Psalms (Gelineau)	
Twenty-seven Twentieth Century Hymns	Weinberger
More Twentieth Century Hymn Tunes	Weinberger
Hymn Tunes Made New (Dickinson)	Novello •
Twelve New Hymn Tunes (Malcolm Williamson)	Weinberger
Thirty Twentieth Century Hymn Tunes	Weinberger
The B. B. C. Hymnal	
The Baptist Hymn Book	
The School Hymn Book of the Methodist Church	Methodist Youth Dept.
Congregational Praise	Independent Press

(b) *Choral Development – Descants and part singing*

Hymns in Harmony (Hogben)	Boosey & Hawkes
Eight Hymns/Anthems for Juniors (2 part)	Schirmer
The Descant Hymn Books (Shaw)	Novello (two volumes)
Forty-one Descants to Familiar Hymns (Winn)	O.U.P.
Twenty-six Hymn Tunes arranged for SSA	O.U.P.
The Descant Carol Book, Vols. 1, 2 and 3	Novello
The Kingsway Book of Descants	Evans *

(c) *Instrumental Activity*

Hymn Tune Descants for Recorders (Knight) (Books 1 and 2)	Universal *
Fifty Songs of Praise arr. for Recorders (Dinn) Book 1 – Seasons and Festivals Book 2 – General	O.U.P.
A Second Fifty Songs of Praise (in two books as above)	
Carols with Chimes (Junior standard – optional percussion, etc.)	O.U.P.
More Carols with Chimes	O.U.P.
Forty-two Hymn Tunes for School Ensemble Books 1 and 2 (Rainbow)	O.U.P.
Forty-five Hymns from Songs of Praise for School Orchestra (Beney & Bryce)	O.U.P.
Fifty Hymns from Songs of Praise for Brass (Beney & Bryce)	O.U.P.

(d) *Seasonal Collections*

Oxford Book of Carols	O.U.P.
Oxford Book of Carols for Schools	O.U.P.
English Traditional Carols (2 or 3 part)	O.U.P.
Merrily on High (part singing)	O.U.P.
(Juniors) Merry Christmas	O.U.P.
(Infant and Juniors) The Clarendon Book of Christmas Carols, Books 1 and 2	O.U.P.
Carols of Today (Modern Composers)	O.U.P.
Kingsway Carol Book (Russell)	Evans
Queensway Carol Book	Evans
Penguin Book of Christmas Carols Carols 1400–1900	Gordon Frazer
Everymans Carols (McMahon)	U.L.P. •
Treasury of Easter Music	Blandford Press
Treasury of Christmas Music	Reed
Carols for Choirs (Jacques and Wilcocks)	O.U.P.

Books on Worship and Background to Hymnology

Prayers and Hymns for Little Children	O.U.P.
Prayers and Hymns for Juniors	O.U.P.
Gateway to Worship (Cox)	Religious Education Press
Oxford Book of School Worship	
Book 2 – Junior	S.P.C.K.
Book 3 – Senior	S.P.C.K.
Historical Edition of Hymns Ancient & Modern	Clowes
Handbook to the Church Hymnary (Moffatt & Patrick)	O.U.P. •
Companion to Congregational Praise (Parry)	O.U.P. •
Songs of Praise Discussed	O.U.P. •
The Music of Christian Hymnody (Routley)	Independent Press •
The Revised Psalter	S.P.C.K.

Service Books and Prayers

Buckmaster, C.	Give Us This Day	P. Smith
Bull, N.	A Book of School Worship	Harrap •
Clifton	The Junior Hymn Book	Hamish Hamilton
Cropper, M.	Prayers on the Sermon on the Mount	S.C.M. •
Doidge, R.	Boys and Girls at Worship	S.C.M. •
Dunkerley, R.	Prayer Time in the Junior School	U.L.P. •
Ferguson, M.	The School Assembly	R.E.P. •
Ferguson, M.	Sing Praise	R.E.P.
Fisher, A.	An Anthology of Prayers	Longmans
Fyfe, E.	Prayers for Today	Batsford •
Hayes, E. H.	Junior Worship	R.E.P. •
Head, David	Stammerer's Tongue	Epworth Press •
Head, David	He Sent Leanness	Epworth Press •
Holloway, B.	Prayers for Children	U.L.P.
Holloway, B.	Prayers for Younger Children	U.L.P.
Milner White	Daily Prayer	Penguin •
Prescot, D. M.	Senior Teachers' Assembly Book	Blandford
	Oxford Book of School Worship (Parts 2 and 3, Junior and Senior)	S.P.C.K.
Prescott, D. M.	Infant Teachers' Assembly Book	Blandford
Prescott, D. M.	Junior Teachers' Assembly Book	Blandford
Rose, Margaret	The Morning Cockerel Book of Readings	Rupert Hart-Davis
Martin, Ed. H.	Book of Prayers for Schools	S.C.M. •
Matthews, H. F.	Book of Worship for Schools	Epworth
Quoist, M.	Prayers of Life	Gill and Son
White	Prayers in Poetry	U.L.P. •
	New Every Morning	B.B.C.
Oldham, J. H.	Devotional Diary	S.C.M. •

Books of Readings

Briggs, E.	The Daily Bible Reading	O.U.P.
Bull & Phillips	New Testament Readings for Schools	Harrap *
Callister, F.	Bible Plays for Morning Assembly	Epworth *
Jarvis, M.	Bible Readings and Prayers for a School Year	S.C.M. *
Vipont, E.	The Bridge	O.U.P.
Vipont, E.	The Highway	O.U.P.
Vipont, E.	Two Minute Bible Readings	S.C.M. *
	A Story and a Hymn (B.B.C. Broadcasts at five to ten)	Mowbrays *
Taylor, L.	Book of Christian Days	Blackwell
Taylor, L.	Book of Prayers for School (A Calendar of Great Men and Women)	S.C.M. *

Books of extra-Biblical Readings

Astle, C.	The Path and the Prize	MacMillan
Baillie, J.	A Diary for Readings	O.U.P.
Blackburn	A Treasury of the Kingdom (An Anthology for School and College Assemblies)	O.U.P.
Bouquet, A. C.	The Lectionary of Christian Prose	Longmans
Daffern, T. G.	Poems for Assemblies	Blackwell
Fletcher, M. F.	A Time for Decision (Monthly readings for young people)	Blandford
Green, B and Gollancz V.	God of a Hundred Names (also "Year of Grace" and "New Year of Grace")	Gollancz
Gill, G. C.	A Glorious Company	Epworth *
Luff, S. G.	Early Christian Writings: an Anthology for Home and School	S.P.C.K.
Martin, H.	A Treasury of Christian Verse	S.C.M. *
Pain, G. S.	Youth at Worship	Methodist Youth Department
Taylor, L.	A Book of Christian Days (Saints Days and Festivals)	Blackwell

Suggested Prayers and Passages for use in Assembly

The Prayer of St. Chrysostom.

'Almighty God, who hast given us grace at this time with one accord to make our common supplications unto Thee; and dost promise that, when two or three are gathered together in Thy name Thou wilt grant their requests: fulfil now, O Lord, the desires and petitions of Thy Servants, as may be most expedient for them; granting us in this world knowledge of Thy truth, and in the world to come life everlasting'.

II Corinthians 13

'The grace of Our Lord Jesus Christ and the love of God, and the fellowship of the Holy Ghost be with us evermore'.

In addition, there are many prayers attributed to people of all denominations, extracts from the Psalms, and passages of prose contained in famous speeches. Nor do they need to be specifically religious, e.g., Abraham Lincoln's, 'With malice towards none, with charity to all . . .'.

Many suggestions may be found in the Books of Readings and the Books of extra-Biblical Readings mentioned in the bibliographies.

INTRODUCTION TO THE PRIMARY PHASE

Many teachers continue to use traditional methods of religious education because they cannot see any practical alternatives. The difficulties of Bible teaching are admitted and there is a growing awareness that current research casts doubts upon the value of a straightforward biblical presentation. There are three main areas in which doubt and difficulties arise. They are:

(1) The intellectual immaturity of the child.

(2) His, or her, limited experience of life and living.

(3) The language and imagery of the Bible.

It seems clear that any real religious development may be impeded if formal religious ideas are presented at too early an age. The alternative is to deal with ideas, language and experience within the reach of children. We cannot avoid children thinking in crude terms of God, the Bible, and even Jesus Himself, but we must keep this to a minimum and not obstruct the way ahead: we must allow room for bridges to be built and ideas to grow and develop.

The changes in educational theory and practice

The question naturally follows, 'How do the changes in our educational thinking affect our teaching in religious education?'. It seems that we have to present a child mainly with those truths which are within his capacity and experience and that the techniques to be used cannot differ to any degree from those which are acceptable in other subjects which are concerned with his coming to terms with the realities of life. If we are concerned with the development of our pupils as individuals, it is impossible to isolate 'instruction' in religious matters from the whole field of education, any more than could, or should be done with the literary, historical, scientific and aesthetic elements which together comprise the field of human knowledge and inquiry. Classroom work and an acquaintance with the relevant biblical and historical evidence naturally form part of it, and this is the part with which an Agreed Syllabus has to deal. Beyond this lies the impact and implications of Christianity in the contemporary world for the individual and the community in which he lives.

Broadly speaking, children pass through three main stages of learning and of forming concepts: the intuitive, the concrete and the final stage, which may not even be attained by all, of logical abstract reasoning. The speed at which they pass through them varies greatly with invididuals and may vary also from one field of knowledge to another. The 'intuitive' corresponding broadly to the nursery and infant period; the 'concrete' which is associated with the acceptance of ideas as literally true, may cover most of the junior period and in many instances continues into the secondary stage. The stage of abstract reasoning and inquiry may begin at almost any point in the secondary school; it may even in exceptional cases make its appearance with older juniors. The danger at the junior stage is that, by accepting all biblical stories as literally true, especially those which call for informed understanding, he will accept primitive or distorted religious concepts.

How the Bible is used

In all syllabuses we have to deal with the question of the authority of the Bible in the presentation of our work. Any differences that may exist on this issue are no longer confined to denominational interpretations since all orthodox Christian churches accept the need for understanding the works or actions of biblical figures, or the message of biblical records, in their original form before we can understand their significance for us today. The question as to how and when the Bible should be used in a primary school is more difficult to answer. If we accept the evidence of recent research as well as the support given to these findings by practising teachers of experience, the Bible is not a book which can be used as a text-book with young children. It was written for adults who can bring to it an experience of life and a maturity of outlook which young children cannot be expected to possess.

It will be seen that at each stage in the primary section references to passages in the Bible are given. These are not intended for the children to refer to : they are for the teacher to use as the basis for a story to be told or to be woven into a story as far as this is appropriate. There are occasions when the use of a quotation in a conversation may be a useful way of conveying the meaning.

Morality and Religion

Most teachers are concerned about giving their pupils a good moral training and in this they look for the sanctions of religion to help them. This is frequently mentioned as a reason for introducing them to the Christian faith. Ruth Batten has said that 'Primary school children should learn Christianity through the atmosphere of their daily lives'.

Children in early childhood have their own way of expressing their moral values based on mixed motives. On the one hand, there is a natural desire to avoid the causes of adult disapproval ; on the other hand, there is normally an acceptance of what authority, in terms of parents or teachers, thinks is right or wrong. As children progress through the junior school, more rules become necessary but it has to be remembered that many are made for the sake of social convenience and the maintenance of law and order, and are accepted for their evident commonsense ; only harm can be done by linking these with religious sanctions. It is when we allow situations to arise in which moral judgments have to be made that religious insights become meaningful. Morality begins in the free acceptance of a series of judgments on certain aspects of social and individual behaviour. All this is a matter of growth and there are stages in the growth of morality just as there are in the growth and development of religious concepts. The merging of security in freedom calls for a delicate balance. If there is too much freedom allowed, the consequences can be disastrous ; if, on the other hand, security is based on too much protection and authority, then children will fail to grow up as they should and become unable to make sound moral judgments for themselves. It is the spirit rather than the letter of the law by which a school educates its pupils.

Aims of the Primary Syllabus

It is hoped that the notes which follow will help teachers to formulate their own schemes to meet the needs of the children they are teaching. Their purpose is not to impose a method but to offer to all who teach, and who may feel the need for a fresh approach to the teaching of scripture, material and themes which are in keeping with trends in educational thinking about most aspects of the work in primary schools.

Religious education has, to a large extent, remained something apart from other fields of study and for this reason is often regarded as something which has to be treated in isolation. With the trend towards 'cross-subject' teaching religion can be treated as part of the natural experience of every child and, far from being a form of indoctrination can meet the deepest needs of all children in terms of their growth and development.

What are the main tasks in helping forward the development of children between 4 and 7 and the end of the primary school at 11 years of age ? The American psychologist Robert Havighurst (1) suggests that there are nine.

(1) Learning physical skills necessary for ordinary games and in carrying out simple tasks.

(2) Building wholesome attitudes towards oneself as a growing organism.

(3) Learning to get along with others of the same age and learning to adjust oneself emotionally with other people.

(4) Learning an appropriate masculine or feminine role in social terms.

(5) Developing fundamental skills in reading, writing and calculating.

(6) Developing concepts necessary for everyday living and so forming simple concepts of social and physical reality.

(7) Developing conscience, morality and a scale of values ; learning to distinguish right from wrong.

(8) Achieving personal independence.

(9) Developing attitudes towards social groups and institutions.

If we accept these tasks as fundamental aims in the primary stage of education it will be wrong to try and distinguish too sharply between the aims of education in general and the more particular aims of religious education. The latter is not just one 'subject' among many but rather a matter of approach and the 'quality-giving' factor in all our work. The Christian teacher will be vitally concerned in helping children to achieve their fullest development physically, mentally, morally and spiritually. Each field of study will have its contribution to make to the fulfilment of these tasks. Although religious education does not have anything to contribute directly to the development of physical skills, it does have a great deal to say when these are considered in relation to building wholesome attitudes towards oneself as a growing organism. Personal relationships are at the very heart of Christian teaching. So too there is a concern with evaluating the male and female roles rather than with the process of achieving them. Religious education will have something to say on the need for and the use of the skills of reading, writing and calculating. Obviously religious education has much to contribute in the development of conscience although it has no monopoly in this field. The achievement of personal independence and a sense of social responsibility calls for a careful balance between too much freedom and too much obedience to a blind compliance with authority ; this involves spiritual as well as intellectual development within a situation where value-judgments can be made.

The Religious Development of Children

Clearly, if religion is concerned with all these tasks in connection with a child's development it has a far more fundamental role than the imparting of what has been called religious knowledge. It is concerned with the giving of values at each stage of development. Can children cope with these tasks at the same time as they cope with stages of mental and physical development? In his book *Religious Thinking from Childhood to Adolesence* (2) Dr. Ronald Goldman reviews the research that has been done.

From these conclusions it may be seen that there are 'thresholds' of ability which it is dangerous to anticipate. It is possible to do more harm than good by pressing children to accept material or terminology which they are not ready to accept and the arrangement of the content of this syllabus is an attempt to put these principles into practice. Much help may be gained from the work undertaken by Violet Madge as related in her book *Children in Search of Meaning* (3).

(1) Havighurst, Robert   Human Development and   Longmans, Green & Co. *
                            Education

(2) Goldman, Ronald   Religious Thinking from   Routledge, Kegan Paul *
                            Childhood to Adolescence

(3) Madge, Violet   Children in Search of   S.C.M. Press
                            Meaning

An Outline of the Primary Syllabus

Children 3–5 years

Themes on:

Homes and families
The Seasons and Festivals of the Year.

Children 5–7 years

Themes on:

The Seasons (continued).
Birthdays and Christmastide.
Homes, friendship and helping others.
Stories which can be used as part of a shared experience.

Children 7–11 years

For children 7–9 years.

Stage One   Term One
  Our family and our relatives.
  Jesus and His family.

  Where and how Jesus grew up.   Term Two
  Learning about God.

  Family rules.   Term Three
  Prayer and worship.

Stage Two   Term One
  Joy and Thankfulness.

  Jewish Festivals.

  Meals Jesus would have shared.   Term Two

  Easter.   Term Three
  Men and women Jesus knew.

For children 9–11 years. Introduction

Stage Three   Term One
  The character of Jesus.
  Men and women who have shown the qualities that Jesus expected
    of His followers.

  Obedience and Forgiveness   Term Two

The work that Jesus began continues in the work of the Holy Spirit.

Stage Four. The Church's Book

Learning about the 'books'.
The lands behind the 'books'.
Journeys in Bible times.
Rivers, wells and water.
How signs and symbols have a special meaning.
The 'Light of the World'.
The Work of the Church goes forward.
Some aspects of the work of the Church today.

THE PRIMARY SYLLABUS

CHILDREN 3–5 YEARS

At this stage, it is difficult to make a distinction between religious education and the whole way in which children learn about life. In this, their generalised experience is connected with a growing awareness of God as Creator and as the Person who cares about His world. One of the most felt needs is for security and this grows out of situations where there are good parent–child and teacher–child relationships. Most of the teaching can be connected with every-day situations in the classroom where activities and experience help the child to a greater awareness of the world around him. His experience of the natural world through tending growing things, following the changes in the seasons, hearing about interesting people, can be an introduction to God's creation.

The religious ideas contained in much of the Bible cannot be fully understood by young children and so their religious education must consist of the enrichment of their general experience rather than any kind of formal instruction. Bible stories therefore need to be selected with much care and should be introduced as part of a shared experience within the school community. In the classroom this will include activities such as painting, work with clay, movement and at a later stage free-writing. Whatever is done by children should be accepted at their level of development and will often lead to imaginative and creative work.

Worship and Young Children

The sense of wonder, which is an attribute of young children's developing experience of the world around them, can be the essence of worship. It cannot be confined to a set time or place. For this reason many situations in the classroom can provide the opportunity for simple acts of worship which are appropriate to the needs, experience and language of young children. The term 'School Assembly' may suggest a too formal approach to this activity; even so, to come together as a community can be a way of expressing thankfulness and a sense of joy in offering worship to God. These occasions can sometimes be the means of bringing the work of the classroom into a wider setting.

Suggested Themes

These suggestions are intended to help teachers to stimulate young children to understand, through an experience of 'their world', what is meant by God's care, and the friendship of Jesus. Sometimes work on these themes may provide the topics to be used in worship; on the other hand, the corporate act of worship may lead to classroom activities. In all these activities children will be participating fully in their own religious education. What matters most is not the use of religious words but the quality of the relationships in the classroom and in the school community.

Books for Further Reading by the Teacher

Goldman, R. J.	Religious Thinking from Childhood to Adolescence	Routledge, Kegan Paul *
Goldman, R. J. Madge, V.	Readiness for Religion Children in search of Meaning	Routledge, Kegan Paul * S.C.M. Press

Homes and Families

This is an important theme developed in the later stages in the junior school. It is part of the basic experience of young children in their play, perhaps in a 'Wendy' house or in some group activity. By playing together and working together in imaginary situations, they are learning to develop ideas of family relationships. Little more than the encouragement to invent and explore the possibilities of creative play within the group is needed at this stage.

The Seasons and Festivals of the Year

(a) Autumn   The theme of God our Heavenly Father, His love and care
God's wonderful world and the countryside.

The town scene : the local park and tending school plants.

Observing pets and their making ready for the winter.

These topics can be brought together as a useful experience by means of Harvest Festival.

(1)   As a way of teaching co-operation between home, school and the child.

(2)   As a means of gaining information about natural things through nature study introduced in an appropriate way.

(3)   Awakening a sense of awe and wonder.

(4)   As a means of providing an opportunity for service to others.

Enjoyable experiences, shared with others, provide an opportunity to express thanks for the gift of life (saying their 'thank you' prayers in simple language).

Stories that might be told in the teacher's own words.

The story of Ruth – reapers and gleaners – Ruth 2 vv. 2–17.

(b) Winter and The time when the world rests.
Christmas   Animals that rest : the dormouse and squirrel.

The trees in winter. Ice and snow.

Ploughing and preparing the land.

A bird table.

The Christmas Story told in the teacher's own words and dramatised within the framework of the joy of birthdays. There is no need to go into great detail with very young children, not only because they will hear the Gospel stories many times in future years, but because these stories contain ideas and concepts which are too difficult for them to understand at this stage. The opportunity to express their delight in their own way and at their own level by painting, in clay, and in movement is what matters most. Any intellectual understanding of the Incarnation is beyond them.

Christmas is best approached as a present-day experience, although it is essential that a foundation should be laid for a deeper understanding later on of Jesus the 'Light of the World'.

The joys of Christmas : warm clothes, warm fires, games in the snow. We can look for stars at night (but not too late at night), frosty patterns on windows, walls, pavements and cobwebs.

The giving and receiving of presents.

Worship with candles (electric torches) and a corona of evergreens.

(c) Spring   The time when the world awakens. Sowing seeds, spring-time as
and Easter   a joyous time.

Birds returning from abroad and the growth of plants.

Spring and Easter : carols such as, 'Spring has now unwrapped the flowers, Day is fast reviving'.

The first Palm Sunday ; in story form told by the teacher in her own words. Mark 11 vv. 1–10.

The more detailed story of Easter is beyond them at this stage and in any case this will be dealt with later on.

(d) Summer and Whitsuntide	There are many themes to be explored. Signs of summer: warmer weather, sunshine and showers, flowers, blossoms on the trees.

The enjoyment of summer in and out of school.

The time for holidays.

People we meet on holidays.

All these can be linked with the theme of thanksgiving for God's gifts.

Whitsuntide as the time when the coming of the Holy Spirit is remembered, is best dealt with through the theme of those who have followed Jesus in the past and those who show His love and courage in their lives today.

The first Whit-Sunday was the birthday of the Church but the festival is a reminder of the power of Jesus at work in the world today. The lives of Christian people and incidents in the life of Our Lord told in the teacher's own words may be used.

Jesus as a Loving Friend (references for the teacher only)

of children	Mark 10 vv. 13–16
of fathers and mothers	John 4 vv. 46–54
of the hungry	Mark 6 vv. 30–44
of the sick	Luke 4 vv. 38–40
of those who need help	Mark 4 vv. 35–41

CHILDREN 5–7 YEARS

It is important that there should be continuity in method and approach as between the nursery and infant stages in this as in all fields of experience and learning. As in the nursery stage, religious education should continue to be an integral part of school life. One of the main features is the development of the child's physical skills as the transition from babyhood to childhood is made. With this comes the need to explore the natural environment, to gain greater control in play-centred activities and to make progress in the more difficult skills of reading and writing. It is likely that, before leaving the infant school, the majority will be able to read suitable material and to express themselves orally in a more logical sequence of thought as well as writing.

Well-printed books of quality, arranged and made easily accessible to the children, become increasingly necessary and with these, Bible stories should be included. It is essential that the greatest care should be shown in the selection of pictures and visual aids. Harm can be done by the inclusion of inartistic and misleading pictures in illustrating biblical material. Suggestions about books and pictures are made at the end of this section.

Throughout infancy there is a basic need for security realised in the child's dependence on adults for affection and support. To this extent all adults standing in a close relationship to children, mediate the unseen power and nature of the godhead. To them God partakes of the known and experienced character of parents, teachers, and other adult figures who form part of their experience of life. This is not saying that God is an idea projected outwards from the child's experience: in a theological sense all activity begins and ends with God. He speaks to men, breaks into the reality we know as our world but He does so through the totality of our experience, including the experience of childhood. Part of this experience includes two crises, The one is the realisation that adults do not have unlimited powers : they are fallible and their powers are limited. The other experience is that of becoming aware of death. Not only do the pets we cherish die, but sometimes our closest relations are taken from us. This is the beginning of a long process by which all of us come to terms with the insecurities of life ; and to the young child this marks a turning point in the change from infancy to childhood.

The organisation in the infants' school often makes for a good deal of overlapping of age-groups. For this reason the material which is given covers the total range of 5–7 years. It is for the teacher to select whatever is appropriate for the children in her class. Much more than the telling of Bible stories is needed.

Suggested Themes

If religious education is to be regarded as an integral part of school life, then it must be related to the child's experience in all its forms. One way of doing this is through themes which have a bearing on the changing seasons and indirectly on the main festivals of the church.

1. Late Summer and early Autumn

This is the time when harvests of many kinds and places can be of interest : the foodstuffs we get from far off lands as well as those we produce ourselves. The religious content should be seen in the wider context of God providing for man's needs. This could take the form of a project ending with a Harvest Thanks-giving : This can be seen as preparing for the service when we say 'Thank you', and when we show our thanks in a practical way. We do this by giving thanks to God by remembering how dependent we are upon those who gather the harvest and by sharing our harvest gifts with others.

Stories from the Bible to be told in the teacher's own words.

Food in the wilderness.

The draught of fishes.

The harvest psalm.

God as Creator.

Man works with God to produce wheat and food. God creates : we have to help and work with Him. The story of Creation is a poem not to be taken literally.

Some of the Nature Psalms are appropriate at this stage.

The story of Jesus blessing the bread and so showing the fruitfulness that follows when man and God work together.

Sources for work on the Seasons

Stories about harvest from present-day sources, e.g. :
Harvest-tide Stories, Krall, B.
Harvest-time in many Lands, Krall, B.
(N.C.E.C. Publishers)

Exodus 16 (see Peake's Commentary revised edition Black, M. and Rowley, H. H., Nelson)

Luke 5 vv. 1–11

Psalm 65 vv. 9–13

Genesis 1

Psalms 104 and 148

John 6 vv. 1–14

2. Birthdays and Christmastide

The idea which links the child's experience with the Nativity is that of birthdays ; the giving and receiving of presents accompanied by joyous activities. The celebration and enjoyment of Christmas at home and at school are fundamental experiences for young children. Detailed consideration of the Nativity stories is not necessary at this stage but it is essential that a foundation should be laid for a deeper understanding of Christ as the 'Light of the World'. At this stage the enjoyment of Christmas should be mainly an emotional experience rather than an attempt to give an intellectual understanding of the Incarnation.

Tell me about Christmas — *
Jones, M. A., (Collins)
Christmas-tide Stories (3 volumes) *
Jones, M. A., (R.E.P.)
The World's Christmas — *
Wyon, O., (S.C.M.)
(Stories from Europe, Asia and Africa)
The Christmas Mouse —
Wenning, E.
(World's Work series pub. 1959, Holt, R. & W.)
Shekerjian ed. A Book of Christmas *
Carols pub. A. Barker.
(good background information)

The story of the Nativity (in the teacher's own words with an occasional quotation).

Luke 2 vv. 1–20

3. Themes on homes, friendship and helping others

This can be introduced at any stage in the work, but particularly in one sense in connection with homes and families.

Twelfth Night and parties.
The Epiphany ceremony.
(Lighting candles — electric torches.)

Above all this calls for some practical activity by the class in helping others. This can involve some sacrifice of time and effort, especially by the seven year olds.

Sources for work on homes :

All God's Children — Webb, P. *
(Oliphant)
Let's look at Houses and Homes
Morey — Muller
St. Matthew 2 vv. 1–12
(To be told in the teacher's own words with the occasional quotation)

Followers of Jesus.
Gladys Aylward and the Chinese children. Stories from news-letters, magazines, etc., and from the publication — 'All these by faith' *
Reason, J., (Lutterworth.)

4. Springtime

Children will link their experience of growing plants, young animals and the return of life in town and countryside with the general theme of Springtime. Stories about the things Jesus saw in Palestine and to which He refers. Passages about :

Stories about the Springtime :

Eastertide and Springtime Stories — N.C.E.C.

Fig trees

Luke 13 vv. 6–9

Flowers

Matthew 6 vv. 28–29

Birds and animals

Luke 12 vv. 6–7
Luke 13 vv. 34.

5. Good Friday and Easter

The story in outline is all that is necessary at this stage. The Crucifixion should be told without stressing the brutality and suffering.

Palm Sunday. Jesus rides into Jerusalem.

Luke 19 vv. 28–40

Jesus washes his disciples' feet.

John 13 vv. 1–10

Good Friday and Easter—continued

The Last Supper.	Mark 14 vv. 12–31

(The stories to be told in the teacher's
own words with quotations where
suitable.)

Mary in the garden	John 20 vv. 1–18
The journey to Emmaus	Luke 24 vv. 13 ff.
By the shore	John 21 vv. 1–14

The Resurrection is best seen in the
setting of the return of life in Springtime.
The assurance of the Risen Lord should
be emphasised rather than the death on
the Cross.

The hymn, 'There is a green hill . . .' used
in worship may convey the meaning of
the Passion far more than the telling of
the Gospel stories to young children.

6. Summer and Whitsuntide

This is the time of year children enjoy most of all. There are many themes that can be explored and only a few examples given. Whitsuntide, the festival of the Holy Spirit, falls in summer time but it cannot be dealt with in any detail at this stage. The main emphasis needs to be on the effect of the Holy Spirit on those who have shown His love and courage in their lives in recent times: the best way of introducing young children to this is through the lives of Christian people. Stories from such sources as:

Cousins, M.	Tell me about the Saints	Hutchinson
Krall, B. C.	Stories of Favourite Saints	R.E.P. *
Reason, J.	All these by faith	Lutterworth *

(and stories from missionary magazines, newsletters and books).

The telling of stories about people who have shown love and courage is only a part of the experience: use has to be made of the child's direct experience. The signs of Summer.

The warmer weather, sunshine and flowers, the flowers and blossom. The time of year when holidays come round; the things we do at home, in the longer evenings, at the seaside or abroad. The people we meet on holidays: fishermen, their nets, boats and work, the farmers, their animals and their implements.

All these are part of the growing awareness of the world into which the child is born and the world to which they belong, and it is through this total experience of life that God speaks to children. It is by this experience that children can be introduced to stories about such people in the Bible who have shown love and courage. With this background of experience they can be introduced by means of the teacher's own words to the following characters and situations in the Bible.

Connected with the experience of people we meet on holiday:

Stories about fishermen. The fishermen who followed Jesus, Simon, Andrew, James and John.	Mark 1 vv. 16–20
Stories about shepherds. David the shepherd boy.	I Samuel 16 vv. 14–23 I Samuel 17 vv. 34–35 I Samuel 19 vv. 8–18
Stories about farmers. The sower (simply told as a story without attempting to deal with the deeper religious meaning).	Mark 4 vv. 1–9

7. Thinking and helping others

Children enjoy quiet thought and will be helped by opportunities of using a 'quiet corner' where they can look at books and enjoy things of beauty which appeal to the sense of sight and touch. Although not always providing us with evidence that this is useful it should not be assumed that children, when so employed, are achieving nothing of importance. On the contrary such opportunities are, for many, of great value in developing an awareness of the deeper things of life.

Children enjoy words and enjoy communicating their ideas (e.g. at news time). Their spiritual development is enriched by all that is attempted in communicating ideas through paint, clay, music, language and other creative activities (e.g. making a home in a 'Wendy' house, caring for pets and helping other people). They enjoy 'doing' and need only the opportunity for writing short letters to sick people and looking after younger children and those who are new to the school. This comes fairly easily when schools are organised so that, at some stage, children of all ages work together.

8. Stories which can be used as part of a shared experience

There are some biblical stories which may be used as part of the background to other sections. While it is impracticable to suggest that children should only experience what is solely within their grasp, we must exercise responsibility in the choice of planned experiences. Some Bible stories can easily create misunderstanding and impede comprehension at a later stage. The theological significance of the story of the Good Samaritan is beyond young children, for example. It also has a simple meaning as a story to be dramatised, written about and used in connection with the section on helping others, merely as a story in the setting of a wider experience which can give it an immediate meaning. There should be no attempt at moralising or interpretation.

Stories told by Jesus:

The Good Shepherd	John 10 vv. 11–15
The Good Samaritan	Luke 10 vv. 25–37
The Lost Sheep	Luke 15 vv. 1–7
The Lost Coin	Luke 15 vv. 8–10

Stories told to Jesus:

Joseph and his dream	Genesis 37 vv. 5–12
Joseph and his coat (with long sleeves)	Genesis 37
Joseph the slave in Egypt	Genesis 39 vv. 1–6 ; vv. 20–23 ; Genesis 40
Joseph the leader in Egypt	Genesis 41
Moses, the baby	Exodus 1 and 2
Moses, the Leader	Exodus 3
The birth and call of Samuel	1 Samuel 1 to 3
David the shepherd boy is chosen	1 Samuel 16
David and Jonathan	1 Samuel 19 and 20

Bibliography for the Nursery and Infant Section

Barnard	The Nursery Song and Picture Book	R.E.P.
	A Book of Christmas Carols	Barker *
Cousins, M.	Tell me about the Saints	Hutchinson
Kitson, M.	Infant Praise	O.U.P.
Kitson, M.	Infant Prayer	O.U.P.
Krall, B.	Harvest-tide Stories	N.C.E.C. *
Krall, B.	Harvest-tide in many lands	N.C.E.C. *
Krall, B.	Stories of Favourite Saints	R.E.P. *
Jones, M. A.	Tell me about Christmas	R.E.P. *
Jones, M. A.	Christmas-tide Stories (3 vols.)	R.E.P. *
Morey, J.	Let's look at houses and homes	Muller *
Pain, G. S.	Prayers and hymns for little children	O.U.P.
Reason, J.	All these by faith	Lutterworth *
Webb, P.	All God's Children	Oliphant *
Wenning, E.	The Christmas Church Mouse	World's Work
	The Infant Teacher's Assembly Book	Blandford
	Prayers for younger children	U.L.P.
	My small corner	International Bible * Reading Association

N.C.E.C. – National Christian Education Council (formerly the N.S.S.U.).

Teachers' Books

	The Religious Education of Children 3–7 years	C.E.M.*
Goldman, R. J.	Religious Thinking from Childhood to Adolescence	Routledge*
Goldman, R. J.	Readiness for Religion	Routledge*
Madge, V.	Children in Search of Meaning	S.C.M. Press

Sources of material, visual aids and addresses of organisations can be found in Appendix E.

CHILDREN 7–9 YEARS

The years from seven to nine mark a natural stage in a child's development. The change from infancy comes only gradually and it is desirable that there shall be continuity in method and approach as between the two departments if these are separated, or within the school if infants and juniors are in one department. At all stages experience and understanding go hand-in-hand but this is particularly important with the younger children when attempts to teach matters which are not related to the child's experience will lead only to bewilderment.

Children are now ready to begin to relate the basic facts of their experience to certain religious truths although this cannot be the full Christian faith as adults understand it. Nevertheless, they are beginning to be conscious of a 'something' or 'someone' bigger than themselves. This need for something bigger than themselves has two forms of expression. One is in the need for adult authority and the other is in the means by which they learn to become less centred in their own affairs and directed away from themselves to form friendships of a more lasting kind, and discover the meaning of the school as a community. They are beginning to learn that Christianity is a social religion very much concerned with relationships between people.

There is a growing sense of awe and wonder when confronted with certain natural phenomena: an embryonic sense of what Otto calls the 'numinous'. With this goes a deepening awareness of the way people behave to one another and to them. The human love of parents, the fact of wrong-doing and suffering both in himself and in others, is often felt acutely. Sympathy for others can easily be roused if only for a brief period. Stories of people who have been concerned with helping others are a source of interest and appeal and this naturally leads to the fact that Jesus loved people, helped them in their difficulties and could always be trusted and relied on. Out of these attitudes can come an awareness of the need for, as well as the means to, worship.

Children also enjoy making and looking at pictures. They are making good progress in reading and in free-writing and there is a real need to see that the library books we offer them are of good quality and that they can be stimulated to explore their ideas in writing and in other artistic ways. We should be very careful that at no time do we provide pictures or books, or select stories, which gave a false or sub-Christian idea of God. A weak or sentimental image of Jesus must always be avoided and special care is needed in the choice and use of Old Testament stories.

Above all, children at this stage have an intense curiosity and are always (unless inhibited by unnatural means) asking questions. As far as possible we must satisfy this curiosity.

What are the main needs of young children aged 7–9 years?

By taking note of the insights gained from recent psychological research into the process in religious education we are able to make our material even more relevant to the situation of the children we teach, even more fitted to their needs and suited to their abilities than a necessarily Bible-centred approach can hope to be. This is not to suggest that the Bible plays an unimportant role in the syllabus or that there is an attempt to impart any teaching which is not fully rooted in the Bible.

How are the basic human needs of young children to be met and supported by religious teaching?

1. They need security and they feel the need to belong somewhere; above all to be loved and protected even when they are straining after independence. They need to feel a sense of solidarity through 'identification' within the group.

2. They need to be able to play out their problems with children of their own age and away from adult pressures.

3. They need to hear stories about people with whom they can identify themselves in order that they can find out what it is like to be another person. With this comes the opportunity for developing sympathy for other people and to imitate those worth imitating.

4. They are now able to feel guilt, to accept blame and to apologise. They have the capacity to apportion blame amongst others quite rationally. Good and bad are seen much more in terms of right and wrong and much less in terms of parents' wishes, but the moral code is still full of unalterable 'blacks and whites' and the idea of 'being fair' is uppermost.

There is, therefore, a need to help children to come to terms with their moral weaknesses and to be assured of forgiveness (usually within the family but also in school). For this they require the opportunity to lead a life regulated on established custom and order as the 'right way' of doing things. The child needs to be assured of a pattern of behaviour which gives security while recognising his psychological needs.

During this period he comes to accept the fact that he himself will die though at some very distant time far and away beyond his ken; so he loses an interest in death. This transition marks a crisis in a young child's life. He is reaching the final stage when reality is separated from fantasy and he has ceased to have any interest in 'fairy stories' (and Father Christmas). He accepts the fact that 'seeing is believing' and loses to a great extent his interest in the unseen and in the over-simplified image of God which does not fit in to any of the categories which he can accept. Prayer and 'wishing' are largely the same thing to him although he often resorts to many forms of spontaneous prayer when in great need or danger. He often has a strange belief in luck and superstitious rituals although he has moved away from a belief in fairy stories and magic.

It is important, therefore, that nothing in our religious teaching should in any way prevent the child from pressing forward to a new and more realistic view of the world around him. His interest in the world is

becoming more of a mental activity over and above the physical exploration of earlier years: there must be no confusion injected into this new
approach to reality. This means that there should be no attempt to present
religious truth in the guise of scientific truth (cf. the Creation story). He is
already able to distinguish between the literal and the symbolic use of
words although in a limited way, and he should be encouraged to do so
(cf. the two meanings of the word 'heaven' for example).

He needs, therefore:

1. To be helped to find God in the natural order and patterns of life; to accept life as
   basically friendly and to connect God with truth, beauty and goodness.

2. He should be supplied with a great variety of 'images' relating to God.

3. He should be helped to value the Bible as a real source of help in decisions of a
   moral kind (i.e. the evaluation of his 'world').

STAGE ONE

TERM ONE

Outline of Topics	*Suggestions for the Teacher*	
Our Family and our Relatives	The child's interest in homes, families (and animals) can be used to give a framework of belief and practice. When environmental studies or 'cross-subject' teaching are developing, the topics	
1 The child ('Myself')	which are suggested need not be taken in the order as it is given but can be linked with the general work of the class as the situation demands.	
	Relationships within the family and beyond can lead to some understanding of the human race as part of the family of God. Where biblical references are given these are for the teacher only. Stories are best told in the teacher's own words : dramatisation can also play a part.	
	A starting point can often be a collection of snapshots of individual children at different ages beginning with infancy. These may be arranged in a folder or book to show the relationship to other members of the family.	
	The story of Jesus blessing the children.	Luke 18 vv. 15–17
2 My father and mother	Some practical work could be done on the theme, 'How do fathers and mothers show their care for children ?'	
	The birth of Jesus, the flight to Egypt and settling in Nazareth can be used to show the care with which Joseph and Mary worked to make a home for Jesus.	Luke 1 vv. 26–33 Luke 2 vv. 1–20
3 Grandparents and ancestors	A discussion arising from this may lead to a link with places in the locality with which grandparents were connected in some way : local chapels, meeting rooms, churches or other centres of worship. This will show the previous generation's contribution to the life of the community. It can also help to deal with one of the crises of childhood when they are facing the loss of a relative. Death or separation are best dealt with as the need arises but it cannot be avoided ; young children are often concerned about both aspects. In some localities there may be interesting monuments to see and hear about.	
	On not being anxious God makes provision for us On famous men	Matthew 6 vv. 25–35 John 14 vv. 1–2 Ecclesiasticus 44 vv. 1–7

Outline of Topics	Suggestions for the Teacher	
4 Cousins and other relations	The interest becomes nation-wide and world-wide as more distant relations are remembered. Such questions as 'How do we keep in touch?' or, 'How do we remember them?' leads to the thought that there is something more than the physical presence of people: we remember them as persons. This can lead to the writing of letters, writing about, friends and relatives, and on writing about people, whom we have never seen.	
5 Other people; other races	Stories about people who are working abroad at the present time; links with missionaries, engineers, doctors who have gone to help in other countries. How far this can be extended will depend on circumstances and the links which can be made with other subjects.	Church magazines, local papers and other sources of information.
	God is concerned for all people regardless of their colour, race, or creed.	Acts 1 v. 8
6 The work of the family	The family cares for its members. Caring about people is at the heart of the Christian faith. It was shown to be so in the life of Jesus and is an essential part of the work of the church. Children can be helped to see this in being kind and helpful and in showing love for others. There is a great deal of suitable material: children can be helped to look for examples of friendship in everyday happenings at home, in the street (helping others to cross the road safely), and at school.	
	Caring for sick or unfortunate people: the work of doctors, nurses and hospitals.	
	Jesus helped a sick mother	Luke 4 vv. 38–41
	Healing a sick man	Luke 5 vv. 12–16
	This may involve children in many practical activities: writing letters to sick people, those in hospital, special schools, children's homes and helping to collect things for refugees or to alleviate world hunger.	
	Addresses are given in the Appendix 'E'.	
7 Doing jobs for the family	How can we help at home? Making a list of things we might do. Helping outside our homes with children's organisations such as Cubs and Brownies.	
	Learning how some grown-ups help the community.	
	On being helpful to all who are in need.	Matthew 25 vv. 31–40

Outline of Topics	Suggestions for the Teacher

8 Families making their homes

Different ways of making a home is a theme developed in the following books:

Gibson, A. : Homes of the World — Chatto & Windus *
Rudge, K. and Edwards, P : Man Builds Houses — Hamilton (Star Series) *
Morey, J. : Let's Look at Houses and Homes — F. Muller
Webb, P. : All God's Children — Oliphants *

9 The family at worship

The school assembly. The children's part in this : preparing a service. The main Christian festivals that are held and the stories behind them. Worship can arise out of the everyday happenings in the classroom as well as occasionally bringing the teaching in the classroom into a broader context in the school assembly.

10 Learning about God

The concept of the Fatherhood of God develops from the idea of the family. Talking about God to young children has many pitfalls but the attempt cannot be delayed. They will meet the word many times outside the classroom and they will fill it with their own content unless guidance is given. Their ideas are strongly anthropomorphic but this need not cause alarm : it cannot be avoided. The teacher's task is not to ignore it but to refine it. The difficulty is not that they think of God as a man (at this stage) but simply that they think of Him as the wrong sort of man.

How Jesus taught us to think about God. — Matthew 8 vv. 23–27
— Mark 6 vv. 30–44
He cared for His friends and followers. — John 13 vv. 3–9
By caring for those who are unliked and unwanted. — Luke 18 vv. 1–10
By teaching us to care for others. — Matthew 7 v. 12
That God cares for animals and all beautiful things. — Matthew 6 vv. 25–34

Jesus used the example of the shepherd in referring to His work in leading us to God. The stories and incidents in which Jesus is portrayed as a shepherd are not easy for children in urban areas to understand. Some of the children will be unfamiliar with the countryside and they need an introduction to the rural and the agricultural background of Palestine in Bible-times. The theme of sheep and shepherds will prepare the way for many of the sayings and some of the parables.
Lambs in springtime : sheep are often 'foolish' and cause the farmers endless trouble by breaking through hedges and fences and straying.
They give us wool for many purposes.

38

Outline of Topics	Suggestions for the Teacher	
	The shepherd is the protector of the flock.	
	Some Bible-stories about sheep and shepherds:	
	Wells and the watering of sheep:	Genesis 24
	Abraham's kindness to Abimelech	Genesis 21 vv. 25–34
	Jacob's kindness to Rachel	Genesis 29 vv. 1–14
	David the shepherd boy	I Samuel 16
	A lost sheep	Luke 15 vv. 4–6
	A good shepherd	John 10 vv. 1–5
	A bad shepherd	John 10 vv. 12 ff.
	A book on this theme:	
	Dingwall, R.: Sheep and Shepherds	Rupert Hart-Davis

Jesus and His Family

The village of Nazareth can be introduced as a not too intrusive comparison.

1 Home and family life

Our houses as compared with those in Palestine.

The kind of house in Nazareth.

The steps leading to the flat roof from outside the house where people could sleep or work.

It was an additional space, a spare room.   Mark 13 v. 15

Lighting in the house

Slits in the walls as compared with our windows. At night the 'candle' – most probably a rushlight burning in oil c.f. our word 'kindle'.   Matthew 5 v. 15

Going to bed

The demanding neighbour. The family slept on mats on a raised part of the floor. The animals (if any) were given space in the same room.   Luke 11 vv. 5–10

Shopping arrangements

The modern supermarket compared with the market places.

The well – a story.   Genesis 24

A day in the life of a modern family c.f. with the work of Joseph and his sons. The implements he would make or repair. Children at play.   Luke 7 v. 32

The work of Mary and the family	Luke 13 vv. 20–21
Making flour and bread	Matthew 24 v. 41
Skin bottles and earthenware jars	Mark 2 v. 22
The clothes they wore	
Repairs to clothing	Mark 2 v. 21
Garments were made from wool, goat's	Proverbs 31 vv. 10–31
hair or camel's hair homespun and	
woven on simple handlooms. Rich	Matthew 3 v. 4
people used silk from the far east.	

2 Clothing

The men wore a shirt of wool or linen from head to ankle; a cloak of striped wool at night or in bad weather. To protect them from the sun they wore headsquares. Round their waist they had a girdle of leather with slits for knives or coins. On their feet they wore sandals of leather with a thong and tied round the ankle. The women wore a veil ; they usually had rings on their fingers, bracelets on their arms, and strings of coins as part of their head-dress.   Luke 15 vv. 8–10

3   Birthdays

The emphasis should be on the joy which the family feels on the arrival of a new life. This can be seen to be the reason for the celebrations associated with birthdays.

Celebrating birthdays : each birthday is a beginning. Postage stamps to celebrate the beginning of a movement, stage, or organisation. The King or Queen has a birthday : a royal salute. Non-birthday presents : presents are often given by the one whose birthday it is in thankfulness — the sovereign's birthday honours. Foolish ideas about stars and birthdays.

4   The celebration of Christmas

The beginning of a new era : the meaning of Anno Domini. The Nativity.

The animals, sheep, shepherds and oxen.   Luke 2 vv. 8–20

The great interest shown in birthdays and the promise of things to come (not to be taken in detail — it shows the great interest taken in a special birthday).   Matthew 2 vv. 1–17

There are many ways of celebrating this event in a way that gives it special significance to children. It can provide an opportunity for remembering God's care for us, and all his creation, by expressing care for people.

Simple ceremonies of all kinds can be devised. How Christmas is celebrated in other lands.
A festival of homes.
A nativity play.

5   The Flight to Egypt

This helps to round off the cycle of stories ; the story of the Massacre of the Innocents is of doubtful value. While Matthew says Jesus was born before Herod's death, Luke, by mentioning Quirinus suggests that it was after. In place of the slaughter of the Bethlehem children, Luke gives the story of Simeon and the return to Nazareth. This story might provide a link with the care that has to be given in choosing the right place and circumstances for making a home ; what father and mother do for us when we are very young.

40

Outline of Topics	*Suggestions for the Teacher*	
	This could lead to some practical work for refugee children.	Matthew 2 vv. 16–23
6 Simeon's Song of Praise	Although this does not fit in easily with Matthew's account it has a special significance for children as it gives us one of the great hymns of the Church.	
	An expression of hope for the world.	Luke 2 vv. 25–35

Books of Reference

Johnson, L.	Christmas Stories round the World	Warne
Pearson, N. F.	Stories of Christmas Customs	Ladybird
	The Christian Year Picture Book 1	S.P.C.K.*.

TERM TWO

Where and how Jesus grew up	The intention is to give background information about the life and times when Jesus lived, as a preparation for the deeper understanding of the Bible later on. The topics provide many opportunities for dramatisation by the children, model-making and art, as well as writing.	
1. The Village	An imaginative picture of Nazareth where Jesus lived. Wells and water supplies; what happens where the water is scanty and rainfall uncertain. The importance of water to us, and ways in which we get our water; washing, bathing, cleaning, drinking, watering the land and the animals.	Luke 14 v. 21
	Examples from the Bible: Quarrels about wells	Genesis 21 v. 2
		Genesis 26 vv. 12–22
	A thirsty child	Genesis 21 vv. 14–20
	A drink of water for David	II Samuel 23 vv. 13–17
	Foot-washing after a journey	Genesis 24 v. 31 ff.
		Luke 7 v. 44
2. The weather and farming	Dust and the animals: it can be bitterly cold at night in winter in Palestine.	Luke 2 v. 8
	The former and latter rains (October and April). Corn and bread: to show how essential is bread and to prepare the way for the teaching of Jesus about the 'Bread of Life'.	
	Joseph and the famine in Egypt	Genesis 41
	A boy helps Jesus with bread	John 6 vv. 1–13
	Bread for widows	Acts 4 vv. 32–37
		Acts 6 vv. 1–6
	A useful book for pupils:	
	Hughes, M.: The Importance of Bread	Rupert Hart-Davis

Outline of Topics	Suggestions for the Teacher

3. The School   School was usually held in the Synagogue but occasionally in a special building. It was for boys 6–15 years of age only : girls were taught at home by their mothers to cook, sew, embroider and grind corn. The boys learned to read and write. They began by making letters in sand (John 8 vv. 6–8) writing from right to left using a stylus and wax tablets as they grew more expert. One of the first passages Jesus would learn would be the Shema.

'Hear, O Israel : the Lord Our God is one Lord : and thou shalt love the Lord thy God with all thine heart, and with all thy soul and with all thy mind.'   Deuteronomy 6 vv. 4–5

We know that Jesus knew the books (scrolls) of the Law, the Prophets and the Psalms.   Luke 4 vv. 16–20

The boys faced their teacher in a semi-circle, sometimes standing, at other times squatting on the floor.

4. The Synagogue   This was a rectangular building with seats on either side. The women and young girls usually sat in a gallery near the entrance. Men and women never sat together. At the far end the scrolls were kept and in front of them a veil. A platform was placed in front of the Ark where the scrolls were kept. A man (any boy over the age of 13) from the congregation read from them ; the preacher sat down to make the address, the service would include prayers, the reading, and saying of the Shema.

5. A Day of Worship   How we spend our Sundays. The Jewish Sabbath in the time of Jesus. This was the seventh day of the week (our Saturdays as now with our Jewish friends – not Sunday).   Luke 6 vv. 1–5

A trumpet was sounded three times to announce the beginning of the Sabbath (at sunset on Friday). All work ceased and the Sabbath lamp was lit. On the Sabbath people were told, 'Hasten to the Synagogue with quick steps' and go home with 'slow lingering steps'.

A Sabbath day's journey (about 980 yards)   Acts 1 v. 12

Books of reference about Jewish customs :

Simpson, W. W. : Jewish Prayer and Worship   S.C.M.*
Wouk, H. : This is my God   Cape *

42

Outline of Topics	*Suggestions for the Teacher* *

Learning about God

Children become interested at an early age in the stars and heavenly bodies as well as the clouds, the wind and all the phenomena of nature. They are fascinated by growing things both great and small. Questions of many kinds are asked : how was the world made ? Are there any more worlds where people live ? These are fundamental questions leading to the concepts of God and his creation. The beginnings of religious thought are to be found in the sense of awe and mystery associated with these questions.

1 God as Creator

As in the remote stages of history, when men thought of God in human form, so young children picture God as an adult figure. This is related to their experience of adults who represent power and authority. This is an anthropomorphic view of God which, in time, has to be refined. Poetry has a large part to play in this process and many of the psalms reveal this in their portrayal of the awe and wonder with which the Hebrews viewed creation. The best way to experience the creative activity of God is to provide opportunities for children to be creative themselves. Such passages as the following could be read and the children encouraged to express their reactions in plastic media, colour or by music and movement. Some may wish to memorise short extracts or use them in choral verse speaking.

Bless the Lord O my soul	Psalm 104 vv. 1–9
Make a joyful noise unto the Lord	Psalm 100 vv. 1–5
O give thanks to the Lord	Psalm 136 vv. 1–9

Practical work can be linked to any situation in the school where plants or animals are taken care of. So far as this is possible this work should be linked to the kind of exploration arising from the children's activities.

God's care for his creation.	Matthew 10 vv. 29–31

2 God's care for us : he supplies our needs

A theme on the harvests of the world could be arranged bringing in the seasonal work of the farmer. God and man working together for our good.

The power to grow is in God's creation.	Mark 4 vv. 28–29

These topics could be brought to a focal point by means of a Spring festival of plants and flowers celebrating the return of life after the winter. In olden times in Palestine the Spring festival was celebrated at the time of the full-moon and the lambing season.

3 What Jesus taught us about God	The image of God is linked in the child's mind with the picture of Jesus as portrayed in his work as teacher, healer, guide and friend. The agricultural background to so many of the stories is not familiar to most children and they need help before they can see the meaning behind the stories. Help of this kind is given in the series :

Dingwall, R. : Sheep and Shepherds	Rupert Hart-Davis

The shepherd's work was of great importance in protecting his flock. God's care for us is shown in the shepherd stories.

The Lord is my shepherd	Psalm 23
Shepherds watching their flocks	Luke 2 vv. 8–20
The lost sheep	Luke 15 vv. 3–7

4 Jesus, by helping those who were in need, showed us how God cares for people	Simon's wife's mother	Mark 1 vv. 29–31
	At the pool of Bethesda	John 5 vv. 2–9
	The epileptic cured	Mark 9 vv. 14–27
	The Samaritan healed	Luke 17 vv. 11–13

5 Jesus taught us to think of God as a loving Father	The Lord's Prayer	Matthew 6 vv. 9–13

'Our Father'	All children have their heroes who are strong and powerful figures ; their ideal is probably an amalgam of many such. What is important is that they shall admire them for their good qualities and not just for their strength. The idea of 'father' should crown them all. Jesus should be portrayed as a strong character whose gentleness grew out of strength as shown in his courage in facing hostile crowds, walking long distances, climbing hills and spending long periods alone in the wilderness.

'Thy Kingdom'	A kingdom is where a king rules : God's Kingdom is wherever his laws are kept and the main law is that of love. It grows from something quite small into a strong and powerful feeling that makes us want to do what is right.

Jesus told a story about his Kingdom : it is about a small seed that grew into a tree.

The grain of mustard seed ; the brassica nigra which grows to a height of some 10–16 feet.	Mark 4 vv. 30–32 Daniel 4 vv. 10–12

Jesus also told us about his rules for the Kingdom : he would be here at our side to make the rules easier to keep.

The oxen yoked together.   Matthew 11 vv. 28–30

Children are not used to the agricultural background and they need descriptions and good pictures to help them : in the 'yoke' the oxen were linked together and a bond of sympathy grew up between them.

6   The Easter Story

The emphasis should be on the risen Lord as seen in people's lives, not in the death and crucifixion which need careful study later. The story should be told in simple language by the teacher. The friends of Jesus lost heart after the terrible events of the Passion : their realisation that Jesus was with them always. 'When two or three are gathered together in my name. . . .

The journey to Emmaus.   Luke 24 vv. 13–35

There are many ways of developing these themes from children's experience. Life and death are often discussed usually in relation to the loss of a pet, a dead animal, or an accident and such moments provide the means of exploring this experience in greater depth ; see 'Readiness for Religion' Ronald Goldman – pp. 90 and 91.

Opportunities for practical work occur in connection with almost every item so that the fullest participation by the children in drama, art and the actual working out of a project is possible.

TERM THREE

Family Rules

This is a continuation of the theme on families : the school as an extension of the family. Children are beginning to break away from simple obedience to father and mother to whom they have looked as the final authority on right and wrong. Some will have turned to other adults (e.g. the teacher) for their guiding moral principles. The school as a community begins to play a larger role in standards of behaviour and 'what is done' and 'what is not done' affects personal relationships.

1   Showing Courage

This may not be the first rule of the Christian community but it is the most likely to win a positive response from children. They are able to look to their own experience for examples of personal courage and may be able to

give accounts of situations in which
they had to be brave. (Going to the
dentist or being lost in a crowd.) They
will accept the fact of other kinds of
courage, not just facing danger of a
physical kind but such things as
standing up for the weaker against the
bully, not stealing when tempted to do
so, keeping a promise when it would be
easier not to.

The story of Gideon and the three hundred. (Gideon has no use for the fearful and trembling : those who lapped like dogs could hold their weapons in readiness. God saves by a few as well as by many.)	Judges 7 vv. 1–8
Jesus faced danger in Judea	John 11 vv. 7–10
Jesus faced hostile crowds at Nazareth	Luke 4 vv. 28–30
Peter is afraid and tells a lie	Luke 22 vv. 54–62
He is forgiven : he shows his courage	Acts 4 vv. 5–20

2 Serving others A fundamental rule of the family.
Children can make their own list of
things they can help in at home. Doing
useful jobs ; giving help to other
children in schools and outside – in
crossing the road, in finding their way
about the school etc. Doing 'good turns'
e.g. Cubs, Brownies, Scouts and
Guides.

Giving for others : the widow's mite.	Mark 12 vv. 41–44
Helping those in need.	Matthew 25 vv. 35–40
The boy who helped Jesus	John 6 vv. 5–12

3 Being fair Learning 'to keep one's head' is a
practical form of this.

Showing mercy : David spares Saul	I Samuel 26
Jesus warns against harbouring resentment.	Matthew 5 vv. 22–24
On not being spiteful : true forgiveness.	Matthew 5 vv. 38–44

4 Being patient The story of John Milton, Helen Keller,
Dr. and Madam Curie, Louis Pasteur.

5 Being cheerful The Christmas Carol	Matthew 5 vv. 11–13
St. Dunstan's for the Blind.	

6 Kindness to animals The story of Peter Scott and the nature reserves in Gloucestershire and Lancashire.	Matthew 12 v. 11
The R.S.P.C.A., P.D.S.A., St. Francis of Assissi.	Luke 14 v. 5

Each of these can be developed as a
topic by children working in groups
preparing booklets on such themes as
'Courage', 'Service', 'Being fair'
'Kindness to animals'. The Bible
references are for the teacher and may
be used to summarise the work or to

give a small link with the Bible as a
place where help can be gained
(working from the child's experience to
the Bible and its teaching).

Many other stories can be added to the
list:

Patrick and his work in Ireland
Bede of Jarrow
William Wilberforce and slavery
Pastor Niemöller in prison
Joan of Arc and her trial
Octavia Hill and her work for others.

Children could be encouraged to look
for the qualities that made them great:
most of the characters possessed all the
virtues mentioned above.

Books for further reading:

Bull, N. J.: The Great Christian Stories	Hulton
Garlick, P.: Conqueror of Darkness	Lutterworth
Prescott, D. M.: Saints for Nowadays	Blandford*

**Prayer and
Worship**

With a growing sense of independence
children look for security of a new kind;
they need to know that they 'belong to
somewhere' and to find a sense of
solidarity within the groups of which
they are members. For this reason
problems arising from adjustments
between individuals ('falling out' and
'making up') become more personal
and even intellectual: this marks the
beginning of a deepening sense of
moral values. They love to hear stories
about people with whom they can
identify themselves in order that they
may feel what it is like to be another
person and so develop a sense of
sympathy and understanding. They also
need heroes to imitate whose behaviour
is worth imitating. This can be dealt
with in the scripture lessons as well as
in the acts of worship which can be
made to centre round great lives. Their
problems can sometimes be dealt with
in the dramatisation of situations as
part of an act of worship (c.f. the B.B.C.
School Services for Juniors). This can
often provide a link with the work in the
classroom.

As the child moves from his world of
belief in God as a kind of superman, he
comes to accept the idea of God's
omnipresence. The more intelligent
children will have reached this stage.
With this comes a new emphasis on
prayer, on God's control of events, and
on God's punishment. There is a
growing awareness that words and
pictures can be used symbolically.

Children can be encouraged to make up prayers, to write poetry as well as to make hymns of a simple kind related to real experience for use in assembly : for example about saying 'Thank you' for many things we take for granted. The words should be the children's own. Although archaic forms of words may have little meaning for children, we should not forget that there are prayers of great simplicity and depth of meaning which have been handed down through the ages. These too have their place.

1 Forms of Prayer

Prayers of thankfulness.

Prayers about the wonders of the world.

Prayers about special occasions such as holidays and birthdays.

Prayers on life themes on which the children may be working.

Prayers in connection with the Christian Festivals.

Two great hymns may be looked at again :
The Magnificat.   Luke 1 vv. 46–56
The Nunc Dimittis.   Luke 2 vv. 29–35

2 The Lord's Prayer

In the previous teaching about the nature of God the basic idea of 'Our Father' has been introduced. Most children are beginning to think less about God as a superman : they are coming to accept his omnipresence, but there is often an increase in personal opinion, of questioning and doubt. There is a new awareness that words can be used symbolically and this opens up the use of the word 'heaven'. The more intelligent can grasp that there are two meanings to this word as in

'Our Father in Heaven . . . .'   Matthew 6 vv. 9–13
'Thy Kingdom come ; thy will be done . . . .'   Matthew 6 v. 10

Jesus doing God's will, making His choice, asking for God's help.
'And do not bring us to the test. . . .'   Matthew 6 v. 13

Heaven is where and when God speaks to us.   Matthew 3 vv. 13–15
Matthew 4 vv. 1–11

The story of Samuel (in teacher's own words).   I Samuel 3 vv. 1–11
I Samuel 3 vv. 15–18

3 Work that children can do in connection with worship

The language and content of worship should be related to the children's experience. School occasions and events may be used as themes and, so too may lessons in the classroom. Preparing the room or hall, and contributing their own prayers and

Outline of Topics	*Suggestions for the Teacher*

readings will help them to feel that they are sharing an experience with others and so to add to their confidence by participation in the service.

Some possible themes :

1 On caring for others, work in connection with Save the Children, Christian Aid or Oxfam.

2 Kindness to birds and animals, bird protection, bird sanctuaries, sick animals and nature reserves. Contact can be made with organisations concerned with these :
The Council for Nature, 41 Queen's Gate, London S.W.7.
Royal Society for the Protection of Birds, The Lodge, Sandy, Beds.
Royal Society for the Prevention of of Cruelty to Animals, 105 Jermyn Street, London S.W.1.

3 Instances of compassion shown by Jesus :

To friends and followers	Matthew 8 vv. 23–27
Giving them rest after work	Mark 6 vv. 30–44
The golden rule	Matthew 7 v. 12

4 The lives of great men and women who have worked for good causes may also be the subject of acts of worship which they can help in preparing.

Books of Reference

Bull, N. J.	In His name : prayers for the church and the world	Lutterworth *
Scott, E.	Stories for School Prayers	S.P.C.K.

The Festival of Whitsuntide

Symbolism is part of the young child's experience. Although it commemorates a phase of history in terms of religious intolerance which is best forgotten, the yearly 'bonfire' still symbolises the sense of community when they gather round. It may be almost entirely a matter of 'fun and games' but there is more than this in the life of a youth, cub or scout in the enjoyment of a camp fire. To the Hebrew, fire symbolised the presence Yahweh : the theophany to Moses.

Outline of Topics	*Suggestions for the Teacher*	
1 How fire, heat and light give us life and the power to do things. The sun warms the earth to make plants grow and give us light to see by.	Moses and the burning bush	Exodus 3 vv. 1–6
	The pillar of fire	Exodus 13 vv. 20–22
	(The stories to be told in the teacher's own words.)	
	Jesus as the light of the world	Luke 2 v. 32
		John 1 v. 4
		John 3 v. 19

Outline of Topics	*Suggestions for the Teacher*
	The story of Whitsuntide. (This festival is difficult to deal with at this age. It is sufficient to show how the power that Jesus gave is seen in the lives of those who follow him.)
2 Stories of those who follow 'The Light'	Children can be encouraged to read about and discover for themselves stories of people who have done great things for the neighbourhood, gone abroad, or worked as missionaries. Press cuttings, articles in magazines and sometimes the relatives of children can provide information which can be the basis of written work. It could be arranged for the children to work in groups in order to produce booklets on special activities such as 'Teachers and Schools in Africa', 'Doctors and Nurses' and any activity which may be of interest to children.

Books for further study

	Eagle Books	Lutterworth [*]
Clarke, E.	Standard Bearers	U.L.P. [*]
Krall, B. C.	Stories of Favourite Saints	R.E.P. [*]
Rhodes, M. G.	A Little Book of Saints	Mowbrays [*]

STAGE TWO

Outline of Topics	*Suggestions for the Teacher*	
Joy and Thankfulness	This can be introduced in a variety of ways in art, music and movement and appropriate readings.	
1 For creation	The 'Creation' as linked with music and movement by Heinz Kuhne. (MacMillan, London). The most important phrase is, 'In the beginning God'. No attempts should be made to link geological epochs as we know them with this story. Any resemblance is fortuitous; the writer was beginning to see the basis for a systematic and orderly Creation but not in our scientific way of looking at it.	Genesis 1 vv. 1–31
2 For Home	Things to be thankful for, but very often taken for granted. The food we eat, the comforts of home life (perhaps contrasted with a home in a less fortunate situation – in one of the under-developed countries of the world). The part father and mother play in making a home. This can be linked with environmental and other studies connected with 'homes'.	
3 For Nature	There is an obvious link at this stage with nature study, harvests and other activities coming within the experience of children. Jesus' interest in nature: his perception for what was beautiful.	
	(i) The lilies of the valley (a lily in the New Testament may be a flower such as the iris, gladiolus or the poppy-anemone which in Spring paints the plains and valleys of Palestine with bright scarlet).	Matthew 13 vv. 4–9
	(ii) The Sower – as a story (it is not necessary to moralise about this parable and its treatment as an allegory is out of place at this stage. Jesus almost certainly took this scene from life and put in much detail as a matter of observation).	Matthew 13 v. 3

Jewish festivals

Long before Jesus could go to school or even attend the Synagogue He would be impressed by the religious atmosphere of His home by the observance of the *Sabbath* and the festive seasons.

Outline of Topics	_Suggestions for the Teacher_	
	The Sabbath is observed by Jews on Saturday.	Genesis 2 v. 2 Exodus 20 vv. 8–10
	The Christian Sunday is the first day of the week when we remember the Resurrection.	Luke 24 vv. 1–2
	The festivals can be used as the basis for simple dramatisation in order to illustrate some of the main points in Jewish history mentioned in the New Testament. In some cases they form a link with Festivals of the Christian Year.	
1 The Jewish New Year	This comes in the Autumn. The Head of the family would spend time casting up his accounts for the year.	
2 The Day of Atonement	A very solemn day reminding the family of the Day of Judgement (settling their accounts with God).	
3 The Festival of Tabernacles	To commemorate God's bounty and care in providing a harvest, in this case the harvest of fruit, oil and wine. In Palestine there are two periods of harvest. This is the second one and comes when the weather is mild and it is pleasant to be out of doors. The people erect 'booths' or tents made of branches from trees and they live in them, or at any rate have meals in them, for a whole week. This is to remind them of their wanderings in the wilderness when they had no permanent homes. At the end of the festivities (towards the end of October) the rainy season begins ; these are the 'former rains' of the Bible times.	
4 The Passover	This commemorates their national deliverance from slavery in Egypt. Year after year it recalls as a living drama, the great fact of their escape under the leadership of Moses.	Exodus 14
	'And Israel saw the great works which the Lord did against the Egyptians, and the people feared the Lord ; and they believed in the Lord and in his servant Moses.'	Exodus 14 v. 31 Deuteronomy 6 vv. 20–25
5 The Feast of Dedication		John 10 vv. 22–41
6 'Festival of Lights'	This can be linked with the Christmas festivities. It commemorates the restoration of the Temple and its services after the desecration by Antiochus Ephiphanes in 164 B.C. He	

Outline of Topics	Suggestions for the Teacher	
	was a foreigner who tried to root out the Jewish religion after invading the country. He placed an altar to Zeus in the Temple in the eyes of the Jews 'the abomination of desolation'.	Matthew 24 v. 15

The Festival was a time of great rejoicing when the houses were lit with candles. The celebrations also brought to mind the Jewish hopes for a restoration of kings descended from David who would rid them of the Romans. This is connected with the excitement of the Jews when they heard of Jesus. They asked, not unnaturally, was He the promised Messiah?

These Festivals can be introduced in a variety of ways: as an occasion for dramatisation or writing about episodes from different points of view. Some indirect teaching on the Hebrew tradition and their way of looking at history in terms of their special mission to the world could be given.

Teacher's books of reference

Deans, A. C.	The World Christ Knew	Eyre & Spottiswoode *
Mathews, Basil	The World in which Jesus lived	O.U.P.
Bouquet, A. C.	Everyday Life in New Testament Times	Batsford
Carter, W. A.	Sons of the Law	Church Mission to the Jews

TERM TWO

Outline of Topics	Suggestions for the Teacher	
Meals Jesus would have shared	The central importance of bread as a life-giving food can be introduced by a theme on the actual process of making bread now as compared with the times when Jesus lived. There could be a link with the science teaching by means of a practical illustration with yeast and flour.	
1 **How bread is made**	How flour is made today by factory methods. Millers of different times and places. Grinding the corn in the time of Jesus.	
	'You shall make loaves of fine wheat flour'.	Exodus 29 v. 2
	The threshing floor: grinding by hand.	
	The leaven: bread in the time of Jesus was principally in the form of thin cakes baked upon the hearth or in the oven.	
	The poorer people ate bread made of barley meal and used oil instead of butter.	

Outline of Topics	Suggestions for the Teacher	
2 How did they eat ?	A meal in the time of Jesus may be compared with our modern way of dining at tables etc. There were no chairs : the family reclined on cushions or squatted on their haunches. The well-to-do reclined comfortably on cushions or couches. The food was placed on a low bench and could include the meat of goats, lambs and calves. The people washed their hands before meals (but the disciples were accused of forgetting to do this!). The head of the house would cut a piece from the whole loaf, or cake, or wafer and say the Blessing. Then he would bless the wine.	Mark 7 vv. 1–8 Psalm 24 v. 1
3 What was the meal like ?	Very different were the meals of the poor who often ate locusts fried in flour : the locust referred to here is the seed or sweet pulp of the carob tree used as food by many people in the Near East. Eggs were a common article of diet. Sometimes the diners dipped their bread in goat's milk. The more prosperous would have soup made of vegetables. Bread and cheese were often eaten. Cucumbers, lentils, beans and peas were eaten in the proper season. References to food and meals are made in the accounts of John the Baptist and The Prodigal Son.	Matthew 3 v. 4 Luke 15 v. 16 and 23
4 Some very special occasions when Jesus shared a meal	Meals were very important as these were occasions when the family and their friends met together. Hospitality was one of the most prized and sacred virtues. Jesus shared in many family situations :	
	The marriage at Cana	John 2 vv. 1–12
	The feeding of the Five Thousand	John 6 vv. 1–14
	Martha and Mary at Bethany	Luke 10 vv. 38–42
	At the house of Simon the Pharisee	Luke 7 vv. 36–50
5 Stories Jesus told about meals	This can be linked with the children's experience of family occasions such as birthday parties and Christmas reunions. The theme of two great stories is that a forgiving spirit and forgiveness are a reflection of God's love for men.	
	The Great Supper	Luke 14 vv. 16–24
	The Prodigal Son	Luke 15 vv. 11–32
6 The Passover Meal	The story can be taken a little further than when it was mentioned in the earlier lessons. It was the Jewish Festival associated with the greatest gladness. It is especially a children's	

Outline of Topics	Suggestions for the Teacher	
	festival. Jesus would usually have taken part in this at home. It commemorates two things :	
	(i) The 'passing over' of the homes whose lintels and door-posts were sprinkled with the blood of sacrifice.	Exodus 11 v. 4 ff.
	(ii) The deliverance of the people of Israel from slavery.	Exodus 13 vv. 3–10

7 What was 'The preparation for the Passover'

The general cleaning up and packing in order to be ready for the journey is still re-enacted and is said to be the origin of 'spring cleaning'. All leavened bread was removed from the house. On the evening before the Passover, the head of the family, a light in one hand, and a pair of tongs in the other, searched the house for any scraps of food or leaven.

John 19 v. 14

The removal of the dead before the Passover was part of this preparation.

Mark 15 v. 42
Matthew 27 v. 62

Once or twice in their lifetime Jews also went to Jerusalem to observe the Passover. They attended services in the Temple.

Easter

The triumphal entry to Jerusalem. (Note the curious attempt to interpret the prophecy Zechariah 9 v. 9 quite literally.)

Matthew 21 vv. 1–11

The Last Supper

Matthew 26 vv. 26ff

The trial and crucifixion

Matthew 27

The Resurrection

Matthew 28 vv. 1–10

Side by side with this should go the experience of Springtime : life returning after the apparent deadness of winter. This can be symbolised by a *Spring Festival.* The brutality and other details of the Crucifixion should not be dealt with or dwelt on at this stage. Better to experience the Resurrection in terms of life as the children experience it.

Books of reference for the teacher

Carter, W. H.	Sons of the Law	Church Mission to the Jews
Rattey, B. E.	A Short History of the Hebrews	O.U.P.
Deursen, A. van	Illustrated Dictionary of Bible Manners and Customs	Marshall Morgan

TERM THREE

Outline of Topic　　*Suggestions for the Teacher*

**Men and women
Jesus knew**

1　Roman
　　soldiers

Jesus would have seen Roman soldiers
individually, and marching in
companies along the two main
highways which passed near Nazareth.
Imperial couriers accompanied by
Roman soldiers would also be seen.
Although the busy little town (with
some 15,000 inhabitants at the time of
Jesus) was in a hollow, the low hills
which he could climb gave a view of the
plain of Esdraelon across which
travellers went in caravans and where
so much Jewish history had been
decided in battles. The traveller's main
preoccupation was commerce.

The Centurion's servant	Luke 7 vv. 1–10
The Centurion who watched	Luke 23 v. 47

See the following articles giving
background information :

J. W. Bowman : 'Life and Teaching of Jesus'	Peake's Commentary 1962 edition
H. G. Wood : 'Life and Teaching of Jesus'	Peake's Commentary 1920 edition

Both articles contain valuable
information about the contemporary
scene.

2　The
　　Tax-
　　gatherers

The tax-gatherer stood not only for
heavy taxation but for the authority of a
foreign occupying power. Naturally, he
was distrusted and despised by patriotic
Jews. The life of a tax-gatherer,
especially a Jewish tax-gatherer, must
have been a difficult and unpleasant
one.

Matthew 9 vv. 0–12

The parable of the Importunate Friend
shows us one side of life which must
have been familiar to Jesus. The people
Jesus knew had no great margin in their
housekeeping accounts ; the supply of
daily bread baked at home was not
enough to meet sudden and unexpected
demands. They were not poor in the
sense of people who are nearly
destitute but they did not find it easy to
make ends meet.

Luke 11 vv. 5ff

Clothes had to last a long time, so :

Sewing patches on old garments	Luke 5 v. 36
Being anxious about tomorrow's bread was part of their daily experience.	Matthew 6 v.v. 25–34

3　The Ruler
　　who was
　　very rich

Not all the neighbours of Jesus
belonged to the poorer classes. Jesus
told stories from His own experience.
He would know, from what others told

Him at any rate, about the local manor-house where the influential owner lived with his retinue of slaves. There were too many foolish men in Galilee whose sole aim in life was getting richer, and richer, and so more influential. The conditions of life for those who served would be familiar. The slaves must wait up for their master when he went out to dine ; the slaves also differed in rank and ability. Some had many talents, others less.

Dives and Lazarus	Luke 16 v. 19ff
The Talents	Matthew 25 v. 14ff
New and bigger barns	Luke 12 vv. 16–21

The moral and theological significance of these stories should not be stressed. It is sufficient at this stage, to present the material in terms of the reality of the situations which Jesus used in his contacts with people. The stories were based on the Galilean way of life.

4 The leader of the Jews : Nicodemus

Jesus grew up when there was a great deal of discussion about the Messiah, when He would come and what He would do. Some looked for a coming of the Kingdom of God through war ; others thought the age of the Messiah would come by keeping the Jewish (religious) laws very strictly. Yet others expected some wonderful supernatural event (the end of the world).

The Galileans seem on the whole to have been less gloomy and less fanatical than the southerners of Judea. Nevertheless, the Zealots were men of great influence ; perhaps the greater friendliness of many of the Jews with Gentiles made the extremists more extreme. Jesus spent his young days in and around Nazareth with journeys to Jerusalem for the feasts and special occasions. The Galileans had a 'country' accent and held lightly to the strict Jewish laws. They were, on the whole, less rigid than the Judaeans.

Nicodemus is a puzzled man ; because he wants to keep clear of any new movement until he knows more about Jesus, who has made a deep impression on him, he comes by night.   John 3 vv. 1–15

There was greater friendliness between Jews and Romans.   Luke 7 vv. 2–10

The 'country' accent of Galileans   **Matthew 26 vv. 69–75**

5 The sick people

Why were there so many sick people ? We have come to accept our medical knowledge as a matter of course. No such things were available in Our Lord's time. Usually, sickness of the mind and sickness of other kinds were regarded as due to evil or demoniacal spirits. The country had been swept by invaders, endured the putting down of insurrections and as an aftermath of the cruelties and sufferings of war, many innocent people suffered. Jesus went about 'doing good'; He put into practice His own principles.

The blind man : Bartimaeus	Mark 10 vv. 46ff
A lame man	John 5 vv. 3–9
The demoniac cured	Matthew 9 v. 32
(and many other examples)	
A leper is cured	Luke 5 v. 12ff
The mission of healing	Matthew 9 v. 35

6   The women folk

What position in society did women have? How did Jesus treat women? Many of His closest friends were women. Their acceptance by Jesus as in no way inferior to men was quite revolutionary '... in Christ Jesus there can be no male nor female'. Women, as were slaves, were often regarded as the property of someone, with no special claims to live a life in which a free choice was open to them. Jesus always acted with kindness, courtesy and understanding to women, many of whom became His disciples. This would be regarded as very unusual and eccentric.

Mary of Magdala, Joanna, Susanna	Luke 8 vv. 1–3
	Luke 20 v. 1–2
Mary and Martha	Luke 10 vv. 38ff
The woman of Samaria	John 4 vv. 7–9
His mother and other women when he died.	John 19 vv. 25–27

7   The men with power

The ruling aristocrats belonged to the Sadducees, the more worldly-minded of the Jewish leaders. When the Sanhedrin (strangely enough a Greek word meaning a 'council') met as a court of law, to try someone, they sat in a semi-circle with the accused in the middle.

Caiaphas, the High Priest A.D. 18–36	John 11 v. 49
	Matthew 26 vv. 3–4
He condemns Jesus	Matthew 26 v. 65

Herod Antipas (deposed A.D. 40). He was crafty, cruel and loved luxury. He married Herodias, the wife of his brother Philip (not the Tetrarch but another). For this he was rebuked by John the Baptist.

He puts John the Baptist in prison	Luke 3 v. 19

Outline of Topics	*Suggestions for the Teacher*	
	He has him killed	Matthew 14
	He is curious about Jesus	Luke 9 v. 9
	Pontius Pilate (A.D. 26 to 36). A sample of the baser sort of Roman.	
	Full of brutal contempt for the people he ruled, he brought the idolatrous signs of the army into Jerusalem (graven images) ; he was far from squeamish of bloodshed and crushed riots mercilessly : he ordered continual executions. At last the Samaritans (of all people) complained to the Emperor. He was removed and it is believed, banished to Gaul. By contrast he has been canonised by the Abyssinian Church (June 25th) no doubt to emphasise their view that the Jews were mainly the guilty ones. Legend has been busy.	Matthew 27 v. 2, vv. 11–14 Luke 3 v. 1 Luke 23 vv. 1–25 Luke 23 vv. 50–52
8 The closest friends of Jesus	It is suggested that children might make short biographies of the Apostles. How they became friends of Jesus.	
	What was their work for Jesus ?	Matthew 10
9 The Twelve	Simon – renamed Cephas–Peter, missionary to Rome and crucified there, and	Matthew 4 vv. 18–22
	Andrew. They lived in Bethsaida and afterwards at Capernaum. Their father's name was Jonah.	
	James the elder – beheaded by Herod A.D. 44, and	Matthew 4 v. 21
	John the beloved disciple – laboured among churches in Asia Minor, especially Ephesus. They lived at Bethsaida and later at Jerusalem. Their parents were Zebedee and Salome.	Matthew 4 v. 21
	James the less or younger, and	Jude 1
	Jude. Their parents were Cleophas and Mary. Both lived in Galilee.	Jude 1
	Philip. Lived at Bethsaida.	John 1 v. 43
	Bartholomew, surnamed Nathaniel. Lived at Cana in Galilee.	Matthew 10 v. 3
	Matthew, surname Levi – father named Alphaeus. Tax-gatherer.	Matthew 9 v. 9–12
	Thomas, surnamed or nicknamed Didymus 'the twin'. Lived in Galilee.	John 11 v. 16
	Simon (known as Zelotes). Lived in Galilee.	Matthew 10 v. 4
	Judas Iscariot. Lived at Kerioth in Judaea.	Matthew 26 v. 14

N.B. The term surname is used in its modern sense. Surnames were not in general use until much later. Most people would be known by the place where they lived — Simon of Bethsaida, or by their occupation as in Simon the fisherman.

Books of reference for the teacher

Bouquet, A. C.	Everyday Life in New Testament Times	Batsford
Carpenter, E.	Life in Palestine when Jesus Lived	Lindsey Press
Josephus	The Jewish War	Penguin Classic
Perowne, S.	The Life and Times of Herod the Great	Penguin Classic

Some simple introductions to the characters referred to in the outline:

Prescott, D. M.	Stories of Peter	Blandford
Krall, B. C.	Friends and Followers of Jesus	R.E.P.*

CHILDREN 9–11 YEARS

What are referred to as the characteristics of the junior become more obvious at about the age of nine. Children develop at different rates and in different ways but continuity in the way we present the material on which ideas and concepts will be formed is always necessary: there should be no sudden break in method at any stage in a child's development.

The emerging characteristic is that of greater detachment from the situations which are presented to them; they are more objective in their attitudes and they become more concerned with concrete facts than with impressions. The phase of fantasy is passing into one of greater realism. Questions become characteristically down-to-earth. 'Is it true?' means to the nine-year-old and upwards, 'Were these real people? Did it really happen?' This is not mere curiosity but a genuine search for reality. In dealing with questions to do with the Bible the need is therefore for facts, not for the abstract ideas with which we as adults are concerned. The ideas of 'faith', 'courage', 'love' are seen and understood in actual situations as shown in the action and the life of people. An element of hero-worship enters in and it becomes necessary to show Jesus as someone strong and vitally concerned with the affairs of every day. Those incidents which show him walking long distances, climbing mountains, suffering hardship and facing angry crowds will help to correct the impressions of weakness which an over-emphasis on his works of mercy may give. We must remember that although the juniors will accept what is presented with the authority of an adult as 'facts', they have, as yet, no subjective experience to support the meaning of the incident in depth. We should help the child, particularly at this age, to form a realistic idea of what kind of a book the Bible is: its message is concerned with religion and the values we derive from this but it has nothing to say about truth in a scientific sense. It is written by many different people with no knowledge of the kind we call 'scientific': it gives the 'truth' in a religious sense.

Children at this stage are beginning to develop a greater sense of what is fair. Ideas of justice are still seen in terms of black and white; there are no halftones. So, many of those stories which have a special significance in theological terms, the parable of the Labourers in the Vineyard for example (Matthew 20 vv. 1–16) are rejected as unfair and should therefore be left to a later stage. It is little use discussing the point that precedence in service gives no claim for priority in the matter of a reward in the Kingdom of God until the child is ready to see more deeply into the nature of the Kingdom.

There is too, a growing readiness to co-operate with others. For this reason they are able to appreciate the idea of a Church as a Fellowship made up of Followers of Jesus.

What are the main characteristics of the older junior as far as moral growth is concerned?

Many of the earlier characteristics persist and this is a period of consolidation. Apart from exceptional cases the standards of the group become of increasing importance. Heroes are not necessarily 'good' people but people who exercise power, physical or otherwise, and there is interest in communities as well as individuals.

There is some refinement in the ideas of 'right and wrong' while these are still conceived in terms of obedience to a set of rules; a few will think of wrong as mainly concerned with selfishness. Parents and adults (in most normal circumstances) still have a determining effect on behaviour but increasingly because the child is afraid of disapproval or punishment or does not wish to upset his parents or teacher. With some, a certain sophistication may develop, as the child comes to feel sure of eventual forgiveness; this can have the effect of moral irresponsibility.

1. There is not much interest in death though there is a heightened interest in the frailty of life as shown in a concern about accidents and illness.

2. With a growing sense of 'reality' as opposed to 'fantasy' there is a tension between 'natural' and the 'supernatural'. The world is understood in terms of 'natural events' and 'natural causes' though God can be seen as supreme over nature working through events.

3. The Bible may be dismissed as 'untrue' because of the miracle stories it contains. So interest in God may show itself in a deep sense of awe but it may equally show itself in certain individuals by complete apathy. Where symbolic language has been forced into a false literalism there is outright rejection of all belief in God or talk about him.

4. Interest in Jesus shows a new sense of questioning or even scepticism where ideas of a theological nature have been presented at too early an age.

5. There is a growing concern for an orderly arrangement of facts, e.g. cause and effect as seen in mechanical contrivances. This leads to a desire to know more about the sequence of events in a history story. This is not a sense of history although it may well lead on to this. With this comes a growing interest in the poetical and historical sections of the Bible.

6. There is a developing awareness of the nature of problems that arise between people, in friendships and within the family. There is a greater sense of personal identity (learning about the strength and the weakness, the possible powers as well as the limitations of oneself). It should also be possible to cultivate a sense of obligation to the family, the school, the neighbourhood and the community in general.

What are the main moral and religious needs of late middle childhood ?

1. There is a need to hear about 'heroes' who are good as well as powerful and more discussion should be allowed.

2. They must be helped to realise the cost of forgiveness and that 'fairness' often involves punishment.

3. There is a need to show that 'reality' includes experience of beauty, awe and goodness which are not wholly described in terms of fact but are none the less real. This has to be dealt with at the level of experience because it is still too early to talk about them as abstractions.

4. Ideas of 'God acting' in abnormal situations should be avoided as far as possible.

5. There is a need to lead them to distinguish between certain elements in the make-up of the Bible in which some are factual and others symbolic.

6. To see oneself as a dependent being, ultimately dependent on God and existing for God. This is fundamental but it cannot be achieved through preaching but rather through example, through implication, through atmosphere and encouragement in worship. The religious teaching at this stage should consist predominantly of factual objective information.

STAGE THREE

TERM ONE

**The character
of Jesus**

It is not too early to begin the theme of what it is that makes people really great. Hero worship comes naturally to children of this age. They are in the process of building up ideals based on the attraction of those who have displayed the qualities young people admire. Standards are inevitably related to the immediate experience of much that is presented in mass entertainment of all kinds. While this is by no means always harmful, contrasts and comparisons should be made as between much that is trivial and superficial and the more enduring qualities of great men and women, past and present. There is a link here with many classical stories and legends (such as the Iliad and the Odyssey) and the developing theme of the greatness of Christian men and women who have shown fortitude of a different kind. The qualities as revealed in the historic life of Jesus can be shown as greatness in its fullest sense. From an appreciation of his full humanity we grow to see the nature of his divinity.

1 How did
Jesus show
that He was
brave and
courageous
as well as
good?

There are examples of His courage at almost every point in His life. His capacity for enduring hardship in the wilderness, in facing opposition, and, in the purely physical sense, His journeyings on foot.

Mark 1 v. 12

He goes fearlessly to Jerusalem

Mark 10 vv. 32–34

In the Garden at Gethsemane

Mark 14 vv. 32–42

2 How did
Jesus show
His
goodness
(or purity)?

Everyone who met Him felt His goodness (and by contrast their own failings and shortcomings).

Matthew 3 v. 14
Luke 5 v. 8

3 Did He ever
show anger?

He was angry at the extortionate behaviour of the money-changers. No coin with an image on it could be accepted in payment for offerings made in the Temple (the law against graven images). So the Roman coins had to be changed for Jewish. The money-changers made a fortune out of this trading in currency.

Mark 11 vv. 15–17

Peter's lack of understanding

Mark 8 vv. 27–33

At the hard-heartedness of many of the Pharisees.

Mark 3 vv. 2–5

Outline of Topics	Suggestions for the Teacher	
4 Where did Jesus show His humility?	At His baptism.	Matthew 3 vv. 13–17 Mark 1 vv. 9–11
	When He washed the feet of the disciples (a slave usually performed this service to his master).	John 13 vv. 1–11
	In not resisting His enemies by force.	John 18 vv. 1–12
5 What standards did He expect from His friends and followers?	He made demands for the highest standards.	
	The Rich Young Ruler	Mark 10 vv. 17–21
	On all who wanted to be His disciples	Luke 9 vv. 57–62
6 When did He show sympathy and kindness?	The Widow's son at Nain Jairus' daughter	Luke 7 vv. 11–18 Mark 5 vv. 22–24 ; 35–43
7 Could He see the funny side of life?	He could make jokes and puns :	
	'Adding a cubit to his stature'	Matthew 6 v. 27
	'The eye of a needle'	Matthew 19 v. 24
	'The mote and the beam'	Matthew 7 v. 3
	He was always ready to cheer people up :	
	'He was moved to pity'	Matthew 9 v. 36
	'Do not be afraid'	Matthew 28 v. 10
	'Do not be afraid ; only have faith'	Mark 5 v. 36
8 Was He able to share other people's happiness?	He joined in family occasions	
	The marriage at Cana.	John 2 vv. 1–11
	He wept over Jerusalem	Matthew 23 v. 37

Men and women who have shown the qualities that Jesus expected of His followers

The following are only suggestions and can be added to or replaced by other biographies :

St. Francis of Assisi (remembered in churches on 4th October)	The work of St. Francis who saw in nature and all creation the work of God.
William Penn of Pennsylvania	A man of peace and integrity who was able to make peace with the Indians in America.
John Wesley	A great preacher and evangelist who, many historians think, may have saved England from Revolution.
David Livingstone	A man who expressed his Christian faith by dedicating his life to the service of his fellow-men in Africa.

Saint Nicholas

Christmas provides the possibility **of dramatising one of the** lives dealt with this term ; or the story of St. Nicholas is an obvious choice. He was Bishop of Myra in Lydia (in Asia Minor). Remembered on the 6th December but subsequently on Christmas Day. Santa Claus is a corruption of the Dutch 'Sintaklaus' as used by the Dutch settlers in North America. Legend has it that he gave presents by stealth and this is said to be the origin of giving presents in secret at Christmas time. Nicholas lived through the persecution of Diocletian (c. 300A.D.).

Books of reference for the teacher

Turner, H. E. W.	Jesus, Master and Lord	Mowbray
Robinson, W. Gordon	Introduction to the New Testament	Arnold *
Barclay, W.	The Mind of Jesus	S.C.M.

Simpler books for use with children, which could be used as a basis for the teacher and children to share.

Wightman, E. M. C.	Stories about Jesus	Lutterworth
Brett, S. R.	Lives to Remember	Black
Crozier, E.	Life and Legend of St. Nicholas	Duckworth *
Latham, R. O.	Trail Makers	Lutterworth
	The Children's Books of Famous Lives	Odham's Press *
	The Eagle Omnibus Books (Nos. 1—6)	Lutterworth *,

TERM TWO

Outline of Topic   *Suggestions for the Teacher*

Obedience and forgiveness

1 What do we look for in choosing a captain ?

Someone who can play well himself : who can make up his mind quickly : who can make fair decisions and one who knows the rules himself.

2 Obedience to the rules

Obedience to the rules must be maintained otherwise the team breaks down. So we accept the rules : this means obedience to the referee or to the captain.

3 The need for rules

Rules have to be made which we can understand and accept because they fit in with our deepest needs.

School rules.

The Ten Commandments (in a simplified form).

(a) Laws about God.

(b) Laws about living together.

The two-fold law of Christ.   Luke 10 v. 27

Outline of Topics	Suggestions for the Teacher	
4 When rules are broken	The stories of Sir Galahad and the Knights of the Round Table. There is a breakdown of good fellowship when the rules are broken. Children can do some thinking and work about this :	
5 Friendships :	They have already had to face the problem of broken friendships and they may call upon their own experience in getting to understand more about forgiveness :	

(a) Examples of people who have not born a grudge – examples can be drawn from their own knowledge of situations.

(b) Discussing their reactions when they are hurt, insulted or offended : coping with the urge to retaliation, revenge ; or forgetting the occasion, forgiving the offender and returning injury with kindness.

Forgiveness and reconciliation are great themes of the Bible. Some examples taken from the Bible and other sources :

	(i) Joseph forgives his brothers.	Genesis 37
	(ii) David and Saul.	I Samuel 24
	(iii) St. Patrick though captured and enslaved becomes a missionary.	
	(iv) John Wesley forgives his enemies and the people who attacked him.	

The friends of Jesus often fell short of the standards He demanded : Jesus had much to say about forgiveness :

Some of His sayings.

To expect God's forgiveness we must forgive others.	Matthew 5 v. 23–26 Matthew 6 v. 14
Forgiveness goes beyond set limits.	Matthew 18 vv. 21 ff
Forgiveness does not always mean 'being let off'. The Prodigal Son suffered many things.	
The father who forgave his son.	Luke 15 vv. 11–32

6 One of the reasons why quarrels begin	The disciples had not grasped the meaning of the Kingdom : they were seeking special privileges in an earthly kingdom. The other disciples were indignant at their requests.	Mark 10 vv. 35–45
7 Stories from the Old Testament	The story of Jacob and Esau How the quarrel went on The two are reconciled	Genesis 25 vv. 27–34 Genesis 27 vv. 1–41 Genesis 33 vv. 1–16
8 Jesus taught us a great deal about forgiving	Peter asks about forgiveness The great commandment	Matthew 18 vv. 21–35 Matthew 22 vv. 35–40

Outline of Topics	Suggestions for the teacher	
9 The greatest act of forgiveness	At this stage the Passion narrative can be introduced to coincide with Easter.	
	The Last Supper	Matthew 26 vv. 14–29
	In the Garden of Gethsemane	Matthew 26 vv. 36–56
	The trials before Annas and Caiaphas	John 18 vv. 12–14 ; 19–24
	The trial before Pilate	John 18 vv. 28–40
	Peter's courage fails him	Mark 14 vv. 27–31 ; 47–50 ; 66–72
	The Crucifixion – the great cry of forgiveness.	Luke 23 v. 34
	The Resurrection	Mark 16 vv. 1–8
	Peter is forgiven : he is reconciled and given work to do.	John 21 vv. 9–19
10 After forgiveness, there is work to be done	The Commission and promise to the Apostles.	Acts 1 vv. 6–8

It is suggested that some appropriate stories be introduced at this stage to show how the work of Christ has, in fact, continued to the present day.

Books of reference for the teacher

Thompson, D. W.	The World He Loves	Lutterworth*
Neill, Stephen	The Unfinished Task	Lutterworth*

Books for use with children :

	Eagle Books,	Lutterworth*
Firth, C. B.	Pioneers in Religion and Science	Ginn *
Garlick, P.	Six Great Missionaries	H. Hamilton *

TERM THREE

Outline of Topics	Suggestions for the Teacher
The work that Jesus began continues in the work of the Holy Spirit	To the child the word 'spirit' may suggest something unreal and far away. The problem becomes, 'How do I get to know someone I have never seen?'.

(a) We can share some of their experiences by seeing or hearing :
A painting by a great painter tells us something about the painter. One of Lowry's paintings of a Lancashire scene could illustrate this. A piece of music by a great composer reveals a side of his character or personality (but by no means all). Beethoven for example.

(b) We can read about them : if they are famous, the things they did to make them famous, or remembered.
In this we we learn something about the 'spirit' or personality of a person we have never met.

Outline of Topics	*Suggestions for the Teacher*	
Getting to know Jesus	Holy Spirit means 'spiritually perfect' and devoted to God. At the beginning of His ministry, 'Jesus, full of the Holy Spirit returned from the Jordan'.	Luke 4 v. 1
	He goes aside and is alone : he makes great decisions. 'Men shall not live by bread alone'.	Matthew 4 v. 4
1 By learning about His life and work	He came to Nazareth and joined in the service at the synagogue.	
	'The spirit of the Lord is upon me, because He has anointed me to preach good news to the poor'.	Luke 4 vv. 16–22
	And at Capernaum.	
	'. . . and they were astonished at His teaching, for His word was with authority.'	Luke 4 v. 32
2 Through worship	By deepening our understanding of the life and teaching of Jesus we are helped to live fuller and better lives.	
	Followers of Jesus first got the name Christians at Antioch.	Acts 11 vv. 19–26 Acts 13 v. 1
	'For where two or three have met together in My name, I am there among them.'	Matthew 18 v. 20
3 Through prayer	Jesus always prayed : He prayed especially when decisions had to be made or when great crises had to be faced.	
	'. . . he continued in prayer to God.' (The choosing of the Twelve Disciples.)	Luke 6 v. 12
	The moment of decision : the vision of the purpose of life.	Luke 9 vv. 18–36
	In Gethsemane.	
	''Pray that you may be spared the hour of testing.'	Luke 22 vv. 40–46
	He taught us to say : The Lord's Prayer 'Father Thy name be hallowed.'	Luke 11 vv. 1–10
	The main point to be discussed : the need for praise and thanksgiving.	Psalm 117
	The glory of Creation and the Fatherhood of God.	Psalm 100
	'Thy Kingdom come' Working for God's Kingdom means supporting the work done in churches and in missions : working for social justice and the Christian way of life : standing for the right things in our work and play : doing what we can to help others who are sick or ill.	Matthew 28 vv. 18–20
	'Give us each day our daily bread.' Thinking of the needs of others : in our homes and in our family : learning to be unselfish : and so remembering the total needs we have of body, mind and spirit.	Luke 4 vv. 2–4

Outline of Topic	Suggestions for the Teacher

Outline of Topic   *Suggestions for the Teacher*

'And forgive us our sins.'
Admitting we are often wrong : learning
to like even those we have disliked.

Matthew 5 vv. 43–48

'And do not bring us to the test.'
Asking for guidance and protection.

Luke 22 vv. 45–46

4   Seeing Jesus
in the lives of
others

Some study, by means of stories and
dramatisation of the lives of Christian
men and women. The following are
only suggestions :

Wilfred Grenfell (Labrador).
Mary Bird (Persia).
Abraham Lincoln (U.S.A.).
Amy Carmichael (South India).
Booker T. Washington (U.S.A.).
Ronald Ross (India and West Africa).
Sundar Singh (India).
William Carey (India).
David Sheppard (East London)
Helen Keller, (U.S.A.).

Work that children may do

Children can discover some of the meaning of the Lord's Prayer through activities
which illustrate the ideas which are difficult.

1   'Thy Kingdom come'.
'Give us each day our daily bread'
These are comparatively easy to interpret through practical steps in one case,
learning to work for the good of others (supporting good causes such as
Christian Aid and similar activities) and in the second, by appreciating our
dependence on resources of food and other necessities not forgetting our
spiritual needs in terms of 'bread'.

2   'And forgive us the wrong we have done'
'And do not bring us to the test'
These may present difficulties. The idea of God 'testing' people may create a
wrong impression and be a cause of stumbling to young children. *Conscience*
can be seen as providing us with a means of 'testing' what is right and what is
wrong.

Children can discover ways in which we are prevented from doing wrong or
kept from harm. '. . . do not bring us to the test', can be a way of asking God to
help us to make wise decisions. They can think about their own quarrels and the
quarrels of older people and the 'test' of character they create.

3   Acts of worship can be worked out by the children to bring many of the points
made in the notes above.

Books of reference for the teacher

| Simcox, C. E. | Living the Lord's Prayer | Dacre Press * |
| Robinson, H. W. | The Christian Experience of the Holy Spirit | Collins |

STAGE FOUR

At this stage it is intended to give the pupils an introduction to the Bible as 'the Church's Book' and to prepare the way for deeper insights into its meaning.

TERM ONE

Outline of Topics	Suggestions for the Teacher
'The Church's Book' **What is the Bible?**	The Bible is made up of many books written long ago about the adventures and experiences of a people who were very gifted. They had a deeper understanding of the ways and needs of men and women than any of the peoples living at that time. They knew very little about science and had none of the modern machinery and apparatus which scientists use today; but they took a deep interest in what was happening in the world around them. In all their mistakes and frequent tragedies, as well as their successes and joys, they found that God was speaking to them and teaching them. Finally, they realised that He had given them a special task in giving this knowledge to the world; they only partly succeeded and in the final test they failed. It is a true Book because it is about life and true to life. It contains stories, history, hymns, poetry, books on law, and letters. It is in two parts. The earlier part tells us how God revealed Himself to the Hebrews, what happened to them over many centuries and the work that God expected them to do in spreading this knowledge round the world. The second part is about the life, work and teaching of Jesus of Nazareth and those who followed Him in the early days of the Christian Church. Another set of books, not always found in our Bibles is the Apocrypha. This contains writings which are not considered as important as the rest and which are sometimes placed between the earlier part, called the Old Testament, and the later part which is called the New Testament.
Learning about the books	It is suggested that pupils should be given the opportunity of finding out for themselves about the books by looking up references.

Outline of Topics	*Suggestions for the Teacher*	
1 Stories about the beginning of the world	The Creation (The second account)	Genesis 1 and 2 vv. 1–3 Genesis 2 v. 7 ; vv. 15–25˙
	The Fall of Man	Genesis 3 vv. 1–21
	The Great Flood	Genesis 6 vv. 7–22 ; 7 vv. 1–24
	God's Promise	Genesis 9 vv. 8–17
	In these stories the writers were saying that God was Creator of all things and had to be obeyed. To flout His authority was to court disaster. They are not scientific explanations but a guide to spiritual truths.	
2 Stories about men of the Bible	Abraham and Isaac Abraham was a puzzled man : he wanted to be obedient to God, but learned that God did not want obedience through cruelty.	Genesis 22 vv. 1–19
	Joseph and his brothers	Genesis 37–45
3 Books about Law ; Exodus, Leviticus, Deuteronomy	Only a reference to these is needed at this stage ; they show how the Hebrews tried to work out a system of rules which would help them to be obedient to God. They were so complicated that they became a burden : Jesus had much to say about them.	
	Moses the Lawgiver	Exodus 20 vv. 1–17
4 Books on history as the Hebrews saw it ; Joshua, Judges, I Samuel, I and II Kings	These are histories written about God's ways with men and especially the Hebrews in their relationship with God.	
	Joshua the Leader	Joshua
	Gideon and the Three Hundred	Judges 7
	David	I Samuel 16 vv. 6–13 II Samuel 1 II Samuel 4 and 5 vv. 1–5 II Samuel 9
	Solomon	I Kings 3 vv. 3–14
5 Books of poetry ; Psalms, Proverbs	A selection of a few of the more literary and helpful of the Psalms.	
	The Song of Deborah	Judges 5
	David and Jonathan	II Samuel 1 vv. 19–27
6 Letters ; Romans, Corinthians	Read the letter about the runaway slave.	Philemon

Outline of Topics	*Suggestions for the Teacher*	
7 The Gospels	An introduction to the order of the Gospels in the Bible with a reference to Jesus in the Temple at Jerusalem. The pilgrim journeys to Jerusalem for the special occasions of national and religious festivals can be introduced by the selection from the psalms.	
	'Little Psalter of the Pilgrims' (These were sung by the pilgrims as they journeyed on their way to Jerusalem.)	Psalms 120–134
	Jesus and his parents at the Passover.	Luke 2 vv. 41–52
	These passages are meant to give the pupils the opportunity of finding out for themselves about the composition of the Bible and where the main divisions come : it is suggested that the Revised Standard Version or the New English Bible be used. It is not intended that the passages should be dealt with in any detail.	

The lands behind the books

Some knowledge of the geography of Palestine is essential. The atlas and maps of the Holy Land should be available and supplemented with good pictures and illustrations in order to show the nature of the terrain where Jesus lived and worked. In many ways the land has not changed, except in a political and economic sense, from what it was in the days when Jesus walked through it with His disciples. The hills and valleys, the plains, lakes and rivers are there, just as they were then ; good modern photographs can be very helpful. A useful book for class purposes is :–

Sanders, E. M.	The Holy Land, Part One –The Land	Geo. Philip *

Journeys in Bible times

Pupils may discuss some modern ways of travel by road, rail, ship or by air. Some comparison of speeds and distances as between ancient ways of travel by camel, donkey and by foot as compared with our modern way of travel. The horse was not in general use in the ancient civilisations except for hunting and in war.

Outline of Topics	*Suggestions for the Teacher*	
	From Ur of the Chaldees to Canaan	Genesis 11 v. 31
	Dothan to Egypt	Genesis 12 vv. 1–9
	Egypt to Canaan	Deuteronomy 8 v. 2
	Palestine to Egypt and back	Matthew 2 vv. 13ff ; and 20
	Jerusalem to Golgotha	John 19 vv. 16–1d
	Jerusalem to Damascus	Acts 9 vv. 1–8
	Palestine to Rome	Acts 27 vv. 1–44

What the books tell us about prayer

The library we call the Bible tells us about God's actions with the Hebrew people : they made mistakes and did things contrary to God's wishes.

Outline of Topics	Suggestions for the Teacher	
1 How people in the Bible prayed	Nevertheless, they asked for God's help, forgiveness and for guidance .The prayers are often in the form of conversations : listening is as important in a conversation as talking. Here are some examples :–	
	Abraham asks for a son	Genesis 15 v. 2
	Moses seeks God's presence	Exodus 33 v. 12
	David asks for God's blessing on his family	I Chronicles 17 vv. 16–27
	Solomon asks for wisdom	I Kings 3 vv. 5–9
	Elijah restores the widow's son	I Kings 17 vv. 20–24
	Hezekiah prays to be made well again	II Kings 20 v. 3
	The circumstances in which the prayer is made provide an opportunity for dealing with the situation in Jewish history in which they occurred.	
2 Prayers that Jesus made	In His suffering in Gethsemane	Matthew 26 v. 39
	His cry of suffering	Matthew 27 v. 46
	He prays for His murderers	Luke 23 v. 34
	He commits His spirit to God	Luke 23 v. 46
	He prays for the Church	John 17
	The Lord's Prayer	Matthew 6 v. 9ff
3 The followers of Jesus prayed	In making a choice	Acts 1 vv. 24–25
	They were continually watchful and in prayer.	Acts 6 vv. 1–7

Books of reference for the teacher

Murray, A. V.	How to know your Bible	Allen & Unwin *
Neil, W.	The Rediscovery of the Bible	Hodder & Stoughton

Books which children may use :

What is the Bible ?	Readiness for Religion series	Rupert Hart-Davis
Parker, C. M.	How the Bible Matters	
Rolls, E.	What Use are Books ?	

TERM TWO

Outline of Topics	Suggestions for the Teacher
Rivers, wells and water · 1 Why water is important	Water is very important to us. We use it in our houses and in every department of life. There is much discussion about supplies of water to our own area and to all big cities (cf. the scheme for supplying Liverpool and Manchester with additional water supplies). Even so, we have a plentiful rainfall which sometimes makes it difficult for us to understand how precious water is in countries where water is less plentiful and badly distributed.

Outline of Topics	*Suggestions for the Teacher*	
2 Water in Palestine	Water and water supplies have always been important in Palestine and frequently the cause of disputes (cf. the continuing argument about water and the use of the River Jordan for irrigating parts of Israel).	
3 Stories about water and wells	Abraham and Lot separate	Genesis 13 vv. 8–11
	Abraham and Abimelech	Genesis 21 vv. 25–32
	Rebekah and the well	Genesis 24 vv. 1–50
	Hagar and her child	Genesis 21 vv. 14–20
	Water for David	II Samuel 23 vv. 13–17
	Hezekiah and the conduit	II Kings 20 v. 20
4 In what way is water indispens- able ?	This does not call for much imagination. Lists of the essential needs of men may be drawn up under different headings : for domestic use, in industry, and above all in agriculture. Experiments could be made by measuring the water needed, weekly, for growing plants, or the statistics given for the water consumption of cows in order to produce milk. This could lead to a link with the science teaching.	
	Examples of the water needs of animals and men as mentioned in the Bible could be looked up by the pupils :	
	The shepherd and his flock	Psalm 23
	The hard life of the shepherd	Genesis 31 vv. 38–40
	Settlements where water could be found. The *Negev* (a map reference is needed) until recently an arid land, but schemes of irrigation by the State of Israel have made agriculture possible.	
	Abraham and his countrymen were nomads, mainly because they had to move about in search of water. They passed through the Negev to Kadesh where there were springs of water ; here they lived for some years.	Genesis 20 v. 1
	Children could make a list of some of the fruits mentioned in the Bible, and discover whether we import any similar fruits today from Palestine.	
5 Rivers and lakes (seas in the Bible)	Which of the disciples were fishermen ? Where did they fish ? Pupils could find out about fishermen in Bible times.	
	The call of Peter and Andrew.	Matthew 4 vv. 18–20
	An unexpected catch. (It is possible to detect a shoal of fish from the sea-shore : the appearance of the surface of the water changes)	John 21 vv. 4–8

Outline of Topics	*Suggestions for the Teacher*	
6 Water was used in curing disease	What have we learned about the importance of being clean? Children could discuss the importance of cleanliness and what happens if a child is left unwashed and uncared for. Disease and misery follow.	
	Naaman is healed of his leprosy. (Much of what was called leprosy in Bible times was not the dreadful disease we read about today although there were many lepers with the serious type of the disease.)	II Kings 5 vv. 1–14
	The man born blind.	John 9 vv. 1–11
	The cripple at the pool of Bethesda	John 5 vv. 5–9

How signs and symbols have a special meaning

There are road signs which are symbols. Pupils can use the road signs and give their meaning; the children can see that the signs, by means of pictures, show us clearly what they want us to do.

1 What do we mean by symbols?

There are other ways in which symbols are used. Every country has a flag. It is designed to represent something of the history of the country it stands for.

There are symbols that show the value of different products.

The wool trade uses many signs: one in particular shows that wool is good to wear.

Pupils can be encouraged to find out other symbols for themselves; British Rail, Britannia on a coin and so forth.

Map symbols can be brought in to develop this in a more advanced way.

2 There are Christian symbols

The early Christians used the sign of the 'fish'. It had two possible meanings; the disciples were fishers of men.   Mark 1 v. 17
The letters of the Greek word for fish give us the first letter of the phrase, 'Jesus Christ, Son of God, Saviour'. In the dark days of persecution, when the Romans were condemning Christians to death, or imprisonment, many fled into secret hiding places such as the catacombs in Rome. They used the sign of the 'fish' as a secret symbol to tell others what they stood for.

The 'halo' was used in Christian art as a sign of great holiness or perfection; in ancient times the circle was regarded as the most perfect form or shape. In Christian art it became a 'spiritualised' symbol of holiness.

There are many such symbols used in the Christian Church.

The Manger reminds us that Jesus was born humbly and for all men.   Luke 2 v. 7

The Cross teaches us that Jesus died for us (pupils may think of ways in which the cross has become a symbol — the Red Cross etc.).   Matthew 16 v. 24

The Empty Tomb tells us that Jesus overcame even death itself for us.   John 5 v. 24

Water is used to show that we are cleansed and that we can become members of Christ's Church. It is used as a symbol ; there is nothing magical about it. In many churches a special service is used to admit children and grown-ups into membership.

John the Baptist and Jesus.

Jesus made Himself one of the company of His own countrymen when He came out to meet John the Baptist ; He shared in their way of life by joining the crowds to be baptised. But He remained sinless, perfect, 'Son of God'.

John baptises in the Jordan.   Matthew 3 vv. 5–6
Jesus is baptised.   Matthew 3 vv. 13–15

Afterwards the disciples baptised many people.

Philip and the Ethiopian.   Acts 8 vv. 26–38

Water is often used in the Bible for cleansing in the sense of renewing a right spirit, or making well and strong.

Jesus speaks of Himself as the 'source of life' :

'If anyone thirsts, let him come to Me and drink.'   John 7 v. 37–38

The Book of Revelation was written in the very early days of the Christian Church at a time of extreme danger. The writer himself had been exiled to Patmos (cf. the way people in Russia can be exiled to Siberia). Martyrdom of Christians was frequent as part of the clash between Christianity and Caesar-worship. The writer believed that God must come to the rescue of His people.

'... the water of life, bright as crystal ...'   Revelation 22 vv. 1–5

'... He will guide them to living water ...'   Revelation 7 v. 17

Water is being used, as in great poetry, as a symbol of life.

Young children are capable of writing poetry on similar subjects in order to express their own feelings in terms of symbols of this kind. They should have opportunities for doing so and include them in an anthology of verse containing chosen passages from the Bible as well as their own poems.

Books of reference for the teacher

Rowley, H. H.	The Student's Bible Atlas	Lutterworth
Hilliard, F. H.	Behold the Land ; a Pictorial Atlas of the Bible	G. Philip
Gröllenberg	The Shorter Atlas of the Bible	Nelson˙

Simpler books for children :

Sanders, E. M.	The Holy Land	Geo. Philip ˙ ˙
	Westminster Smaller Bible Atlas	S.C.M. Press

TERM THREE

Outline of Topics	*Suggestions for the Teacher*	
The Light of the World	An attempt must be made to interest the children in the symbolism of 'light' as an introduction to the Festival of	
1 Thinking about 'light' and power	Whitsuntide. To do this we have to help children to understand that, in our language, we use pictorial phrases to explain what we mean. This will help them to realise why 'light' and also 'fire and wind' were used as the symbols standing for the Holy Spirit.	
2 Fire and Light	Some discussion on the uses to which fire has been used down the ages as a source of light.	
	Burning wood, flaming torches, candles, gas lamps, lanterns, oil lamps. Electricity as a source of light is a recent invention. To give light, electricity is used to heat a thin wire. Until then, apart from the sun, a naked flame was the only source of light. Children can draw or write about all the ways of making light other than the light of the sun. This can provide a link with the science lessons.	
	How is fire (in the sense of heat and light) used in language ?	
	'warm hearted', 'a warm smile', 'to be enlightened'.	
3 Jesus as 'the Light of the World'	'. . . a light for revelation to the Gentiles'.	Luke 2 v. 32
	Some recapitulation is needed of the main points in the life of Jesus.	
	(a) The Passion narrative stressing the following points : The disciples misunderstood the reasons for Jesus dying. They were afraid :	
	Fear of captivity and authority.	Luke 22 vv. 54–62
	They were unable to sustain a life of prayer and service.	Mark 14 vv. 32–42
	They were sad and faint-hearted.	Luke 24 vv. 13–35
	They did not understand about the nature and person of Jesus.	Luke 18 vv. 31–34
	They did not understand the part they had to play.	Luke 22 vv. 24–38
		Luke 22 vv. 44–53
		Luke 24 vv. 47–53

(b) Jesus commanded His disciples to
    wait for the coming of the Holy Spirit
    which would enlighten men and give
    them power.

It would bring comfort.	John 14 v. 16
Be a reminder.	John 14 vv. 25–27
Give them power.	Luke 24
Help them to be witnesses to the truth.	John 14 vv. 4–6

(c) The story of Whitsuntide.   Acts 2

    This is the day the Church went into
    action. The statements about time are
    not to be taken too literally, but the
    promise given in the earlier situations
    was fulfilled. (Pentecost is fifty days
    after Easter and ten days after
    Ascension.) In the Psalms, winds are
    referred to as 'God's messengers'. Also
    in the Book of Job.   Job 38 v. 1

    (See Peake's Commentary 1962
    edition : 'Contemporary Jewish
    Religion' by W. D. Davies p. 705.)

    The effect on the disciples.
    How the disciples changed at
    Whitsuntide.

Before	*After*	
They were afraid	They went out to meet the crowds.	Acts 2 vv. 5–14
They were unable to pray.	They led a life of prayer.	Acts 2 v. 42
They were sad.	They were full of joy.	Acts 2 vv. 46–47
They misunderstood.	They began to understand.	Acts 3 vv. 14–26

The work of the Church goes forward	Paul is converted.	
	The spread of the Gospel to the wider world.	Acts 18 and 21
	To Rome.	Acts 27 and 28
	Christianity comes to England.	St. Alban c. A.D. 303
		St. Patrick A.D. 432
	The Celtic churches.	St. Columba A.D. 597
	St. Augustine lands in Kent.	St. Aidan A.D. 651

The church of the Middle Ages – care
for the sick, development of farming,
the establishment of Schools. This work
could be linked with the local history of
places in the County : see the
Appendices B and C.

There could be a link with the history
teaching in the form of a project leading
to some study of the local churches.

The Reformation and what followed.

The closing of the monasteries.
The new preaching.
Some of the Reformers — Martin Luther.

The Prayer Book.

The Elizabethan settlement and those
who could not accept it.

The 'coming together' again as seen in
the growing friendship between
churches.

**Some aspects
of the work of
the Church
today**

What churches are
there in the
neighbourhood?

What are they
concerned with?

1   Worship

Today, although each church worships
regularly, the congregations do so in
different ways. They all look to the
Bible for their final authority in the
matter of belief and practice. In this
country we have freedom to choose our
own ways of worship.

From the first, Christians came together
to pray and worship.

The letter sent by Pliny the Younger to
his uncle.

'Documents of the
Christian Church'
Bettenson, O.U.P.

Sunday is the first day of the week, not
the Jewish sabbath which is
remembered on Saturday.

We should worship, '. . . in spirit and in
truth'.

John 4 v. 24

In an act of worship we do two things in
a general way.

(a) We join together to deepen our
knowledge of the things we believe
in.

(b) We gain strength and power to go
out in to the world to put this into
practice.

Children can be encouraged to work
out their own forms of worship in
assembly by developing a theme of
their own choosing.

Themes suggested by the idea of 'light'.
Themes suggested by Biblical topics
within their understanding. Themes
connected with practical activities to do
with school or wider interests.

Outline of Topics	*Suggestions for the Teacher*	
2 Caring for people	How to help the sick, aged or lonely. Helping with activities in the neighbourhood such as 'Christian Aid Week'.	
3 Teaching and learning	By studying the Bible. By work in Sunday Schools or church. By joining with other people in helping with a good cause.	
4 Prayer	There should be a connection with the children's experience. This is not to limit them to the trivial or purely personal.	
	Jesus and His need to pray at the beginning and end of the day.	Mark 1 vv. 35–38 Luke 6 v. 12

Books for teacher's reference

Elphinstone-Fyffe, J.M.	An Illustrated Calendar of the Christian Year	Church Information Office*
Foster, John	Beginning from Jerusalem	Lutterworth
Slack, K.	The Ecumenical Movement	Lutterworth *
Slack, K.	Many Churches — One Church	S.C.M.*

INTRODUCTION TO THE SECONDARY PHASE

At whatever age the transfer from primary to secondary school takes place and whatever the form of the organisation, a fresh approach to the teaching of the subject is called for. Two factors have to be considered: on the one hand the pupil is anticipating that he will have fresh and exciting ways of learning more about himself and the subjects and skills he will be called upon to master, and secondly, a new dimension in his ability to think calls for a deeper enquiry into the nature of truth. With their growing insights into the meanings of biblical language and terminology many will bring a more discerning attitude to the knowledge they are gaining.

On the other hand, the effect of continuing social change on the pupil has also to be considered in devising a syllabus or scheme of work. There is no longer a tacit acceptance of inherited religious beliefs or patterns of behaviour: an increasing number react against dogma or dogmatic statements especially when these are associated with a remote period of history. With this goes a rejection of authority in matters of morality and a vacuum, so far as values are concerned, in the day-to-day making of decisions.

A new situation has developed in family as well as in community life. The settled circumstances in which relatives lived in fairly close association has been replaced by a type of anonymity in which the individual becomes depersonalised. Birth and death are treated clinically and have less impact on the young. Parental values and established standards are less willingly accepted and in seeking to find a way out from a bewildering situation there is a tendency to look for relief in mass entertainment in which the attempt is often made to shock in order to achieve notoriety. For the most part the society in which children move and have their being wishes to live a day-to-day existence in which the deeper issues of life are avoided.

If school is to be a preparation for life it must take into account the trends for the future and the kind of life which children now in schools will live as adults. It seems probable that the society of the future will experience large scale movements of population involving resettlement. As new methods of automation in industry are applied there will be an increase in leisure and a growing surplus of the less skilled workers: the place formerly occupied by hewers of wood and drawers of water will be taken by machinery. With this will go a vast expansion of consumer goods with the intensified sales techniques for the disposal of them and a move towards larger units at all levels of human activity with the grave danger to the individual of loss of identity. It is likely that the sense of the insecurity of life will remain as long as world tensions and conflicts continue: to many this will be a cause of anxiety or a desire to escape from the harsher realities of life.

While all aspects of education must be concerned with this problem, religious education has an important part to play in helping the children in our schools to establish constructive attitudes in this complex situation. The particular function of religious education is to open the way for the individual to make an encounter with God. In our county schools it is clearly within the province of the teacher concerned with the presentation of the Christian faith to deal adequately with what Christianity has to say about the problems posed in the previous paragraphs dealing with the changing situation in society. For this reason the syllabus has been devised so as to give some prominence to personal relationships and the practical difficulties with which young people are confronted.

The study begins with an introduction to the origin and nature of the Bible. One of the difficulties is the biblical approach to truth. This, in many ways, is so alien to the climate of thought in which young people grow up today that it can form a barrier to the communication of the truths which have to be grasped. For this reason an attempt must be made to explain the way in which the biblical message was intended for adults with a very different kind of culture and way of life. Too often it has been assumed that the ability to read was sufficient in itself; that given this literary skill the contents would be self-explanatory. This cannot be true today. Children need much help before they can begin to see the relevance of the Bible to the problems of the present age. It has been truly said that, 'The issues with which the Bible deals are perennially fresh and urgent; the nature of man, the choice between taking life seriously and letting it happen, between a large view and a small view of human destiny, the meaning of conscience, and experience of absolute obligation in which men are made aware of God.' (1) These issues are not self-evident. They have to be brought into line with the pupils' experience; they are not explained in the same terms as so much of the phenomena of their environment can be explained.

There is no single way of teaching any subject and the use of the material and the method to be used in its presentation will vary to some extent with the interests of the teacher as well as the age and ability of the pupils. There is room for experiment in any given situation. For example, some may prefer a method by which a contemporary movement is taken as a starting point for an enquiry into the historical reasons for the present situation; it would be possible to make an interesting excursion into church history beginning with the Ecumenical movement and working backwards to the cause for disunity. Similarly, it is often necessary to deal with a topic of interest which may be a matter for general discussion in the press, or out-of-school, but which has a close link with some aspect of religious education.

Suggestions for drawing up a scheme of work

In the making of a scheme of work the first step is to gauge the ability of the pupil and then to make a realistic plan based on the number of periods available for religious education. When doing this, it must be kept in mind that there are interruptions in the course of study due to half-terms, the incidence of examinations, and possibly for other reasons; it would be generally agreed that a minimum of two periods a week is required to do justice to any subject and if it is to have even parity of esteem religious education should have no less. The planning of the scheme should take into consideration the links that may be possible with other subjects and with the festivals of the Christian year.

Next in importance is to take note of the key points in each part of the Syllabus. It is arranged so that themes are introduced several times but each time in a new way. It is a basic principle of good teaching that we return to a main point again and again, but each time there is a need to approach it from a new angle. In this way for example, it could be claimed that, with a growing knowledge of the circumstances, and the life that ensued, a deeper insight into the nature of the Person of Christ may be built up.

---

(1) Loukes, H., Teenage Religion, pp. 150–151 S.C.M. Press

It is not easy to make a scheme which does justice to the aims and purposes of a Syllabus but which, at the same time, serves the needs of the children being taught. For this reason, the Syllabus has been arranged so that a given theme runs through the sections suggested for each stage. There are five stages corresponding to the five years in the life of a pupil in a secondary school; a further section is added, with suggestions for more advanced work in sixth forms, but it may be that some of these topics could be dealt with within the framework of the earlier sections.

The place of external examinations

Different views are held about the place of external examinations and with the introduction of new ways of examining perhaps an even greater prominence may be given to them. Many have grave doubts about the desirability of examining religious knowledge lest attention should be focussed on minor points to the exclusion of weightier matters.

It will be unfortunate, to say the least, if the syllabus to be followed in order to meet the needs of an external examination has the effect of limiting or, in some cases nullifying, the intentions of the Agreed Syllabus. That this could be a possibility is evident from experience in other subjects where the need for the preparation of the less able pupils (many of whom are probably unable to benefit by an external examination) has led to the examination syllabus replacing the school syllabus even in the first and second year. It is most undesirable in any case, that the work for an external examination should occupy more time than can be given in the fifth year, thus allowing the Agreed Syllabus to be followed for at least the first four years; the teaching in the Agreed Syllabus should, in any case, be the foundation of the work to be examined.

An outline of the Secondary Section

The intention of the Agreed Syllabus is to offer to teachers a source from which they may make a scheme of work suitable for the pupils they have to teach. This recognises that in the first place, the Bible is supremely and authoritatively 'the word of God' for all those who call themselves Christians. But, as no less an authority than Dr. C. H. Dodd pointed out some time ago, its authority rests upon a confirmation based on experience. If we do not realise this the mistake can be made of offering a kind of Bible-centred teaching which may do more harm than good. Moreover recent research has indicated that many aspects of biblical truth require an experience of life and living which is beyond the reach of children. Failure to appreciate this can lead to a merely verbal response which defeats growth in their ability to understand the inner spiritual truth of the Bible.

With this in mind the work has been arranged in stages rather than in years in order to make it easier for teachers to draw up a scheme of work in keeping with the needs of the pupils they are teaching. Special care needs to be taken in the choice of passages for study and the basis on which a selection should be made is not 'Can the children understand this passage of scripture?' but rather 'What conception of God as revealed in Christ are the children likely to apprehend by this scripture passage, and is it within their range of interpretative ability?'

There are creeds based on a theology evolved within the history of the church down the ages; these are summaries of Christian belief and allow for a wide variety of interpretation. Their importance, however, in the education of growing children must always be limited. What is more important, within the framework of an Agreed Syllabus, is to show that religious truth, or Christian insight, is 'normal experience understood at full depth' (Professor Jeffreys). (1) While such truth or insight comes within the context of the church teaching, its acceptance by a child must come from within his own experience and the insight he has gained into this by study of the scriptures. It cannot be imposed from without.

The secondary syllabus is divided into three parts and each part into stages.

---

(1) Jeffreys, M. V. C., 'Glaucon', Pitman, 1961, p. 118.*

Part One

Stage One – for those 11 to 12 years

        The Story of the Bible.
        The Sources of Christianity.
        The Beginnings of Church History.

Stage Two – for those 12 to 13 years

        What the Bible is about.
        What the Old Testament has to say.
        The Life and Times of Jesus.

Part Two

The Main Syllabus

Stage Three – for those over 13 years

        Becoming an Adult in the Community.
        What do we mean by the 'Law and the Prophets' ?

Stage Four – for those over 14 years

        Christianity in the Modern World.
        What do Christians believe ?
        The Christian Community.

Stage Five – for those over 15 years

        The Church in action.
        Personal relationships and responsibility.

The Alternative Syllabus

        Some consideration of the needs of the pupil (13 to 16 years).

Stage Three – for those over 13 years

        Growing up in the home.
        Growing up in the neighbourhood.
        Our responsibilities in the world.

Stage Four – children over the age of 14 years

        Becoming an adult in the community.

Stage Five – mainly for the non-academic child staying on to 16

        Contributing to the community.

Part Three

        The Sixth Form – changes in the Sixth Form.
        Suggestions for an approach to the subject of Religious
        Education. Further suggestions.

At this stage, a beginning should be made with an introduction to the Bible as the basis of study. This implies that we should give the pupils some idea of its nature and its message. What is meant by biblical truth? It is, to the ordinary boy or girl, very different from truth as we see it in our search for verification; this arises from the quest for a solution in the scientific sense. To many the scientific approach may mean little more than the acceptance of rules which appear to be capable of universal application. By pursuing a line of investigation, and proceeding stage by stage, we arrive by logical deduction, at a solution which gives us a positive answer. It is in the nature of things that this attitude comes to the fore in looking at the certainties or uncertainties of life, the existence of God, and the nature of His world in terms of creation. To the pupil questions become 'Is there a God to be found?' and 'If there is one, what then?'. These are useful questions but one to which there is no simple answer; one of the first things that has to be learned is to ask the right questions in the right way. The main biblical theme is about how God reveals Himself to us; all activity begins and ends with God. The Bible is concerned to show us how God, through the ages, has revealed Himself to men in the history of the Jewish people, through His prophets, and through His great acts of redemption.

The story of the Bible

The Bible is made of many books, and these in turn are based on ancient writings. Throughout the Bible there is one main theme, the revelation of God to man and God's purposes for us and His creation. In revelation it is God who reveals and Who is revealed.

It contains legends, stories, poetry, allegory, history of a special kind, law, philosophy, political criticism and many other things in the Old Testament; letters (the earliest records), expositions of the Christian faith, as well as records of the life and sayings of Jesus insofar as the authors thought they were important, in the New Testament.

It was written over a period of about a thousand years and the interpretation of the history it records covers a much longer period. Over the period in which the writings were made the materials used advanced from stone and clay to papyrus and parchment.

Apart from a few verses in Aramaic, the Old Testament was written in Hebrew, and the New Testament in Greek. Over the centuries translations have been made into many languages including English. In recent times, scholars have done much research into the meaning of the original records and new translations have been made of the English Bible. The Bible in whole or in part has been translated into over a thousand languages and into most of these during the nineteenth and twentieth centuries.

The Bible of Jesus and the early Christians was the Old Testament but no list of the books it might have included exists. Many scholars have looked into the origin of the books of the Bible. Some ancient Jewish writings were put into a section called the Apocrypha; these were considered as worthy to be read but not to be quite as valuable as the other books.

Before any books were included in the New Testament or even written down, the Christian Church used the Old Testament as its Bible. It had also its tradition of what was remembered about the life and sayings of Jesus. As those who had known Jesus personally grew old and died, it became necessary to write down what was remembered about Him and His teaching. The followers of Jesus carried the Gospel to parts of Asia Minor, Greece and thence to Rome and the accounts of their travels and experiences were written down in the Acts of the Apostles.

The oldest writings in the New Testament, those which were written down first, were letters sent to groups of Christians who had formed churches in Greece or in Asia Minor, and in the fourth century A.D. the list of New Testament books, as we have them today, was accepted by the Church.

All through the variety of style and the difficulties of translation the Bible reveals a clear purpose – to show us progressively the character of the Living God and how He has acted in history and, of course, continues to act.

Suggestions for books in connection with 'The Story of the Bible'

Pupils' books of the easier kind (good for background information) :

Sanders, E. M.	The Holy Land Book 1 : The Land, the People and their work Book 2 : Background and Customs	George Philip *
Hilliard, F. H.	Behold the Land : a Pictorial Atlas	George Philip

Pupils' books ; more advanced :

Gadd, K. M.	Ancient Civilisations	Ginn *
Mathews, H. F.	Bible Cavalcade	Epworth *
Smith, J. W. D.	Bible Background	Methuen
Van Deursen, A.	Illustrated Dictionary of Bible Manners and Customs	Marshall Morgan
Youngman, B. A.	Background to the Bible	Hulton Educational Publishers
Woolley, L.	Digging up the Past	Penguin

Reference books, mainly for teachers :

Bruce, F. F.	The English Bible	Lutterworth
Barclay, W.	The Making of the Bible	Lutterworth
Dodd, C. H.	The Authority of the Bible	Fontana
Herklots, H. G.	How the Bible came to us	Pelican *
Kenyon, Sir F.	The Story of the Bible	Murray
Parmelee, A.	A Guide to the Bible	E.U.P.
Van Allman	The Vocabulary of the Bible The Cambridge Bible Commentary	Lutterworth C.U.P.
Harrison, R. K.	The Dead Sea Scrolls (Teach Yourself Books)	E.U.P. *

The Bible as a library: the Old Testament

(a) The Law (Torah)

The Law was an account of God's will and purpose first to His 'chosen people' the Jews, and through them to the rest of the world; in this way it was to be equally binding upon all peoples. The work of scholars has shown that many of the early stories in the Book of Genesis, such as the story of Creation, the Fall, and the Flood have parallels in other ancient literature, but when the Old Testament stories are compared with them it is the differences, not the similarities, which are impressive.

The writers of these early books did not have our modern scientific knowledge of the universe. Perhaps the most important statement they make is the opening sentence, 'In the beginning God . . .'. God is declared to be the beginning and end of all activity; He is both Creator and Sustainer of the universe, which is rational and based on an orderly system of law. Indeed, science could not have developed without a belief in an ordered system of creation. What the writers had in mind was a belief in the directing power of God (Yahweh). The value of the narratives is not scientific but religious.

For a fuller interpretation of this cycle of stories see :

A. Richardson	The Bible in an Age of Science	S.C.M.
A. Richardson	Genesis I–XI	S.C.M.
Clarendon Bible	In the Beginning – Vol. 6	O.U.P.

The Law was, in one sense, an attempt to create an orderly life in keeping with the needs of a community of the Middle East, living in the circumstances of climate and the civilisation of that age. Today, Jews, who are the descendants of these peoples, accept the laws of the country in which they have settled. They are loyal members of the community and many of them hold high positions in local and national affairs. They do, however, keep to their customs and laws in religious matters: they have their own New Year and follow a religious calendar as well as our own secular calendar. In matters of food they also keep to their own regulations and have a diet which differs in some respects from ours. The exciting story of the discovery of the Book of the Law can be read in II Kings 22.

The Clarendon Bible, Vols. 1–6 :

The Ten Commandments	Exodus 20
Laws of Property	Exodus 22 vv. 1–13
Laws of Eating and Drinking	Leviticus 11
Laws of Cultivation	Leviticus 25
Laws of Inheritance	Numbers 27 vv. 1–11
Laws of Refuge	Deuteronomy 19 vv. 1–10

(b) History

This is rather the interpretation of history from a national and religious point of view, than history as we know it. The reign of David and the period of the captivity are taken as representing the most formative phases of the history of the Hebrew nation, apart from the Exodus, and the giving of the Law. This history becomes important to us in terms of its concern with the religious development of the Hebrews. They formed a small nation which in a political sense was weak and oppressed for most of its history. This history consists mainly in its relations with the foreign powers of Syria (Aram in the Bible) and Assyria in the north, Egypt in the south: after the division of the kingdom, Israel and Judah take up the story.

The high water mark of Hebrew political history is reflected in the period when David ruled and the Kingdom stretched from Dan to Beersheba; its ebb is recorded in the captivity in Babylon. The history of the northern kingdom is found in I Kings and II Kings 1–17. The history of Judah is found also in II Chronicles 10–36 but the writer was so critical of the separation of Israel from Judah, that he left out all references to the northern kingdom, except for occasional points of contact. The writer of I and II Kings was himself a Judean. The unity between north and south was precarious and only really achieved under David and Solomon; politically there was tension and the sense of unity was in their common religion made stronger by the centralisation of the worship at Jerusalem after the building of the Temple. The obelisk of Shalmanezer III, now in the British Museum, is an important piece of archaeological evidence of the history of this period. There are many references to the northern kingdom in Amos and Hosea; to Judah in Isaiah and Jeremiah.

The reign of David	II Samuel I vv. 1–12, 17–24
The captivity in Babylon	II Kings 24 vv. 8–17

There is a further development of this period of Jewish history in Appendix A.

Books of reference :

Rattey, B. K.	A Short History of the Hebrews	O.U.P.
Robinson, Gordon	Historians of Israel	Lutterworth
Wright, G. E.	Biblical Archaeology	Duckworth

(c) Prophecy

The prophets were God's messengers. In the passages given below, they speak about the situation at critical times in the history of the kingdoms of Israel (the northern kingdom) and Judah. They were speaking about situations in which they themselves were involved; they had a deeper insight into these situations than their contemporaries and were often speaking out against the prevailing views of those in authority. They showed great courage in speaking out and expressing unpopular views; their statements and denunciations were often introduced by such a phrase as, 'Thus saith the Lord . . .'.

Amos	The prophet is accused	Amos 7 vv. 10–15
Jeremiah	He is given orders to speak out Each has an individual responsibility: the law is 'in their hearts' A reprimand	Jeremiah 1 vv. 4–10 Jeremiah 18 vv. 1–12
Ezekiel	In captivity, he receives his commission 'the word of the Lord came to Ezekiel'. The valley of dry bones and the restoration of Israel	Ezekiel 1 vv. 1–3 Ezekiel 1 v. 3 Ezekiel 37 vv. 1–14

Books of reference :

Fleming, James	Personalities of the Old Testament	Scribner *
Lace, O. Jessie	Teaching of the Old Testament pp. 52–54	S.P.C.K. *

(d) Poetry and Wisdom

The Psalms as we have them were probably written down between 400 B.C. and 100 B.C. although many of them are centuries older in their origin. The word Psalm comes to us from the Greek and means a song or hymn sung to an instrumental accompaniment. Thus Psalm 4 was to be sung to the accompaniment of stringed instruments, while Psalm 5 was to be sung to the sound of the flute.

There were Psalms for special occasions. When families went up to Jerusalem for a festival they joined up with other families to make a pilgrimage. As they journeyed they sang Psalms to help them on their way: such songs are called Songs of Ascent possibly because from whatever angle they approached Jerusalem it meant climbing the Judean hills. Examples of such Psalms are :

Psalm 84	'How lovely is thy dwelling place . . .'.
Psalm 121	'I will lift up my eyes unto the hills . . .'.
Psalm 122	'I was glad when they said to me, "Let us go unto the house of the Lord" . . .'.

Other Psalms are in praise of God as Creator: they offer thanks for the glories and gifts of nature :

Psalm 104 v. 24	'Oh Lord how manifold are Thy works . . .'.
Psalm 19	'The heavens are telling the glory of God . . .'.

Many Psalms see in the universe a sign of God's wisdom and goodness as shown in the material world. Their theme is God's providence and care :—

Psalm 72	'Give the king Thy justice O Lord . . .'.
Psalm 67 v. 4	'Let the nations be glad . . .'.

Most important of all, the Psalms were often recalled by Our Lord. They express much of His thinking and were used by Him at crucial moments in His life, thus :

In the Temptations	Psalm 91 vv. 11 ff
In the Sermon on the Mount	Psalm 18 vv. 25 ff
On the Cross	Psalm 22

There are too, many examples of Hebrew poetry apart from the Psalms. One of the greatest is David's dirge over the death of Jonathan (tradition makes a great deal of David's musical skill – I Samuel 16 vv. 14–23; Amos 6 v. 5).

David's Lament	II Samuel 1 vv. 19–27

Sayings from various periods, some of them worldly-wise, others showing a shrewd estimate of the human situation, are to be found in the Book of Proverbs and Ecclesiastes Proverbs 3 and 8 are examples.

The Jews were very practical people who took life seriously and made sympathetic observations on human behaviour.

Books of reference:

Lewis, C. S.	Reflections on the Psalms	Collins
	The Psalms (Layman's Bible Commentary)	S.C.M. Press *

(e) Stories

A Love Story	Ruth 1–4
The Story of Jonah	Jonah 1–4

Both of these, one a story, the other a parable, deal with the problem of exclusiveness The Jews were not unnaturally inclined to look inwards to their own community and look down on other peoples: both these stories are a challenge to this point of view.

A tragic drama	Job 1–4

Deals with an ever recurring problem, the challenge of innocent suffering.

What might be called a 'tract for the times' 167–165 B.C.   Daniel 1 and 3

On loyalty, and an allegory of the national faithfulness, to encourage the Jews to be loyal to their faith in times of persecution.

Books of reference:

Weimer, R. O.	Jonah and the Whale	MacMillan *
	The Clarendon Bible Vols. 1–6	O.U.P.

The Bible as a library: the New Testament

(a) Letters

In studying the sections from the New Testament it must be realised that there is a fundamental change brought about by Our Lord's crucifixion. The mode of His dying involved the curse of the Law; a crucified Messiah came under the curse of the Law. It is the development of this law which is the main concern of the Old Testament (Deuteronomy 21 vv. 21–22; Galatians 3 v. 13). It was this staggering fact which was '... a stumbling block to the Jews and folly to Greeks' (I Cor. 1 v. 23 N.E.B.). Yet Paul's acquaintance with Jewish literature was that of an expert; he was the son of devout Jews (Phil. 3 vv. 5–7); the Law the Prophets, and the Psalms he regarded as authoritative for his faith and life. When he became a Christian he looked into their meaning with fresh insight.

The usual way in which Paul began his letters	I Cor. 1 vv. 1–3
An appeal for unity and a poem on Christian love.	I Cor. 1 v. 10–13
A final appeal	II Cor. 13 vv. 5–14
A challenge to the relationships in society; a runaway slave.	Philemon

James, the Lord's brother (eldest of the group of younger children named in Mark 6 v. 3) and leader of the church at Jerusalem writes an 'open letter'. Belief without right conduct is worthless: an essay on practical religion.

James 1 vv. 1–27
James 2 vv. 1–13

Books of reference:

Beare, F. W.	St. Paul and his Letters	Black*
Nock, A. D.	St. Paul	Home University* Library
	Understanding the New Testament (Cambridge Bible Commentary pp. 82–98).	C.U.P. *

(b) The Gospels

Only four Gospels, all written after the letters of Paul and probably in this order, Mark, Luke, Matthew and John, have come down to us. We know that when Luke wrote his Gospels : this was an attempt to weave the four into one continuous narrative. It was (cf. Luke 1 v. 1). One of these was almost certainly our Gospel of Mark. Some of these accounts to which Luke refers no doubt provided material for his own Gospel and that of Matthew, but none of them, Mark apart, has survived, presumably because none was held in the same esteem as our four Gospels.

The question is sometimes asked, why should we have four Gospels ? About A.D. 170 an Assyrian Christian, Tatian by name, prepared the first known 'harmony' of the Gospels : this was an attempt to weave the four into our continuous narrative. It was called the Diatessaron. His was the first of many efforts to do this. No single Gospel, however, can take the place of the four Gospels, each with its own understanding of Christ to contribute.

The Synoptic Gospels

The first three Gospels are called 'synoptic' because they give in general the same view of Our Lord's life and are similar in the general scheme and in the selection of materials.

Most scholars believe that Luke and the author of Matthew made use of Mark: two-thirds of Mark, for instance, appears in both Luke or Matthew. Luke and Matthew also have some two hundred verses in common which are not found in Mark. Many scholars are of the opinion that this material, consisting of sayings of Jesus, was found in a written source or sources commonly called 'Q' the first letter of the German word Quelle meaning 'source'.

The Gospel of John

Turning from the synoptics to John, we find ourselves in a new world. Where are the well-known parables ? Why has the short epigrammatic teaching been displaced by long discourses ? How is it that there is no proclamation of the Kingdom, but, instead, teaching about eternal life ? In the synoptics Jesus is concerned about the effect His miracles will have on the people's understanding of His Messiahship : in John, miracles are referred to as 'signs' which indicate the very nature of his Messiahship. Thus, in the fourth Gospel, Jesus is recognised as the Messiah at the very beginning of His ministry.

A comment by C. S. C. Williams gives us considerable help in answering these questions :

'The fourth Evangelist began with what he took to be historical and by profound contemplation of it he uncovered deeper and deeper meanings, often allowing the characters of or events 'on the surface' to fade away into the backcloth of his scene or the conversation to run "into the sand"' (2)

It must be remembered, however, that current New Testament scholarship will not allow us to think of the synoptic Gospels as 'historical' and the fourth Gospel as 'theological'. All four are both.

(c) The Acts of the Apostles

This contains the story of the early church. It is by the same author as the writer of Luke's Gospel and can be regarded as volume two of a work intended to tell the story of the continuing ministry of Jesus through the Holy Spirit. It tells of the spread of Christianity from Jerusalem through Asia Minor and Greece to Rome.

---

(2) Williams, C. S. C.   Introduction to the New Testament p. 330.   A. & C. Black *

(d) The Book of Revelation

Like Daniel (and cf. Mark 13 and II Thess. 2 vv. 1–12) this book is apocalyptic in character. The clash between Christianity and Emperor-worship had caused Christians to be the victims of a reign of terror and Revelation was written to encourage members of the Church to stand firm. This book was intended mainly as a book of consolation and guidance in time of persecution for what might have been called the 'underground' movement of those days. Although the Christians did not take part in warlike actions against the Romans in the same way as members of the 'resistance' in the occupied areas in the 1939–45 war, they suffered a similar fate if they were discovered. Hence the style of writing is often in the form of a 'code' which had a special significance for those who were able to see the hidden meaning contained in the imagery.

The book falls into three main sections:

Christ's message to the Churches	Revelation ch. 1–3
The vision of judgement of God's enemies and the victory of the faithful.	Revelation ch. 4–20
The coming of God's Kingdom on earth	Revelation ch. 21–22

Note on the formation of the New Testament Canon:

This was a long and gradual process: its most powerful motive was to preserve the Church from heresy. The Canon containing the books we now have in the New Testament was not officially sanctioned until the fourth century.

Books of reference:

Grant, R. M.	The Formation of the New Testament	Hutchinson
Robinson, W. Gordon	An Introduction to the New Testament	Edward Arnold *
Williams, C. S. C.	Introduction to the New Testament	A. & C. Black *
Taylor, Vincent	The Gospels: a Short Introduction Understanding the New Testament (Cambridge Bible Commentary)	Epworth * C.U.P.*

Some famous translations

The Septuagint – an early translation of the Old Testament from Hebrew into Greek. A large number of Jews who had settled in Alexandria had become estranged from their own (Hebrew) language; they spoke Greek better than their native language, so a translation of the Old Testament into Greek became necessary. This was done in the 2nd and 3rd centuries B.C. and became one of the original documents used in making other translations.

The Vulgate (3) – Written in Latin this was the Bible of the Western Church for over a thousand years. Confusion had arisen over different versions and Pope Damasus I ordered a monk named Jerome to standardise the texts. He took more than twenty years revising different scripts and he completed his work about A.D. 404.

Some of the great English Bibles

The Venerable Bede (A.D. 672–735) and King Alfred (A.D. 849–899) as well as John Wyclif (A.D. 1320–1384) translated St. John's Gospel into the vernacular. William Tyndale translated the New Testament from the Greek original in A.D. 1525–6. One of the great tragedies of the intolerance and cruelty of the age was his death at the stake in Belgium whither he had fled from England; his writings were scholarly and his translations sound. One of the greatest forces in the English Reformation, his work formed the basis of the Authorised Version A.D. 1611.

The Coverdale Bible

Miles Coverdale (1488–1569) is, next to Tyndale, the man to whom we owe the greatest debt. He devoted the best part of his life to translating the Bible into the 'common tongue'. He was not a scholar in the sense that Tyndale was, but he added a

---

(3) Bruce, F. F.   The English Bible   Lutterworth

touch of genius to the task by using colloquial phrases such as 'Good Luck have you with thine honour' (Ps. 45 v. 5) and 'Tush, say they, how should God perceive it' (Ps. 73 v. 11) for the sake of vividness. We still use the Coverdale version in the Psalms as set out in Book of Common Prayer 1662 (still used in the Church of England). Coverdale's Bible was published in 1553.

The Great Bible

This made its first appearance in 1539. Coverdale supervised the work which was based on Matthew's Bible, the 'Bible of the largest volume in English'. Thomas Cromwell's injunction read as follows:

'That ye shall provide, on this side of the feast of all Saints next coming, one book of the whole Bible of the largest volume in English, and the same set up in some convenient place within the said church that ye have cure of, whereas your parishioners may most commodiously resort to the same and read it; the charges of which book shall be rateably borne between you, the parson, and the parishioners aforesaid, that is to say the one half by you and the other half by them ...' (3)

These Bibles were chained to a desk and so much in demand that a notice had to be fixed saying that the 'reading aloud of the English Bible during divine service' was forbidden – so great was the interest in the scriptures in the 16th century.

The Bishop's Bible 1568

This was a revision of the Great Bible in the light of more scholarly work (the Geneva Bible A.D. 1557–60).

The Authorised Version A.D. 1611

James I summoned a conference 'for the hearing, and for the determining, things pretended to be amiss in the church'. The Conference met at Hampton Court in 1604 and it was decided that a new translation of the Bible be made. The real reason was to do away with the copious notes that had appeared with the previous Bible, some of them very 'partial, untrue, seditious and savouring too much of dangerous and traitorous conceits'. This version was used, and continues to be used in most churches to this day. (3) p. 97.

The Revised Version 1881–5

Better manuscripts had come to light, older than any of the texts previously used. It became clear that the A.V. ought to be revised.

The Revised Standard Version

This is the work of American scholars and has been warmly welcomed. Published completely in 1962, it does away with some of the old forms of speech which we may call 'bible language' (most of the 'thees' and 'thous' disappear and such phrases as 'and it came to pass').

The New English Bible

As a result of a suggestion made at the General Assembly of the Church of Scotland in 1946, it was decided that a completely new translation of the Bible should be made. All the main churches approved, and a committee was set up in 1947. The emphasis was to be in making a translation into 'modern English'. The New Testament was published in 1961 and the Old Testament in 1970.

---

(3) ibid

Suggestions for books in connection with ' The Bible as a library'

Pupils' books about the Bible :

The following books, intended for younger children, may be of interest to the secondary pupils who show less interest in academic work.

Readiness for Religion Series   Rupert Hart-Davis
   Bull, N. J.   Symbols (Series)
                     What is the Bible (Series) vide p. 73.

Pupils' books :

                     The Bible and the Christian Faith   Ginn *
                     (a series).

   Firth, C. B.   A People of Hope
                     (This book deals with the Law, the
                     historical books and the prophets.)

   Latham, L. C.   Poets, Wise Men and Seers
                     (This deals with the Psalms, Wisdom,
                     Literature and Apocalypse in Old
                     Testament and New Testament.)

   Titterton, A. F.   Christ in the Gospels.
                     (This deals with the Synoptic
                     Gospels only.)

All these are useful reference books for teachers.

   Frost, S.   Patriarchs and Prophets   Murray
   Smith, J.   Synoptic Tables   Berean Press

The British Museum has a wide selection of facsimile reproductions of old texts, codices and other documents.

The Rylands Library, Deansgate, Manchester, has a fragment of St. John's Gospel and of part of Deuteronomy. Reproductions may be had.

Material is also available from the British and Foreign Bible Society, 146 Queen Victoria Street, London E.C.4.

STAGE TWO

What the Bible is about

The Bible is a book of great questions. In this section we are finding out what the Hebrews believed about God, the questions they asked, and the way they believed God revealed Himself to them.

What the Old Testament had to say

The Hebrews had learned to believe that there is one God (Yahweh) and one only ; He had acted, so they believed, throughout their history as both powerful and good. In this way they felt that they were different from most of their neighbours.

They also learned from interpreting their national history, that God was profoundly concerned about all human affairs. This is not a general belief of all religions : to many people God was a distant power, often a hard taskmaster working against, and not on behalf of, humanity. At best, He was indifferent and did not care for men and women.

It was because their religion was so different from other peoples round about them that they were bound by a special loyalty to their God. They believed He had a special interest in them and they had a special purpose in the world. All this, to them was expressed in an agreement – a covenant.

To some of the people of Israel this was regarded as a special favour; it gave privileges which set them apart from the 'lesser breeds without the Law'. To other members of the nation it meant that they had special responsibilities and a special mission to show the world the true nature of God. Their knowledge of God was still not complete and they had much to learn.

The Jews who took the wider view were much aware of how the people of Israel had failed to measure up to the duties and responsibilities laid upon them, but they still believed that in spite of their failings God would stand by His word and not reject them. So it came about that they expected God to take strong and decisive action. The coming of Messiah would be the signal for Israel to be made free and throw off the yoke of their new masters, the Romans. Then Israel would be free to carry out her mission to the rest of the world, to show the people that there was one God who was love itself, holy, and righteous.

Jesus was born into this society and brought up in this religion. The only story that has come down to us about His boyhood is when His parents took Him to the Passover Festival at Jerusalem when He was twelve years old. We know from the Old Testament what it was the teachers in the Temple were teaching and what it was that Jesus discussed ; we also know what Jesus meant when He referred to 'His Father'. It is through the life and teaching of Jesus that we know what God is like. The hope was widespread that a Messiah would soon appear and 'restore again the Kingdom to Israel' and many were prepared to follow any leader who would start a national revolt. Some pictured the Messiah as the Son of David, who would do more than restore the Kingdom as they believed it to have been in Solomon's time. Others looked for the coming of a super-human being who would be God's representative 'The Son of Man from Heaven'. These were the familiar expressions of the faith which refused to believe that God's purposes could fail, or that he would forsake those who had put their trust in Him.

When, therefore, Jesus said that the Kingdom of God had come, He meant that these hopes were fulfilled, that in Himself the Kingly power of God was made manifest : that in Him men could see the power of God at work in the world.

Isaiah's wonderful vision	Isaiah 6 vv. 1–8
A King to reign over the nations	Psalm 2
The great commandment	Deuteronomy 6 vv. 4–5
God's promise and the mission which they had to carry out.	Isaiah 42 vv. 6–7

The Life and Times of Jesus

For a better understanding of the life and times of Jesus, it is advisable to deal with the main features of the geography of Palestine. Water supplies were of paramount importance as they are today. Wells and streams, as well as the river Jordan, feature largely in the story. The position of the main cities and the political divisions under the Romans should be shown as an important part of the background.

Some knowledge of the history of the period is essential in understanding the message of the Gospel. Much of the materials can be presented as the need arises, incidentally, in the story. The people, members of a small nation, no longer independent but under the rule of the Roman Empire, were proud of their history and easily moved by the memories of their struggles as recorded in the Old Testament. They were especially conscious of the part their religion had played in shaping their destiny. The calendar, unlike that of the surrounding peoples, was not closely linked to the changing agricultural scene but designed to remind them of the great religious experiences in their stirring history.

The beginning of history was to them associated with Yahweh leading them out of Egypt into the Promised Land — the Exodus (remembered each year in the Passover ceremony). They held firmly to the belief that they were specially chosen by God to fulfil a special purpose; they looked for the coming of a national leader, the Messiah, sent by God to give them freedom and to lead them to their destiny.

Roman rule in Palestine had its advantages as well as disadvantages and drawbacks. On the one hand it gave them peace, great public works, roads, aqueducts and the advantages of civilisation; on the other hand double taxation and the humiliation of being a subject nation.

There was much poverty and unemployment (parable of the Labourers in the Vineyard).

The ruling classes were mainly self-seeking men, so that Jesus compared the masses to 'sheep without a shepherd'.

The Roman Governor and officials were the centre of much intrigue. The Dynasty of the Herods was an affront to the pious Jews. The party of the Pharisees was, in a way, the party of the 'good men' of their day, although it fell far short of being good in the sense that Jesus meant. Other important people were the High Priests and the Sadducees. The Zealots were extreme nationalists. Although not mentioned in the New Testament, there were the Essenes and it is generally agreed that the Dead Sea Scrolls, discovered at Qumran belonged to members of this Sect.

Religion and education centred in the Temple and Synagogue. There was a great contrast between Galilee and Jerusalem.

The Life of Jesus

It must be made clear to the pupils that the Gospels were not written as biographies or 'lives' of Jesus. The Gospels were 'good news', the announcement that in the life and teaching of Jesus, the Kingdom had come.

The pattern of the life might well fall under the following main headings but material from other gospels will be necessary and sometimes preferable:

How was He born? These stories reveal the hunger of the people for a divine wonder.

Some Jews were waiting for a Messiah John the Baptist	Luke 3 vv. 1–22
The prophecy of Simeon	Luke 2 vv. 25–35
The circumstances surrounding the birth of Christ.	Luke 2 vv. 1–20
Bethlehem and the Davidic descent	Matthew 1 vv. 1–16
The flight to Egypt	Matthew 2 vv. 13–23
The Birth Stories as poetry emphasising the divine origin of Jesus	Luke 1 vv. 26–55 Matthew 1 vv. 18–25

How did He train?

The boy in the Temple	Luke 2 vv. 41–52
The last of the Old Testament Prophets : herald of the new age	Matthew 3 vv. 1–12 Mark 1 vv. 1–11
The arrest and death of John	Matthew 14 vv. 3–10
The Temptations – a time for decision	Luke 4 vv. 1–13

How did He begin His ministry?

The preaching mission	Mark 1 vv. 16–20
The mission of the twelve	Luke 9 vv. 1–10
The mission of the seventy	Luke 10 vv. 1–24
The plan for the Kingdom	Luke 4 vv. 14–30 Isaiah 61

Did He perform miracles?

The healing mission at Capernaum	Luke 4 vv. 31–44
In the synoptics faith is a pre-requisite of the miracle :	
at Nazareth none cured	Mark 6 vv. 4–6
at Capernaum all cured	Mark 9 vv. 23–24

The miracles of Jesus are recorded as performed in different ways :

Healing by touch

By contact with the person to be cured	
The leper	Luke 5 vv. 12–16

In the synoptic Gospels, Jesus shows a desire to keep the miracles a secret. Luke 5 v. 14 : '. . . He ordered them not to tell anybody' and so in Mark 5 v. 43.

Healing through faith followed by forgiveness

The healing of the paralytic	Luke 5 vv. 17–26

In this case there is doubt expressed when Jesus claims to have authority to forgive sins. He meets opposition. The phrase 'son of man' is used (cf. Daniel 7 v. 13).

He healed by word of mouth at a distance

The healing of the Nobleman's son	John 4 vv. 46–54

The healing is not done because the father saw a miracle but because he really believed in the power of Jesus as 'the Word'.

In healing he showed a complete understanding of the human mind

The man possessed by an 'unclean spirit'	Mark 5 vv. 1–20

It is necessary to give some information on the prevailing ideas concerning demoniac possession and Christ's willingness to help such people. The incident is recorded by a person whose knowledge of mental disorder was in keeping with the medical knowledge of the age in which he lived. The permission for the evil spirits to enter the swine has been a stumbling block to many ; some have seen this as a contradiction of the teaching on the nature of God. A probable explanation is that the swine were frightened by the commotion accompanying the violence of the demented men and so terrified that they ran head-long down the hill into the sea. Some authorities suggest that the reason the man was not forbidden to tell other people about his cure was because he was a Gentile.

Jesus healed by touch and saliva

The healing of the man born blind

Mark 8 vv. 22–26 ;
John 9

This is of interest as it shows how an event could be treated differently by different writers. In Mark's account there is the detail of an eye-witness (v. 24) : 'I see men but they look like trees . . .'. The miracle is to be a secret.

In John's account, the miracle is made the occasion for teaching about the Jewish ideas of corporate personality and sin (John 9 v. 2) and there is a development of the idea of Jesus as the 'Light of the World'.

The Summary

John gives his reason for the miracles

John 20 v. 30

Books of reference

Lewis, C. S.	Miracles	Bles *
Moule, C. F.	Miracles	C.U.P.*
Richardson, Alan	The Miracle Stories of the Gospels	S.C.M.

Events leading to the Passion

Peter's confession at Caesarea Philippi

Mark 8 vv. 27–33

He already shows leadership (v. 28 was the popular opinion – Elijah being taken up to heaven was to confirm that he had not suffered death in the usual way by bodily corruption).

The Transfiguration

Mark 9 vv. 2–8

A moment of insight on the part of the disciples. Jesus had superseded the old covenant : He was no mere prophet but the Messiah.

The entry into Jerusalem

Words are replaced by action : Jesus is acting out His Messianic mission. This is a royal reception by the crowd who received Him.

The placing of garments or the strewing of articles on the road has, from the most ancient times, been regarded as a sign of the coming of royal personages.

Jesus is acclaimed king

Luke 19 v. 38

The greeting of the crowd echoes the Messianic references in Psalm 118 vv. 26–29 ; II Kings 9 v. 13 (cf. John 12 v. 13).

The author of Matthew's Gospel uses the verse Zechariah 9 v. 9 to show how prophecy was being fulfilled.

Why did they arrest Jesus ?

The struggle with authority.

(a) Cleansing the Temple
    Striking at the heart of Judaism and the vested
    interests of the Temple : 'my house' cf. John 2 vv.
    13–22 and the chronology of the same incident.
    This is an acted parable :

Mark 11 vv. 15–19

(b) The widow's mite. God's and man's arithmetic :
    we ask 'How much has he given ?'
    God asks, 'How much has been left ?'

Luke 21 vv. 1–4

(c) The raising of Lazarus

John 11 vv. 11–44

(d) A day of questions :
     of authority   Mark 11 vv. 27–33
     of tribute   Mark 12 vv. 13–17
     the resurrection   Mark 12 vv. 18–27
     the great commandment   Mark 12 vv. 28–34

(e) Jesus and the Sabbath :
     The cornfield dispute   Mark 2 vv. 23–28
     The man with the withered hand   Mark 3 v.v 1–6
     Further opposition   John 9 v. 14

(f) The betrayal – contrast the woman at Bethany :   Mark 14 vv. 3–9
     possible reasons for betrayal ; the denunciation   Mark 14 vv. 10–11
     of those in authority.

(g) The Last Supper   Mark 14 vv. 12–26
     Moses and the old covenant. Christ the new,: 'Do
     this in remembrance of Me'.

(h) The arrest   John 18 vv. 1–14
     The cup of suffering and the humanity of Christ   Luke 22 v. 42
     Mark's witness   Mark 14 v. 51

(i) The trials   John 18 vv. 19–40
                                  John 19 vv. 1–16
                                  Luke 22 vv. 54–71
                                  Luke 23 vv. 1–25
                                  Mark 14 vv. 53–65

     Pilate's attempt to release Christ. He seeks to
     evade responsibility by allowing the crowd to
     choose between Christ and the murderer. By their   Mark 15 vv. 1–15
     choice the Hebrew nation loses its unique
     position : its unique relationship with God.

(j) The Crucifixion   Mark 15 vv. 20–41
                                  Luke 23 vv. 27–49
                                  Matthew 27
                                  John 19

N.B. The emphasis should be on the victory, never on the details of horror ; on the courage which faced and bore them, rather than on the sufferings themselves. Such saying as 'My God, my God, Why hast thou forsaken me' and, 'It is finished', might be studied to advantage.

Why was Christ rejected ?

It is suggested that pupils should look through the following passages before proceeding to discuss this question.

1   The opening stages of the ministry   Luke 4 vv. 16–22
     He taught in the synagogues   Matthew 4 vv. 23
     What he taught about his mission :
     The work of John the Baptist   Matthew 11 vv. 1–11
     The fulfilment of prophecy   Luke 4 vv. 16–21

     The beginning of conflict with authority :
     He claims to forgive sins   Mark 2 vv. 5–28
     Breaking the Sabbath law   Mark 3 vv. 1–6

2   Jesus no longer teaches in the synagogues. The authorities have turned against Him and He is no longer welcome. He turns to the lakeside at Galilee and to the hills. He is popular with the ordinary people and regarded by them as a famous man and as a hero ; great crowds follow Him and the climax is reached at the Feeding of the Five Thousand.
     He teaches on the hillside and at the lakeside   Mark 3 vv. 7–14 ;
                                            4 vv. 1–3
                                          Matthew 5 vv. 1–2
     He becomes a hero in the eyes of the ordinary   Matthew 4 vv. 23–25
     people.

What the scribes and pharisees thought about
Jesus

The lawyers criticise His actions	Mark 2 vv. 6–12
The learned men (members of the establishment) dislike His eating and mingling with bad company.	Mark 2 vv. 16–17
But the people still follow Him and attempt to make Him king.	John 6 vv. 1–15

3   The people had become so excited and the Jewish leaders so hostile that
Jesus went into the comparative peace of the countryside (the Gentile
world) near Tyre and Sidon. These people would not easily be agitated at
the hopes of a nationalist rising.

There is a further breach with authority over rules and regulations.	Mark 7 vv. 1–13
The deaf man is healed but after being taken away from the crowd.	Mark 7 vv. 31–37
The blind man is led out of the village	Mark 8 vv. 22–26
The Pharisees ask for a sign	Mark 8 vv. 11–13
The testimony of Peter at Caesarea Philippi	Mark 8 vv. 28–33

The following questions might be discussed or made the subject of written work:

What was the reason for the popularity of Jesus?	
'The people were astounded at his teaching for He taught with a note of authority'.	Mark 1 v. 22
'There was a general stir of admiration'	Luke 4 v. 22
Did He appear to the ordinary peasant folk as a deliverer?	
What things did they want to be delivered from?	
Are there any modern parallels to this situation?	
There was also opposition even from His own people.	
Why were the people so 'infuriated'?	Luke 4 vv. 29–30
Why did the people of Nazareth turn against Him?	Luke 4 vv. 21–28

The difference of view over the 'covenant relationship' between the Jews and
Yahweh might be discussed. To many, if not the majority this meant being God's
'chosen people' in the sense of being superior to other nations 'the lesser breeds
without the law'. To the extremists this made a strong appeal. To others, almost
certainly a minority, the idea of being a 'chosen people' meant having greater responsibilities in carrying out God's purpose for the world. The teaching of Jesus was a direct
challenge to the narrow conception of the 'chosen people'.

The teaching Jesus gave was contrary to much that was accepted. He spoke 'with
authority' about:

1   The universal love of God.

'Who is My neighbour?'	Luke 10 vv. 25–37
The incident at Jacob's well	John 4
The centurion's servant is healed	Matthew 8 v. 10
'From east and west people will come...'	Luke 13 v. 29

2   Jesus opposed the conception of 'law' as
keeping to the letter and forgetting the spirit. He
taught that actions should be judged by the
motive behind them.

	The Sermon on the Mount Matthew 5
The Pharisee and the Publican	Luke 18 vv. 9–14
'This people pays Me lip-service, but their heart is far from Me'.	Matthew 15 vv. 1–11
The woman at Bethany	Mark 14 vv. 3–9

Some problems

Can you think of any well-known characters in literature whose actions were a denial of what they professed ?

What do you think Jesus would have said about the 'colour bar' ?
About forms of snobbery whether real or inverted ?
What did Jesus say about the use of money ?
Is a majority always right ?

You are in a factory and belong to a trade union. One man refuses to obey a call for what he considers to be an unnecessary unofficial strike. Someone demands that he shall be 'sent to Coventry'. What should a Christian say about this ? cf. the film, 'The Angry Silence' which has much to say about attitudes in an industrial situation.

Is it wrong to watch television when you could be spending time with a lonely person who is ill and in need of help ? Should we spend eighty pounds (perhaps on the instalment plan) on a motor-bicycle, when there are calls for help from under-developed countries and organisations which are in need of funds (Feed the Minds, Christian Aid, Freedom from Hunger, Oxfam and Save the Children Fund) ?

Have you read the Rubaiyat of Omar Khayam or the book of Ecclesiastes ?

How far does this wordly wisdom fall short of the teaching of Jesus ?

Why was Jesus so critical of the Pharisees, the 'good men' of His day and genera-tion ? and of those in authority ? and of the official idea of religion ?

The healing of the paralytic	Mark 2 vv. 1–12
The rule about fasting	Mark 2 vv. 18–22
The keeping of the Sabbath	Luke 6 vv. 1–11
The belief in Christ as an imposter	Mark 3 vv. 22–26

By being so critical of the official idea of religion, Jesus made many enemies.

The main points at the climax of the Story

(i) The burial : Nicodemus was also there cf. the story of Nicodemus ; he helps with the embalming of Jesus	Mark 15 vv. 42–47 John 3 vv. 1–21 John 19 v. 39
(ii) The Resurrection : the Crucifixion and Resurrection should be seen in close relation to each other. Good Friday was the victory, Easter Day the result of that victory	Mark 16 vv. 1–8 Luke 24 vv. 1–49 Matthew 28 vv. 1–20 John 20 and 21
(iii) The Ascension : the walk to Bethany The disciples are promised the power to bear witness to their Lord	Luke 24 vv. 50–53 Acts 1 vv. 1–11

Jesus had been helping His disciples to realise that He was with them all the time whether they could see Him or not. Finally, by some means He made it clear that they would not see His bodily form again, though in fact He would be with them always. The account of the Ascension is naturally coloured by the frame-work of ideas of the first century and is not ours. Our conception of heaven does not help in a belief in a physical body passing through space to a physical heaven, which is what the disciples probably imaged. The essential fact is that Jesus was with His Father, having triumphantly completed His life's work on earth, and at the same time He was still with His disciples helping them to build the Kingdom.

An alternative syllabus for the life of Jesus

The Gospels can be considered as giving us four portraits of Jesus painted by different artists who each saw Him from their own point of view ; they are a mixture of history with some imaginative constructions.

100

The Gospel of St. Mark

Most probably the earliest impression by an artist who paints with the vividness of an eye-witness. John Mark has given the first hand recollections of Peter the disciple; these are written down. He is concerned mainly with the deeds of Jesus : his 'mighty works'.

(a) The portrait gives details only a very perceptive artist would observe.	
Jesus is 'asleep on a cushion'	Mark 4 vv. 37ff
The one possessed by a demon was 'crying aloud among the tombs and on the hillsides and cut himself with stones'	Mark 5 v. 5
The disciples 'searched Him out'	Mark 1 vv. 35ff
The five thousand 'sat down in rows'	Mark 6 v. 40 N.E.B.
The blind man when he is cured says 'they look like trees'	Mark 8 v. 24
(b) There is an orderly arrangement of the story and the action moves quickly from one incident to another.	
The story moves quickly from the Baptism and the Temptations to the Galilean Mission.	Mark 1 vv. 9–14
The authority of His teaching is dealt with within twenty-four hours.	Mark 1 vv. 21–28
A selection is given of five typical narratives ending with the hostility of the Pharisees.	Mark 3 vv. 1–6
There are more descriptions of the 'mighty works'.	Mark 4 vv. 35–41
The great day at Caesarea Philippi is followed by the first prediction of the Passion with the story	Mark 8 vv. 27–33ff
of the Transfiguration.	Mark 9 vv. 2–8
The crowning events of the Passion and Resurrection are told.	Mark 14 v. 1 ; 16 vv. 1–20
(c) The realism with which the humanity of Jesus is shown : the lack of insight displayed by His disciples.	Mark (at all points)
(d) There is clear evidence that Jesus is the Messiah. At His Baptism He is declared to be 'Thou art my Son, my Beloved ; . . .'.	Mark 1 v. 11
Peter's confession.	Mark 8 v. 27ff
The High Priest's question, 'Are you the Messiah . . . ?' is answered explicitly.	Mark 14 v. 61ff

The Gospel of St. Matthew

This is a less colourful picture. We see less of the 'man of action' and much more of Jesus as Teacher. The artist aims at giving a living presentation of Jesus and His message which is put clearly and in fewer words than Mark. The touches of an eye-witness deeply moved by what he remembered, and which included much detail about the situations in which Jesus found Himself, are lacking. For example, in the account of the blessing of the children, Mark's phrase, 'and He put His arms round them, laid His hands upon them and blessed them' (Mark 10 v. 16) is omitted. This Gospel is a portrait of Jesus as the fulfilment of revelation, as the Messiah.

(a) The order of events is often changed from that in Mark to bring a group of sayings together as a topic. Thus :	
The Sermon on the Mount.	Matthew 5–7
The sayings on greatness and forgiveness	Matthew 18
The parables of the Kingdom.	Matthew 13
The description of the Last Things.	Matthew 24–25

(b) The Christian message is the fulfilment of Old
Testament religion : the pleasure the writer
shows in telling about the :
Triumphal Entry to Jerusalem.   Matthew 21 vv. 1–11
Many Old Testament quotations are given such   Matthew 12 v. 18ff
as in Isaiah.   Isaiah 42

(c) There is a deep concern for the 'Last Things' and
the return of Christ. This is seen in the parables
only found in this Gospel.
The ten virgins   Matthew 25 vv. 1–13
The sheep and the goats.   Matthew 25 v. 31ff
(Some scholars think that the sack of Jerusalem
in A.D. 70 has added to the sense of doom as felt
by the writer.)

(d) A special interest is shown in the origin and
foundation of the Church.
On Peter as the Rock.   Matthew 16 v. 18ff
(Not to be confused with any special claims
about the authority of a particular church.)
The power to set free and unbind.   Matthew 18 v. 18ff
'... where two or three have met together in My   Matthew 18 v. 20
name ...'.
' ..I am with you always....   Matthew 28 v. 20

The Gospel of St. Luke

Another picture of the Christ as seen through the eyes of one who wanted to convey
the pathos of the story and the gentleness of Jesus ; there is hope for all sinful men and
women and an unbroken confidence in the love of God. There are picturesque
parables with a broad human interest, and the portrait painted is of a Jesus who, in
dutiful love, accepts his destiny even though it ends in suffering and death.

(a) The portrait is of a man whose chief characteristic
is '... peace for men on whom His favour rests' –
universalism.   Luke 2 v. 14
Simeon sees in the infant Jesus ... 'a light that
will be a revelation to the heathen ....   Luke 2 v. 32
The parable of the Great Supper ... 'Go out on to
the highways and along the hedge rows and
make them come in ...'.   Luke 14 v. 23

(b) There are many incidents which show a deep
concern for social relationships, especially those
to do with wealth and poverty.   Luke 6 vv. 20–21
The Beatitudes appear in the form 'How blest are
you who are poor', 'How blest are you who now
go hungry ...'.
Illustrations are taken from finance :
The two debtors.   Luke 7 vv. 41–43
The rich fool.   Luke 12 v. 16ff
The lost coin   Luke 15 vv. 8–10
The unjust steward.   Luke 16 vv. 1–13
The rich man and Lazarus   Luke 16 vv. 19–31
Sayings about almsgiving   Luke 21 vv. 1–4;
                                                           Luke 11 vv. 37–41

(c) Jesus is shown as being particularly gracious to
the outcast, the sinner, and the 'other man – thy
neighbour' – the Samaritan.   Luke 10 v. 30ff
The woman who was a sinner.   Luke 7 v. 36ff
Zaccheus.   Luke 19
The penitent thief.   Luke 23 v. 39ff
The Prodigal Son.   Luke 15 v. 11ff

(d) The attitude of Jesus to women is, for the times,
unusually understanding.

The Widow of Nain.	Luke 7 vv. 11–16
Martha and Mary.	Luke 10 v. 38ff

(e) But there is sternness as well as kindness and
graciousness; sometimes there is severity too.
Jesus makes a stern challenge: 'If anyone comes
to Me...'.   Luke 14 vv. 26, 33, 34

(f) The writer is very much interested in the Passion.

(g) He nevertheless stressed the joy of life; joy in
prayer and the Holy Spirit, 'Do not be afraid, I

have good news for you...'.	Luke 2 v. 10
He prays for Peter.	Luke 22 v. 31ff
And for His murderers.	Luke 23 v. 34
Jesus is led from the Jordan and is led '... with the power of the Spirit.....'	Luke 4 v. 1

The Gospel of St. John

This is a religious picture which fills in details not given by others. Someone writing at Ephesus at the close of the first century or the beginning of the second, with a deep knowledge of Jewish customs, drew a picture of Jesus for Greek speaking peoples. Written on sheets of papyrus fastened together to make a roll; occasionally, by some mischance, the correct order was not preserved and some think this may have happened in one or two places; so there are differences between this Gospel and the others.

(a) In this Gospel most of the ministry is centred at
Jerusalem and three Passovers are mentioned.   John 2 v. 13 ; 6 v. 4 ;
                                                           12 v. 1

(b) The cleansing of the Temple comes at the
beginning of the ministry: the raising of Lazarus
the event which leads the powers that be to take
action: there is no account of the Institution of
the Last Supper.   John 11 vv. 47–53

(c) There is a difference in the way the sayings of
Jesus are expressed.

Suggestions for books in connection with 'What the Bible is about'
These books are mainly for teachers' use.

About the Old Testament

Achtemeir, P. & E.	The Old Testament Roots of Our Faith.	S.P.C.K.*
Martin, H.	The Meaning of the Old Testament.	S.C.M. Press*

About the New Testament

Hoskyns, Sir E. & Davey, F. N.	The Riddle of the New Testament.	Faber*
Manson, T. W.	The Teaching of Jesus	C.U.P.
Richardson, Alan	The Miracle Stories of the Gospels.	S.C.M. Press
Richardson Alan	An Introduction to the Theology of the New Testament.	S.C.M. Press
Taylor, Vincent	The Gospels: A Short Introduction.	Epworth*

The Life of Christ

Bull, N. J.	Jesus and His Teaching.	R.E.P. [*]
Harrington, J.	Jesus of Nazareth. (A fairly simple approach based on the B.B.C. television series of broadcasts under that title.)	Brockhampton Press [*]
Hunter, A. M.	The Work and Words of Jesus	S.C.M. Press
Titterton, A. F.	Christ in the Early Church. (Book 2 in the series The Bible and the Christian Faith.)	Ginn [*]

Sources of Information

For guidance on books :

'Religious Education, a bibliography for the use of Teachers'. Christian Education Movement, Annandale, North End Road, London N.W.11.

Various manuscripts, a fragment of St. John's Gospel dating about A.D. 110. Post-card reproductions may be had. The Rylands Library, Deansgate, Manchester.

Reproductions of manuscripts relating to the Bible may be obtained from the British Museum, National Gallery and the Victoria and Albert Museum.

Biblical illustrations

Some of the best illustrations may be obtained from the following :

Christian Year Pictures (reproductions of Old Master and contemporary art illustrations).

Biblical Teaching Pictures : E. A. Wood.

(Both the above sets of pictures may be obtained from S.P.C.K., 69 Great Peter Street, Westminster, London S.W.1.)

Also, French Bible Pictures designed by the Abbaye de la Rochette may be obtained from the Catechetical Centre, 13–15 Denbigh Street, London W.11

German Bible Wall Pictures by Paula Jordan may be obtained from The Fortress (Lutheran Bookshop), 71 Edgware Road, London W.2.

Nelson's Bible Visual Aids, Set A – The Teaching of Christ. A set of 15 pictures 15in. × 11½in. for use in schools, may be obtained from : Thos. Nelson & Sons Ltd., 35 Park Street, London W.1.

INTRODUCTION TO STAGES THREE TO FIVE MAIN SYLLABUS
(for pupils aged 13 to 16 years)

From this point in the syllabus alternatives are offered. What is intended to be the Main Syllabus is arranged for pupils who will be following an academic course and continuing their studies to the sixth form and beyond. The Alternative Syllabus is intended for the non-academic pupils, many of whom will leave school at an earlier age to enter industry or commerce. The syllabuses are not mutually exclusive.

There are many pupils (not necessarily the less-able or non-academic) who find the language of the Bible difficult and much of its content irrelevant in terms of their own experience. A great deal of what is written about the less-able pupils 13–16 years in the Report of the Central Advisory Council for Education (England) 'Half our Future' applies in the case of religious education to pupils of all abilities and for many of them topics in the Alternative Syllabus may provide a method of approach.

1 Most of the problems concerned with the onset of puberty, independence, the pressure of a secular society are common to both the academic and the less-able pupil, although the academic pupils sometimes develop physically at a slower rate; the more intelligent may, too, have wider interests which enable the adolescents to find the means of coming to terms with their emotional problems. For most of the academic pupils the transition from the sheltered life of school to the world of industry or commerce comes later.

2 The less-able, non-academic pupils will find the content and the method of approach of the Alternative Syllabus more suitable for their needs and abilities.

Stage Three – The Christian Way of Life

Becoming an adult in the community.
What do we mean by the 'Law and the Prophets' ?

Abraham, Moses and Elijah
The Ten Commandments.
Some great prophets and their message.
The new law.
The teaching about the Kingdom of God.
How people have worshipped.

Stage Four – Christianity in the Modern World

What do Christians believe ?
Some problems of the Faith.
Worship and Christianity.

Stage Five – The Church in action

The Church in New Testament times.
The Church spreads.
The Church in the world today.
The trend towards unity.

Personality, relationships and responsibility.
Suggestions for projects, individual and group work.

The emphasis in this section of the syllabus is on the questions related to becoming an adult in the community. A growing desire for independence on the part of the adolescent often coincides with a longing to find a basic authority by which to govern his actions. In this situation young people require to know at greater depth how Christians have responded to this challenge and the way in which experience from the past has fashioned and shaped our sense of values. The starting point may be that of discussion or the study of the sections based directly on the Bible.

Becoming an Adult in the Community

What do we mean by the 'Law and the Prophets'?

In the Bible we read about the adventures of the Israelites and their gradual coming together in tribes to form a nation under Moses and Joshua. In the process God was teaching them about Himself and the Laws which He expected them to keep. They only partially understood what was revealed to them. In this sense the whole nation becomes a church, i.e. a community bound together in order to worship God (Yahweh) and keep His Laws. Life for them was their religion; but they failed fully to understand His teaching.

They were mistaken in their ideas about God because to begin with they expected Him to fight for them against others.	Joshua 10 vv. 10–14
They believed that God was confined to a given piece of land.	II Samuel 26 vv. 19–20
They thought that God could be vindictive as instanced in:	
The tenth plague.	Exodus 11 vv. 4–10
Baldhead and the two bears	II Kings 2 vv. 23–24
They mixed legends and wonder tales with history (cf. Drake's game of bowls, Alfred's burnt cakes and the Knights of the Round Table, Robin Hood).	
An animal talks.	Numbers 22 v. 28
Ideas of magic are introduced — iron floats.	II Kings 6 v. 6
Nevertheless, they were helped to see the truth by special messengers whom we know as prophets. Their work and purpose can be seen in:	
Demanding good relationships because God made the world '... and behold it was very good'.	Genesis 1 v. 31
Showing that God asks for absolute loyalty.	Exodus 20 v. 3
And is always ready to help.	Psalm 46
And to forgive.	Hosea 3 v. 1; Isaiah 1 vv. 16–18

Who were the Lawgivers and the Prophets?

The message came to the nation-church through:

Abraham

Most primitive peoples hold their gods in fear and dread : they thought that their gods were always ready to do them a bad turn. Abraham came to know God as a friend who could be trusted but God also claimed his obedience. The conflict; as a sign of obedience and love Abraham wanted to give God his most valued possession — Isaac his son. He learns that the kind of God he was getting to know could not possibly want the sacrifice of children.

God is one who can be trusted : He claims obedience.	Genesis 12 vv. 1–19
Abraham and Isaac.	Genesis 22 vv. 2–18

God speaks as He speaks today. God is a friend : like all friends He has the right to expect loyalty, co-operation and the keeping of a promise. In return He makes a promise.

The covenant.	Genesis 17 vv. 1–2

Moses

He teaches that God acts upon His promise (a God who loves His people cannot allow them to remain in slavery).	Exodus 20 v. 2
God wants all to be free. Isaac not Ishmael. (God is made to speak as man.)	Genesis 17 vv. 19–21
'You shall not wrong a stranger'.	Exodus 22 v. 21

In all this God is teaching us to value freedom and to use it properly. God's laws :

The Ten Commandments. Religion and social behaviour are linked : this is not a private relationship between the individual and God but a family (i.e. community, church) relationship, each to other and each to God. Moses laid the foundation of	Exodus 20 vv. 1–17
the Hebrew–Christian tradition.	Luke 10 vv. 17–28

Elijah

He came at a time when the lowering of moral standards was leading to the disintegration of the community (i.e. nation-church dedicated to serving God).

He emphasised the distinction between the religion of Israel and that of other nations. All alliances between nations implied an alliance between the national gods. God (Yahweh) makes definite claims upon the obedience of His people. Religion cannot be watered down into what can be accepted easily.

The prevalence of Baal worship.	I Kings 16 vv. 31–32
The central message of the prophet.	I Kings 19 vv. 11–12

107

The period of the great prophets of Israel
continues for the 'writing prophets' from the 8th
century for about 200 years. They leave behind
them a way of thinking about God which religion
has refined but never really transcended.

Amos 760 B.C.

The great work of Moses seemed to have lost its
power to influence and Amos, brooding over the
wickedness of his time in the village of Tekoa in
Judah, asks 'What does Yahweh (God) say about
this ?'.

He uses the analogy of the plumb-line.	Amos 7 vv. 7–9
He goes on to say that although Israel's oppressors had behaved barbarously Israel had behaved just as badly.	Amos 2 vv. 4–5
He despised their burnt offerings and feasts : He looks for justice as between rich and poor.	Amos 5 vv. 21–24

Hosea 745 B.C.

He sees the wickedness in Israel much as Amos did :	Hosea 7 v. 5
he denounces the luxury of the rich : but in spite of all this he stresses that God is ready to forgive.	Hosea 2 v. 23

Isaiah ch. 1–39, 700 B.C.

The writer gives a more vivid picture of the situation. He sees in the lack of social justice, the oppression, the formality of worship, a soulless service to Yahweh : the nation had forsaken God. He stresses that man is as nothing before God because God is Holy and Righteous.	Isaiah 2 v. 22 Isaiah 6 v. 3

Micah 730 B.C.

He sees in the social evils of the times a cause for God's anger.	Micah 2 v. 9-10

700–500 B.C.

There is a long pause in prophecy but the discovery of the Books of the Law and the reforms which follow bring out a renewed emphasis on monotheism.	II Kings 22 v. 8ff Deuteronomy 4 v. 35

Jeremiah 626–585 B.C.

New teaching about God and man:

(i) Religion is found in the hearts of men.

(ii) It is personal – each man belongs to God and God to him.   Jeremiah 31 v. 31ff

(iii) There is no need for intermediaries: each man can speak with God.

(iv) God is concerned with all mankind.

(v) He forgives and pardons our offences.

Ezekiel 592–? B.C.

Writing at the time of the exile: Ezekiel 18 v. 20

Everyone is responsible for his own fate 'All souls are mine . . .'.   Ezekiel 18 v. 4

God has no favourites.

Second Isaiah ch. 40–66, 540–? B.C.

God is in control of the world however differently this may appear.   Isaiah 40 vv. 1–26

God is directing history. He still loves His people.   Isaiah 40 v. 2

The world is to be saved through the Servant of God.   Isaiah 42 v. 1

The Suffering Servant.   Isaiah 52 v. 13 ; 53 v. 12

Books for further reading

Ashe, Geoffrey	The land the Book	Collins
Fleming, James	Personalities of the Old Testament.	Scribners
Lace, O. Jessie	Teaching the Old Testament.	S.P.C.K.
Manson, T. W.	The Servant Messiah	C.U.P.
Fison, J. E.	Understanding the Old Testament.	O.U.P.
Anderson, W.	Law and Gospel.	Lutterworth
Barclay, R. A.	The Law Givers.	Lutterworth
Joy Davidman	Smoke on the Mountain	Hodder & Stoughton

Possible points for discussion

(The key section comes under Moses.)

The purpose of the sections under the headings 'Religion and People' is to show the relevance of Christianity to life as the pupils find it to be. It begins with an introduction intended to show that communities everywhere and at all times have sought for a solution to the problem of learning to live 'in love and charity with one's neighbour'. It is part of God's plan that mankind is free to choose and this freedom – even to be selfish and harbour evil intentions – is only finally over-ruled by God's intervention, at first by individuals, the prophets (messengers) and uniquely in the life and teaching of Jesus Christ. The connection between the testaments can be shown in this way, but the importance of this – the continuous and continuing revelation of God to men – has to begin with our contemporary experience. For most of the time the teaching has to be implicit, rather than explicit (cf. the parable of the Seed growing Secretly).

The questions which follow are the type of question which could be used to open up the problem of the relation between God and man, and man and man, as the Christian sees it.

1 The Ten Commandments (4)

1 Are they outdated in the twentieth century ?
2 How far does the two-fold law of Jesus make the Mosaic Law unnecessary ?
3 Getting a living – is that all there is about a job ? If not, what else comes in ?
4 Why do we need churches ? Can we worship anywhere ?

The Covenant Relationship

The gramophone record of Benjamin Britten's 'Abraham and Isaac' (3 canticles) may be useful in connection with this incident (Argo RG 277). Such questions as :

'Does it really matter what you believe ?'
'Is it easy to do what God commands ?'
'How can we be sure that it is God who commands us ?'
'Can we be mistaken about the commands of God ?'
'Was Abraham behaving as a selfish, cruel father ?'

can be discussed with advantage. The apparently conflicting demands of God are the cause of real anguish on the part of Abraham. Such conflicts can, and do, arise in our own lives.

Some areas of interest for further discussion on present day issues :

1 What are the conditions under which a full and happy home life can exist ? How far do they depend on external conditions and how far upon personal relationships ? Should the Christian be interested in both ?

2 What do we mean by a fair chance and a living wage ? What should the relationship be between a man and a machine ? How, in a Christian country can we find ways of co-operation and learn to think of men first of all as men ?

3 The machine and the more equal distribution of money are giving everyone a chance of more leisure. What has the Christian to say about the right use of leisure ?

A New Age Begins

The nation-church of Israel gave way to a new conception of a world-wide church. There have been two tendencies in the story of Israel. One to turn inwards and regard themselves as a 'chosen people' in the sense of special privilege and so to regard themselves as superior to the 'lesser breeds' without the Law : the other to regard their special relationship as one calling for 'outward looking' responsibilities to the world as a whole. The following are examples of the 'outward looking' view :

Our duty is to share the family-life with all races; to face the risk of persecution which this would involve with courage and steadfastness.	Jonah ; Ruth
The profaning of the Temple by Antiochus Epiphanes is referred to – the Maccabean revolt. The theme of the book is to encourage those who are affected by persecution to meet adversity with courage and so, to eventually overcome the causes of persecution.	Daniel 11 v. 31

---

(4) Purcell, W.	The Plain Man looks at the Commandments.	Collins

The period between the Testaments was a time of great political and religious unrest and distress : a time of Israel's utmost need. The circumstances prevailing at the time of the birth of Jesus Christ help us to understand the Gospels :

The Jews believed that childlessness was a punishment from Yahweh.	Luke 1 vv. 6–7
That Yahweh would avenge unbelief.	Luke 1 v. 20
In the work of John the Baptist there was a renewal of prophecy after a long silence.	Luke 1 v. 17
He is seen as the forerunner of the Messiah.	Malachi 4 v. 5

At the time when Jesus was born the highest religious authority in the land, Annas and Caiaphas lived a life of indulgence, violence and luxury. The special sin with which the Jewish chronicles accuse Annas is that of 'whispering' or, to use the phrase they used, 'hissing like vipers' which seems to refer to their using private influence on the judges in their administration of justice, so that 'morals were corrupted'. Hence Yahweh's blessing had been withdrawn from Israel. It was terrorism (cf. Nazi Germany) which prevented the better members of the Sanhedrin from effective action, e.g. Nicodemus, Joseph of Arimethea and even Gamaliel would be powerless. Add to this the merciless harshness on the part of Roman officials under the Emperor Tiberius and it will be seen that the Jews were driven to the limit of endurance.

Jesus of Nazareth – Jesus (Greek) Joshua (Hebrew) 'Yahweh is salvation'.	Luke 1 v. 31
He was a ruler like David.	Luke 1 v. 32
He was of Davidic descent, born at Bethlehem.	Luke 1 v. 27 ; 2 v. 4
'The virgin will conceive'.	Matthew 1 v. 23
'God with us'.	Isaiah 7 v. 14
Mary shows God's power and insight. (The Magnificat was an expression of her personal feelings.)	Luke 1 vv. 46–55 I Samuel 2 vv. 1–20
A song of praise because Messiah has come : the fulfilment of a national aspiration.	Luke 1 vv. 68–79
The new hope for the world : 'A light that will be a revelation to the heathen'.	Luke 2 vv. 29–32

Some further points for discussion

1 We date our era from the birth of Christ. Suppose you had the opportunity of broadcasting to the world (cf. the Queen's broadcast to the Commonwealth). what message, in order 'to put the world right' as we say, would you give ?

2 Suppose your mother had the dream-house she had always wanted, your father, the car he hopes to own one day, and you, the bicycle or special favour you have craved for. Could you live for a whole year, as a family, without falling out, 'having words' as we say, or experiencing some personal unhappiness ? If not, why do you think this is so ?

3 'A light that will be a revelation to the heathen' was a personal feeling about the Christ event. What mainly, through Christianity, has brought 'light' to the world ?

4 'Life is less like a struggle than an adventure'. In what way could this describe the Duke of Edinburgh's Award Scheme ? Could this be applied to the following of the Christian way of life ?

Books of reference for the teacher

Snaith, N. H.	The Jews from Cyrus to Herod.	R.E.P.
Bevan, Edwyn	Jerusalem under the High Priests.	Arnold *
Bouquet, A. C.	Everyday Life in New Testament Times.	Batsford
Phillips, J. B.	A Man Called Jesus.	Fontana
Dale, A. T.	New World.	O.U.P.

What do we mean by the Kingdom of God ?

What did Jesus mean by 'the Kingdom of God' ? There is no more debatable or debated question in the whole field of New Testament scholarship. This is hardly surprising, since it involves Jesus's whole understanding of Himself and of His ministry.

We need to bear in mind :

1 Jesus did not invent the idea, which has a long history in Jewish thought. The Old Testament prophets had often spoken of the day when God would intervene and usher in a new order of righteousness and peace. In some of the prophets the coming of the New Age was associated with a Messiah, a contemporary hero or a supernatural figure. At the time of the birth of Jesus most Jews thought of the Kingdom in nationalistic and materialistic terms, although they were not agreed on the methods by which God would establish His Kingdom.

2 Jesus spoke of the Kingdom of God as a present, living reality and also as something which was still to come. This is more easily understood if we remember that the Kingdom of God means the *Rule* of God. Put at its simplest; wherever God rules, there is His Kingdom.

'The Kingdom of God' was the central theme of the teaching of Jesus ; the following are some of the most important aspects :

Entrance to the Kingdom is gained by repentance and trust (cf. Matthew 17 v. 2ff) ; it is costly (cf. Luke 14 vv. 28–32) ; nonetheless, the Kingdom is a gift, God's gift (cf. Luke 12 v. 32).

The members of God's Kingdom, then are not the 'righteous' (cf. Mark 2 v. 17) but repentant sinners.

To be in the Kingdom is to have found treasure (cf. Matthew 13 v. 44) ; the pearl of great price (cf. Matthew 13 v. 45ff).

It also means the acceptance of a new way of life (cf. Matthew 5 vv. 1–11) based on grace alone (cf. Luke 6 v. 36).

The time to enter the Kingdom is now ; there must be no excuse (cf. Luke 14 vv. 15–24) ; no procrastination (cf. Matthew 25 vv. 1–13).

Membership of the Kingdom can be lost (cf. Matthew 25 vv. 31–46).

The future of the Kingdom : the parables of the mustard seed (cf. Mark 4 vv. 30–32) and the leaven (cf. Matthew 13 v. 33) illustrate the extent and the methods of the Kingdom's growth.

Some points for discussion

1 The accounts of the Temptation Story (Matthew 4 vv. 1–11 ; Luke 4 vv. 1–13) suggest that all the social reform in the world will, of itself, never bring the Kingdom and Jesus said that His Kingdom was not of this world (John 18 v. 36). Does this mean that a Christian should not concern himself with politics ?

2 'Most people think that one becomes a Christian by living up to the teaching contained in the Sermon on the Mount. The teaching of that Sermon is not for those who want to become Christians but for those who have become Christians'. Do you agree with this ?

3 'For the earliest Christians the central thing was the Cross on the Hill and the Empty Tomb, not the Sermon on the Mount'. Discuss this claim of A. M. Hunter (*Design for Life*, p. 102).

4 In his book, 'Your God is too small', J. B. Phillips writes (p. 86) 'Most people think :

Happy are the pushers : for they get on in the world.
Happy are the hard-boiled : for they never let life hurt them.
Happy are they who complain : for they get their own way in the end.
Happy are the blasé : for they never worry over their sins.

Do you agree with what "most people think"?'

J. B. Phillips goes on to say (p. 87):

'Jesus Christ said:

Happy are those who realise their spiritual poverty: they have already entered the kingdom of reality.

Happy are they who bear their share of the world's pain: in the long run they will know more happiness than those who avoid it.

Happy are those who accept life and their own limitations: they will find more in life than anybody.

Happy are those who long to be truly "good": they will fully realise their ambition."

What do you make of what Jesus taught in the Beatitudes?   Matthew 5

What does the Christian mean by love?

The fulfilment of the 'law and the prophets' is found in the New Testament teaching about love. In the English language there is only one word for what is the most profound of all experiences.

Human love is seen as a response (an echo) of   I John 4 vv. 19–21
God's love to us. 'We love because He first loved
us ...'.

Jesus is the full revelation of what love is.   John 3 v. 16
'God loved the world so much that He gave His
only Son that everyone who has faith in Him may
not die, but have eternal life ....

Love must be shown in practical ways.   Luke 10 vv. 25–37
'Master, what must I do to inherit eternal life?
Love the Lord your God ... and your neighbour as
yourself'.

Love looks beyond the external to the motive.   Luke 7 vv. 37–50
'Two men were in debt to a money-lender ...
which will love him most?'   I Cor. 13

Love is the great commandment.   John 15 vv. 12–17
'There is no greater love than this: that a man
should lay down his life for his friend'.

Love enters into all relationships: it is seen in the teaching of Jesus about the use of money, in the use of our leisure time, and the compassion for the sick and needy and the outcasts.

1 The use of money. 'We can hardly respect money   Prayer before a Five
enough for the blood and toil it represents'.   Pound Note
                                                     Prayers of Life p. 23 (5)

'Sell your possessions and give in charity, ... for
where your wealth is, there will your heart be
also'.   Luke 12 vv. 33–34

Some questions to discuss:

What gives money its value? Would it be possible to do without money and live by exchange and barter?

In what way can Christian love be revealed in the situations where money is needed?

How can money be said to represent 'blood and toil' in terms of the history of a country? in terms of personal responsibility?

Do we think too much about money?   Matthew 6 vv. 25–34

Money gives us a great freedom of choice: the coin or the note represent a power to satisfy our needs and wants over a wide field of activity. So it faces us with the responsibility of decision-making: these decisions are nearly always what are called moral decisions.

---

(5) Quoist, Michel   Prayers of Life.   Gill and Son, Dublin

Decisions of this kind were made in the early days of the church: although the economic situation has changed, the problems they raised have a bearing on many situations today.

(i) The disciples were bidden to 'Take nothing for the journey, neither scrip nor pack, neither bread nor money...'. Luke 9 v. 3
They had to depend on help freely given from those they visited. Can you think of a reason for this?

(ii) Later on St. Paul (and no doubt other disciples) made a point of earning enough to support himself: he made tents or parts of tents and exchanged these for money. Why do you think this change came about? II Cor. 11 v. 9

(iii) In the Acts of the Apostles we read that they had all things in common. 'Not a man of them claimed any of his possessions as his own, but everything was held in common.' Why did they do this? How did this system break down? Acts 4 vv. 32–33

In all these situations important decisions were made: all had to do with relationships between people and were therefore concerned with the idea of Christian love.

2　The use of leisure 'Lord I have time'. Prayers of Life p. 76 (6)

'Be most careful how you conduct yourselves: like sensible men, not like simpletons'. Ephesians 5 vv. 15–17

It seems likely that the time spent by men and women on earning a living will get less and less as new methods of production come into operation in industry. As this comes about the amount of leisure will increase.
What do you think about this?

In the story of 'the Fall' man is made to work by the sweat of his brow as punishment for disobedience. Genesis 3 v. 19
Is work a curse? Can you see the difference between work and play?
Is there any real difference between an amateur and a professional player? Why work? Why worry? Is this a Christian attitude that could be defended?

In Psalm 8 v. 5 the psalmist makes the statement:
'Yet thou hast made him little less than God,
and thou dost crown him with glory and honour'.

The '... little less' implies that man has been given some of God's power: the power to love and the power to be creative. Leisure gives man the possibility of expressing both by living creatively himself. Write down as many ways of recreation as you can: which of these could be said to fulfil the idea of living creatively? How many of these have a value to the community or to other people?

3　The power of love. The prayer of the Adolescent. Prayers of Life p. 38(6)

'May he have a friend, a brother, who will help him to forget himself for others, lest he become a slave to himself, incapable of loving'.

'The man who does not love is still in the realm of death, for everyone who hates his brother is a murderer and no murderer, as you know, has eternal life within him.' I John 3 vv. 14–16

'Dear friends, let us love one another, because love is from God. Everyone who loves is a child of God and knows God but the unloving know nothing.' I John 4 vv. 7–8

---

(6) Quoist, Michel　　　　Prayers of Life.　　　　Gill and Son, Dublin

This challenge was answered in the early church: the letters to the young churches and the history given in the Acts of the Apostles deals with situations, basically, not so very different from our own.

Sharing and helping others.	Acts 2 vv. 41–47; Acts 4 vv. 32–37
Being sensitive to the views and feelings of other people – at home and in the community.	Philemon I Peter 3 vv. 8–13
Showing reverence, charity and concern for weaker consciences.	I Cor. 11 vv. 17–28 I Cor. 13; I Cor. 8
Generosity.	II Cor. 9 vv. 6–11;
Practical Religion.	James I vv. 22–27; 2 vv. 1–4
The need for standards.	Romans 13 vv. 7–14
Striving after perfection.	Ephesians 3 vv. 14–19
Courage.	Acts 4 vv. 1–21
The Christian armour.	Ephesians 6 vv. 11–20
Self-control.	I Cor. 9 vv. 24–27
Joy and peace.	Philemon vv. 4–9
Unity.	Ephesians 4 vv. 1–6
Confidence in God's love.	Romans 8 vv. 35–39
The Gospel is for all men.	Romans 10 vv. 12–15
A vision of the 'City of God'.	Revelation 21 vv. 1–14, 22–27; 22 vv. 1–5

Some questions to discuss

In the Lord's Prayer, men are urged to love their neighbours as themselves. What does this imply? A measure of 'self-love'? To what extent must we love ourselves in order to love others?

In the Beatitudes, we read:

> You have learned that they were told, "Love your neighbour, hate your enemy". But what I tell you is this: Love your enemies and pray for your persecutors; only so can you be children of your heavenly Father...'.   Matthew 5 vv. 43–45

In what way can we love our enemies?

There are opportunities for bringing into the scheme some practical ways of teaching about the Kingdom.

How can young people help others?

Are there ways of doing social work?

Information can be given about:
Christian Aid: 10 Eaton Gate, London S.W.1.
Oxfam: Banbury Road, Oxford.
Freedom from Hunger: 17 Northumberland Avenue, London W.C.2.
Save the Children Fund: 29 Queen Anne's Gate, London S.W.1.

Worship in the Community

What is meant by Worship?

In worship we make our response to the initiative that God takes in drawing us to Himself: it is a response to His revelation made to us in His creation, in the Bible, and above all in the life and teaching of Jesus Christ. Although our response is often feeble, it is due to the stirring of the Holy Spirit. Worship is not only the singing of hymns and the saying of prayers. It calls for all the activities of mind and body and should be the inspiration of our work.

As George Herbert expressed it:

> 'Who sweeps a room as for Thy sake
> Makes that and the action fine...'

Even the most humble actions may express our sense of worship if entered into fully and with right intentions.

Worship in the Old Testament

The desire to worship has found expression in many ways. In the early days men expressed this according to their understanding of what they thought was demanded by God. Early Israelite worship was a reflection of their ideas of Yahweh.

Tops of hills, the 'high places' were sacred and often linked with idolatry.	I Kings 11 vv. 6–10
Stone pillars and wooden poles called 'asherah' (translated wrongly in A.V. as 'grove') were centres of worship.	Judges 6 v. 25ff
These became centres of idolatry and were eventually destroyed.	II Kings 18 vv. 1–6
Altars (mounds of earth) were used as places for sacrifices.	Exodus 20 vv. 21–26 ; Deuteronomy 27 v. 5

Different kinds of sacrifices were made :

	The Priests' Law Book
the burnt offering.	Leviticus 22 vv. 17–20
the peace offering.	Leviticus 3 vv. 1–17
the sin offering.	Leviticus 4 vv. 1–5
the guilt offering.	Leviticus 5 vv. 14–16

This system of sacrificial offerings was often abused and condemned by the prophets :

Amos demands justice not burnt offerings.	Amos 5 vv. 21–25
Hosea teaches that love is needed, not burnt offerings.	Hosea 6 v. 6
Micah calls for love, kindness and humility.	Micah 6 vv. 6–8
Isaiah declaims against burnt offerings.	Isaiah 1 vv. 11–17
Jeremiah urges obedience to the 'Law'.	Jeremiah 7 vv. 21–26

In the Old Testament, the Jewish worship centred round the 'Law and the Prophets'.

(i) The Law as developed from the Pentateuch or the first five books in the Old Testament, together with a mass of regulations (the 'yoke' referred to by Jesus).

(ii) To remind the Jew of the Law and the need to keep it, they wore (and in modern times still wear) a praying shawl with fringes : a phylactery (a prayer box strapped to the arm or forehead) : and a 'mezuzah' stuck to the door of their houses.

    Numbers 15 vv. 37–41
    Exodus 13 vv. 9–10
    Deuteronomy 6 vv. 4–9

(iii) The Ark and the Holy of Holies : the centre of worship at Jerusalem :

Directions for making it.	Exodus 25 v. 10ff
It passes the river Jordan.	Joshua 3 v. 15ff
Is carried round the walls of Jericho.	Joshua 6 v. 11
It is captured by the Phillistines.	I Samuel 4 v. 11
It is restored to Israel.	I Samuel 6

(An interesting account of the ideas of the times with the 'taboo' which surrounded all things regarded as holy.)

The Ark is taken to Jerusalem.	II Samuel 6
It finds its resting place in the Temple in the time of Solomon.	I Kings 8

Worship in the New Testament

Jesus was brought up in the Jewish faith and knew the Law and the prophets. He Himself worshipped regularly in the synagogue or in the Temple at Jerusalem. He was critical of those who stood by the strict letter of the Law and who often neglected to obey the 'great commandment'. Deuteronomy 6 vv. 4–7

(Some may wish to introduce their pupils to the Temple and to the synagogue.)

Matthews, Basil	The World in which Jesus lived.	O.U.P.
Parrot, Andre	The Temple of Jerusalem.	S.C.M. Press *

The Scribes, the Pharisees and the Sadducees were experts in the Law and each in his own way tried to keep it:

The Scribes were indignant at what Jesus said.	Matthew 21 vv. 14–17
They attacked those who seemed to sit lightly to the law.	Acts 4 vv. 5–7
The Pharisees questioned the authority of Jesus.	Matthew 9 vv. 10–15
The Sadducees demanded a proof of the Messiahship of Jesus.	Matthew 16 v. 1 ; Acts 3 vv. 17–26

The New Law

Jesus gave a new version of the Law which contains the old and goes beyond it to 'complete the Law'.

The greatest commandment.	Matthew 22 vv. 34–40
The new Commandment.	John 15 vv. 12–14 ; Matthew 5 vv. 21–26
Jesus makes His promise concerning the Law. (The 'yoke' was the cross-bar to which draught oxen were fastened by the horns or the neck for drawing carts or ploughs. The affection that was believed to exist between a pair of oxen yoked together is used in the illustration given by Jesus.)	Matthew 11 vv. 28–30
Christians met together for the 'breaking of bread' and for worship.	Acts 2 v. 42 ; 20 v. 7

Worship Today

This might be introduced by discussion based on such questions as the following:

Is it possible to be a Christian without going to church?
In what different ways do Christians worship?
Why does the Christian church keep Sunday as a special day for worship?
Do you think any improvements in worship are needed?

The Christian Year

Some information is needed on the main festivals of Christmas, Easter, Whitsuntide and other occasions of special importance in the Church's year.

Sunday

From very early times – the first century A.D. – the first day of the week was known as 'The Lord's Day' in celebration of the Resurrection.	Acts 20 v 7 ; Revelation 1 v. 10

The use of the name Sunday dates from the middle of the second century where it is first found in Justin Martyr's 'Apology' – written in Rome between A.D. 141–161 where he writes:

'On the Sun's day we all make our assembly in common. For it is the first day on which God, changing the darkness of matter (lit. put to flight darkness and chaos) into light and made the world and on the same day Jesus Christ our Saviour rose from the dead.'

By an edict of Constantine, A.D. 321, the 'people shall rest on the venerable day of the Sun' Constantine's legislation in favour of the Church.

Bettenson   Documents of the Christian Church.   O.U.P.

The Christian Sunday is not the Jewish Sabbath although it took over many of its features.

For further information:

Taylor, L.	Books of Christian Days	Blackwell*
	Books of Prayers for Schools	S.C.M. *
	(A calendar of Great Men and Women.)	*
Porter, B. H.	The Day of Light (about Sunday)	S.C.M. *
McArthur, A. A.	The Evolution of the Christian Year	S.C.M. *
Fenn, E.	How Christians Worship	S.C.M. *

The Church at Worship

One of the regular activities of the Church is the coming together of its members for acts of worship.

> 'Where two or three are gathered together in My name, there am I in the midst of them.'

Worship has a twofold function. For those who are taking part in it as members of a Christian congregation, it says something about the faith which, at various times and levels of commitment, they wish to profess. It also says something and does something to strengthen and confirm the faith they profess. Christians do not work and live in isolation. They require fellowship and this means coming together to help one another and to support one another in worship as well as in social activities.

The form which this worship takes has varied within the history of the church and varies as between churches today. Most churches have a form hallowed by tradition, custom and experience. From the earliest times, it has been expressed in forms of liturgies and written forms of service. In more recent times, particularly since the Reformation, many branches of the church have been drawn to more spontaneous forms in which the prayers are extempore and the teaching or preaching (of the Word) has a central position. The different forms express the worshippers' understanding of their belief.

Many questions may arise from this which are related to the history, form of organisation and theology of the various churches. Although the problems need treating with tact and without dogmatism, they must be faced. Such questions as :

> Is it necessary to go to church to worship God ?
> Why do different churches vary in their forms of worship ?

may be dealt with in connection with the churches in the locality.

Prayer forms a prominent part of all acts of worship. The primitive form is an attempt to ask God and to persuade Him to do what we want to happen and to obtain a blessing (God's favour towards us). Pupils may be led to see that Christian prayer is not, however, a means of getting our own way but to ask for the power to do God's will. It should be possible to sum up all our prayers in the familiar words, 'Thy Kingdom come, Thy will be done'.

Prayer is in many ways an art and as with all arts, it is first necessary to learn how to do it, to master the attitudes which are needed, and then to practise constantly. There are four main objects in prayer :

(i) to get to know God

(ii) to offer Him worship

(iii) to learn what is His purpose for us and the world

(iv) to receive strength to do this.

Books for further study

Fosdick, H. E.	The Meaning of Prayer	Fontana
Montefiore, H.	To Help You to Pray	S.C.M. *
Northcote, H.	Man, God and Prayer	Seraph *
Quoist, Michel	Prayers of Life	Gill and Son *

STAGE FOUR

CHRISTIANITY IN THE MODERN WORLD

What do Christians Believe?

Young people in their search for a meaning to life are faced with questions which, although they may not recognise the fact, are theological in character. The Newsom Report, concerned as it is with the non-academic child, states the point of view of young people, academic or otherwise, in stressing the questioning spirit of adolescence.

> 'This happens rather earlier perhaps in modern rather than in grammar schools, partly because their pupils come at a younger age into immediate contact with the unsheltered world outside school and home. It is a major task to steer their new doubting spirit into positive and creative channels avoiding the truculence of "couldn't care less".'
>
> Half our Future 1963, pp. 52ff

There will be some doubts about the existence of God, the person of Christ and the reality of the Holy Spirit. They need to explore and discuss, at this stage, these issues in an atmosphere of sympathetic understanding and encouragement.

How have people thought about God?

What we believe about God will determine our views on the nature of men and society as well as our attitude to other people and life itself. Two questions from Prayers of Life p. 55, Michel Quoist (7) may start a discussion on this:

> 'That face, haunts me . . .'.
> 'Lord forgive me for the face which has condemned me,
> Lord, thank You for that face which has awakened me.'

On our belief as it affects our relationships with one another and with God.

> 'If he does not love the brother whom he has
> seen, it cannot be that he loves God whom he has
> not seen. And indeed this command comes to us
> from Christ Himself that he who loves God must
> also love his brother.'   I John 4 vv. 20–21

From earliest times men have been conscious of a 'something other than themselves' that they desired to get to know and to be reassured about. To primitive man it was usually a power to be dreaded, often hostile or at least indifferent to the sufferings and needs of men.

How did Jesus teach us to think about God?

Look up some of the passages in the Gospels where Jesus spoke of God as Father and consider what was meant by the use of this word. What is meant by the statement 'God is love'? and that God is almighty?

We belong to God's family.	Matthew 5 vv. 44–45
God is concerned about the needs of men.	Luke 11 vv. 1–13
He provides for our needs	Luke 12 vv. 22–30
He is forgiving and shows compassion.	Luke 15 vv. 1–32
Jesus Himself placed His life in God's hands	Luke 23 v. 46

---

(7) Quoist, Michel   Prayers of Life   Gill and Son (Dublin)

Books to read and discuss :

Neil, S.	The Christian's God	World Christian Books
Phillips, J. B.	Your God is too small	Epworth
	Be Honest about God	C.E.M. Study Outline
Walton, R. C.	God and You	S.C.M. Press
	(Thinking Things Through.)	
Wilson, J.	Is there a God ?	S.P.C.K.

Occasionally, a personality known through the press or television may be a point of interest in the sense that they make their belief in God known.

Articles may be found in the papers, or in magazines about topical situations in which men and women declare their belief in God. This should be done honestly and without glossing over situations in which such declarations seem to be at variance with the Gospel teaching : criticism must be charitable.

Pupils might refer to the publication 'Who's Who', 'Crockford's Directory' and the 'National Biography'.

The playing of extracts from the recordings made by Flora Robson and Andrew Cruickshank of the N.E.B. translation of St. John's Gospel may be appropriate here as the quality of the recordings conveys the sincerity of the speakers.

The Gospel of John   Leonark N.E.B. 1, 2 & 3

Did Jesus really live – as an historical character ?

We date our era from His birth : in what way do we show this ? The events in His life are linked with historical personages about whom we have other sources of information.

In the reign of Herod	Luke 1 v. 5
Caesar Augustus was emperor of the Roman	
empire of which Palestine was a part. The	
enrolment.	Luke 2 vv. 1–5
The link with John the Baptist	Luke 3 vv. 1–2
Pontius Pilate governor of Judea	Luke 23 vv. 1–8

There are references to Christianity in very early documents. The Roman historian Tacitus who lived c. 60–120 writes :

The Trial of Pomponia Craecina, A.D. 57.
She was the wife of Aulus Plautius the Roman General, who conquered the southern part of Britain A.D. 43–47 : accused of a 'foreign superstition' and handed over to her husband for trial. The foreign superstition is surmised to be Christianity.
The Neronian Persecution, A.D. 64.
The Christians were made the scapegoats for the fire of Rome in the summer of A.D. 64. The document refers to :
'Christus from whom their name is derived was executed at the hands of the Procurator Pontius Pilate in the reign of Tiberius.

Bettenson, Henry   Documents of the Christian Church   O.U.P.

What did people living in the same time think of Jesus ?

They were often puzzled by what He said and did. For example :

The Crowds	Mark 1 v. 27
The Pharisees	Mark 2 v. 18
The Scribes	Mark 2 vv. 6–7
The people of Nazareth	Mark 6 vv. 2–3

How did people living at the time receive His teaching?

An understanding of His life and teaching came only slowly and partially even to His closest friends.

Peter's confession at Caesarea Philippi (A Jew would have been brought up to know the prophecies in his Bible — part of our Old Testament.)	Matthew 16 vv. 13–16
The Prince of Peace	Isaiah 9 vv. 2–7
The Root of Jesse (the restoring of David's line)	Isaiah 11 vv. 1–10
The return of a King	Isaiah 32 vv. 1–8
The Suffering Servant	Isaiah 42 vv. 1–4; 49 vv. 1–6
A man of sorrows	50 vv 4–9; 52 v. 13; 53 v. 12
The power of Christ to redeem	Malachi 3 vv. 1–3

The Jews thought about the Messiah in different ways and there were Messiahs of other kinds. Reference should be made to the Dead Sea Scrolls, The Qumran community and John the Baptist.

Harrison, R. K.	The Dead Sea Scrolls	E.U.P.

How did the early Church come to understand Jesus?

What did Paul learn about Jesus?	I Cor. 15 vv. 1–5

The early church searched for words to bring a
deeper meaning to the life and teaching:

'I am Alpha and Omega'	Revelation 21 v. 6
'The Word made flesh'	John 1 v. 14
'The image of the invisible God'	Colossians 1 v. 15

What do you think these expressions mean?

How do the Gospels portray Jesus?
(This can take the form of a revision of the 'Four
Portraits of Jesus' as given in Stage 2.)

How has Jesus been portrayed in literature, drama and art?

Jesus as seen in literature and drama.

Sayers, D.	The Man Born to be King A Man Dies

Jesus as portrayed in great art (see the suggestions Appendix E).

Books for further reading:

McLaren, R. B.	What's special about Jesus?	Epworth [*]
Rolls, E. F.	Jesus and the Kingdom	Epworth [*]
	Portraits of Christ	King Penguin [*]

The forgiveness of sins — what do we mean by this?

We are all conscious of wrong-doing from time to time. The word 'conscience' has a meaning which comes from the word to 'know' (Latin con-scire) and we all 'know' moments when we wish we had not done certain things because we know that they are wrong. When, however, the word 'sin' is used in the Bible, it means the action or attitudes which have separated us from God. It means the inclination we all have towards selfishness; and selfishness is a form of evil and the cause of evil. This goes much deeper than wrong-doing.

That men are 'sinful' in this sense, is one of the most obvious facts of human experience.

Sometimes we hear the statement, 'I couldn't care less'.
This could be used in more than one way.

1   In the way the Miller of the Dee used it : 'I care for nobody, no not I' – he was not worried by what other people thought.

2   Or meaning that the speaker was only concerned about himself.

Can you think of any way in which it could stand for selfishness? What happenings in recent times have shown greed, selfishness and cruelty? It is written in Romans 7 vv. 15–20 :

'I do not even acknowledge my own actions as mine, for what I do is not what I want to do, but what I detest . . . for I know that nothing good lodges in me – in my unspiritual nature, I mean – for though the will to do good is there, the deed is not. The good which I want to do, I fail to do, but what I do is the wrong which is against my will ; if what I do is against my will, clearly it is no longer I who am the agent, but sin that has its lodging in me.'

Many have argued against this : those who do so make their stand on a belief in the natural goodness of mankind. What do you think?

Read Genesis 3 and see what is said there about man's selfishness and pride.

What do the Gospels say about Jesus as the Friend of sinners?

Jesus dines with bad characters.	Mark 2 vv. 15ff
The Son of Man comes eating and drinking.	Matthew 11 v. 19
Saving the lost sheep.	Luke 15 vv. 1–7
What did Jesus say about forgiveness?	Matthew 18 vv. 20ff
'Forgive us the wrong we have done	Matthew 6 v. 12
As we have forgiven those who wronged us'.	

If God forgives, why the Cross?

At the centre of Christian belief stands the conviction that, 'God was in Christ reconciling the world to Himself' (II Cor. 5 v. 19). God, then, did not need to be persuaded to love men ; for it was because of His love and on His own initiative that He sent Christ to bring sinful man into a new and right relationship with Himself.

When we say that a man is 'sinful', it means that the relationship between God and man has been broken, i.e. the 'sons' cannot make contact in heart and mind with the 'Father'. In everyday language they are not on speaking terms. 'Sin' is a state of estrangement from God. Many modern men and women do not understand this, but the frustration and anxiety from which they so frequently suffer is often a sign of this estrangement. We are aware of the unhappiness we experience when we are at cross-purposes with our friends or ill-at-ease because of the life we live ; we feel disillusioned, frustrated and fearful. In extreme situations we feel lost and abandoned. God, we feel, has deserted us. To be reconciled to our friends and neighbours and to the immediate task in hand would be 'salvation' : we are, when reconciled, at peace again.

To harbour guilty feelings is wrong. We should not indulge in morbid introspection. Sometimes our moods and feelings of 'sin' can become a matter of undue pre-occupation. While we need to examine ourselves from time to time, it is wrong to brood about ourselves in a self-centred and harmful way.

How is Jesus relevant to this?

This self-realisation brings home to us the need for God's forgiveness and the power, given by God, to be different from what we have been. With forgiveness goes the need for sacrifice ; most frequently this has to take the form of sacrificing our pride and admitting we were wrong. So too it may mean sacrificing our time and possessions in order to put right the wrong we have done.

By sacrifice, we mean giving up something voluntarily ; to the Jews, as to us, this involved a spiritual quality. It was also associated with other aspects of worship, such as the slaughtering of animals as a sacred rite. Such ideas are repugnant to us and we cannot understand how the death of an animal could bring about forgiveness. Men's thoughts about sacrifice have changed. It has been said that 'at-one-ment' (reconciling God and man) is the same as expiation and this is a popular view; usually it is expressed by making Jesus the 'victor over the devil' or as the 'sacrifice', the 'Lamb of God', all of which are often used reverently and appropriately in liturgies and worship. It does not mean that God exacted the life of Jesus to cancel the sins of the world; God gave Himself, willingly, in love, to open up a new means of approach between men and God.

When we compare ourselves with Jesus, He awakens in us a sense of our great shortcomings. When we measure ourselves by the standards of Jesus we discover streaks of cruelty, selfishness and blindness to what is good and true about which we were not aware. God offers us not only the forgiveness we need, but also the power to be different from what we have been. Christian, in 'Pilgrim's Progress', finally sees the Cross, his burden is loosed from his back because, 'Then was Christian glad and lightsome, and said with a merry heart, "He hath given me rest by his sorrows and life by his death".'

What does the New Testament say about the forgiveness of sins?

First are the sayings and parables of Jesus:

Jesus spoke about the man hopelessly in debt, who came to his creditor and begged to be let off because he could not pay; the 'Creditor' was moved with compassion (Matthew 18 v. 27) '. . . the master was so moved with pity that he let the man go and remitted the debt'. It is God who acts to forgive; we must realise that our debts (sins) are unpayable.

Two parables show God's initiative in searching for those who are lost:

The Lost Coin	Luke 15 vv. 8–10
The Lost Sheep	Matthew 18 vv. 12–14

Another parable shows the extent of God's compassion:

The Lost Son	Luke 15 vv. 11–32

The teaching of Jesus about redemption was linked with His teaching about 'The Kingdom of God'. To the Jew, the age in which he lived at the time of Christ, was subject to Satan and the 'power of darkness'. One day God would bring this to an end and usher in the days of the Messiah and the 'Kingdom of God'. What was new in the teaching of Jesus was the 'good news' (i.e. the Gospel) that the Kingdom was 'at hand', already realised in the life, work and teaching of Our Lord.

Secondly what does the 'death on the Cross' mean when we talk about Redemption?

In many places in the New Testament the death of Christ is used in terms of sacrifice and the language of sacrifice has been taken into Christian worship. In the ancient world animal sacrifice was looked upon as part of a sacred rite. Gradually there developed in the prophets and psalmists a more spiritual view of sacrifice, the inner significance of which was seen to be the offering of the will to God in obedience, whereby a new relationship with God could be attained.

The early Christians saw not only who Jesus was, but they perceived what He was doing and expressed it in the thought forms of their own time. As they believed that 'sacrifice' brought a new righteousness (or rightness) with God, they said that Jesus's death upon the Cross was a kind of self-undertaken divine sacrifice which had the effect of obtaining for man a rightness with God which he could not obtain for himself. It should be remembered that there is no obligation on God's part to win man back: He does so because it is His nature to love. When God's active love is truly apprehended, man responds with love to God, often through service to his fellow-men.

Because of Christ's death on the Cross and His resurrection, we know that God accepts us as we are. In the same way the Christian believes that he should accept others as they are. 'Forgive us the wrong we have done, as we have forgiven those who have wronged us.'

There is nothing magical or automatic about this new relationship or 'at-one-ment'. The Gospel of decision, repentance, faith and the Christian life is seen as an extremely close relationship, and a phrase frequently used by St. Paul to express this is the phrase 'in Christ'. In the New Testament itself this relationship is symbolised by baptism and in the Eucharist or Holy Communion, the Family Meal. These sacramental acts are still retained by most churches.

The following are some of the metaphors, or picture-language, used to interpret the Cross:

(i) *Justification:* in the Bible, to be justified means to be restored to a right relationship with a person, in this case, God. This word is the one used for the action of a lawyer in the law-courts in winning his case for his clients.

(ii) *Ransom:* this was the price paid for a slave's freedom (Mark 10 v. 45). The emphasis here is on (i) the voluntary nature and, (ii) the costliness of Christ's sacrifice.

(iii) *Redemption:* like 'ransom' the word redemption is used as a metaphor. It means 'to buy back' and it recalls the bitterness of slavery. When it was used originally, the world was familiar with the slave market: human-beings were bought and sold as chattels. We can imagine what it meant to be told, 'You are free today forever; you can go home'. A slave could be redeemed. Paul was illustrating the work of Christ in words which his hearers could understand.

(iv) *Propitiation:* a term associated with the sacrificial ritual of the Old Testament, and the 'mercy-seat' in the Tabernacle (Romans 3 v. 25 and generally Hebrews).

(v) *Atonement:* this originally referred in Hebrew thought to the name whereby God's wrath could be averted or by which sin is expiated or 'covered'. In the New Testament it refers to God's reconciling acts by the death and raising of Jesus.

'The guilt of sin is removed by sending Christ. The sending of Christ, therefore, is the divine method of forgiveness.'

C. H. Dodd

N.B. It is important that we should not become too involved with theories about the Cross. All of them try to say the same thing in different ways. It is God who is on the Cross and it is He who is willing to go to such lengths to deal with 'sin' for man's sake. Reconciliation is offered to man and it is God who has come to offer it. The depth to which this teaching can be taken depends very much on the circumstances of the class to be taught.

Books for further reading

Richardson, A.	Theological Word Book of the Bible	S.C.M.
Taylor, Vincent	Jesus and His Sacrifice	Macmillan
Van Allmen, J.	Vocabulary of the Bible	Lutterworth

Points for discussion

How can a death on a Cross achieve anything?
How can a death some two thousand years ago do anything for the world now?
Did Jesus have to die?
What sort of God is God if He allowed His 'Son' to die?
If Jesus had to die, why blame Judas?
Why did Jesus pray to God?
Should we forgive someone who seems to be beyond forgiveness?
Is forgetting the same as forgiving?
Does forgiving mean 'being let off'?
Can we make forgiveness too easy — just an easy way out?
How do I know I am in the right and have something to forgive?

Sometimes young people (and others) find consolation in sedatives, tranquilisers, pep pills and other drugs: apart from the dangers of a physical kind, is this a sign of defeat in facing up to life-situations?

Mental illness can be, and often is caused by over-anxiety. People too, can become ill because of their own sense of inadequacy. They feel life is too much for them. Can you suggest a reason for this in Christian terms?

The following books are helpful in dealing with questions that may arise in this, a difficult section of the syllabus:

Sangster, W. E.	They Met at Calvary	Epworth
Selby Wright, R.	Asking them questions	O.U.P.
Joyce, C. A.	Fair Play — Thinking Things Through series.	S.C.M.

What is meant by 'eternal life'?

This presents a difficulty to many in view of erroneous ideas of heaven and 'everlasting life'. It is a subject that can be expanded indefinitely but one that puzzles many young pupils. How far this is dealt with must depend on the circumstances.

Questions that may arise include:

1 As science enables us to move into space we realise how very limited is our knowledge of the universe. Has space exploration taught us anything about life after death?

2 Another approach is through 'spiritualism' and extra-sensory perception. Is there any value in this kind of experience?

3 One of the problems is that of innocent pain and suffering. Why do people suffer especially by physical handicaps? We should consider the lives of men and women who have surprised the world by overcoming their handicaps.

> Beethoven and his deafness;
> Helen Keller and blindness;
> Milton and his blindness, among many others.

Is life after death a compensation for handicaps in this life?

4 What has the Bible to say about 'eternal life'? Most of the ideas are expressed in poetical form:

The vision of the Celestial City: Revelation 21 v. 22 to 22 vv. 1–5. There is a development in biblical thought from the Old Testament to the New Testament.

1 God is to be vindicated by retribution	Psalm 37
2 There is an expectation of a resurrection for some, whether they be good or evil, so that an adjustment can be made.	Daniel 12 v. 2
3 We do not understand the purpose of suffering. Yet, if we could grasp it that purpose would be adequate: the innocent sufferers can bear witness to God through suffering.	Book of Job
4 The suffering of the moment becomes a sacrifice for the guilty.	Isaiah 53

This brings us to the threshold of the New Testament teaching. The centuries had to pass before men were ready to receive the truth of the Gospel of the Cross: the suffering of the Cross is the suffering of divine love, not a price to be paid to win it.

'Not pie in the sky when we die' but life with the Eternal (the French word for God) which can begin here and now by means of the 'at-one-ment'.

For further reading:

	Why does God allow pain and suffering?	Fact Finders C.E.M.
Garlick, P.	Conqueror of Darkness	Lutterworth
	Artist without hands	Epworth *

What is meant by the Holy Spirit?

Sometimes we hear the 'holy ghost' referred to: the meaning is the same. The word comes from Old English 'geist' which means simply, the principal of life, as opposed to death (see introduction).

What does 'to give up the ghost' mean?

'Holy' means morally and spiritually perfect.

What does 'holy ghost' mean?

After Pentecost (remembered each year at Whitsuntide) Christians found courage, hope and a renewed sense of brotherhood in their love for one another. The act of baptism by which they were admitted to the Church was the outward sign that they were living 'in the Spirit'.	Acts 2 vv. 1–7
What is meant by the 'gift of tongues'?	I Cor. 13
	I Cor. 14 vv. 13–19

How were all these beliefs brought together and summarised ?

It was summed up for the earliest Christians, those who lived by 'the Spirit' in the simplest of creeds 'Jesus is Lord'. It was their belief in the Resurrection, that Jesus was with them still though 'in the Spirit', that gave them courage, hope and confidence.

In the first century the substance of their faith was a belief in :

God: as revealed in the life and teaching of Jesus Christ.

The Father: not as a mere 'Life Force' but as having a 'personal' concern for all His creation.

Jesus Christ: the life of Jesus as an historical fact, no mere accident but part of the plan for God's creation.

The Holy Spirit: the sense of living 'in the Spirit' as Jesus taught us to do. Baptism was the outward sign by which men were admitted to full membership of the Church.

The Church: in which we experience the 'Body of Christ' not in isolation, but by sharing in Christ's witness with others.

The Forgiveness of Sins; our sense of right and wrong is made clear in the life and teaching of Jesus. Forgiveness releases the power to live a new life, creatively.

The life eternal: the fellowship with God which is not destroyed by death.

What came to be known as the 'rule of faith' began as a series of questions put to a candidate for baptism by the one officiating in the following form :

> Dost thou believe in God the Father Almighty ?
> Dost thou believe in Christ Jesus, the Son of God, who was born by the Holy Spirit from the Virgin Mary, who was crucified under Pontius Pilate and died, and rose again on the third day, rising from the dead, and ascended to the heavens, and sat down at the right hand of the Father and will come to judge the living and the dead ?
> Dost thou believe in the Holy Spirit in the holy church ?

That such a form of questions existed in the second century is almost certain.

It can be seen how easily this could be translated into its affirmative form as we have it for the most part in the Apostles' Creed. This is recited in the offices of the Roman, Anglican and several Protestant Churches. In the Book of Common Prayer it appears in this form :

> I believe in God the Father Almighty,
> Maker of heaven and earth :
> And in Jesus Christ his only Son our Lord,
> Who was conceived by the Holy Ghost, born of the Virgin Mary,
> Suffered under Pontius Pilate
> Was crucified, dead and buried
> He descended into hell,
> The third day He rose again and ascended into heaven and sitteth on the right hand of God the Father Almighty.
> From thence He shall come to judge the quick and the dead,
> I believe in the Holy Ghost, the holy Catholic Church,
> The Communion of Saints, the Forgiveness of sins,
> The Resurrection of the body,
> And the life everlasting.

The main divergences from the original statement were commonplaces like the 'maker of heaven and earth' or ideas popular in the medieval church, such as the descent to hell and the communion of Saints. Rufinus published a commentary on the Apostles' Creed in the fifth century when it was in general use in the liturgy of the church. Creeds began to be used in the fourth century as a test of belief to halt the spread of heresies.

It will be seen that the oldest (and most venerable) of the statements of belief grew out of the experience of the church ; it expressed the traditional belief of Christians from the earliest times and came to be known as the Apostles' Creed because of its antiquity. Two other creeds have won acceptance at certain periods in the church's history. These were the Nicene Creed formulated at the Council of Nicaea A.D. 325 and the Athanasian Creed, the exact date and origin of which is uncertain. The Nicene Creed is of considerable interest to us today, as it has been accepted in modern discussions on reunion as an indispensable standard of belief in any reunited church (see Appendix B).

What do Christians believe about man ?

This questioning about God and the way He has shown us His purposes in creating the universe is part of the adolescent's search for a meaning to life. It ends as it begins by consideration of 'What is man ?' and goes on to ask as the psalmist asked, 'What is man that thou art mindful of him ?' (Psalm 8 v. 4).

Man is a spiritual being, made for fellowship with God and for those relationships with one other and to God's creation by which he finds fulfilment. Can man be explained in merely biological terms ? Can the psychologist give us all the answers ?

(Some humanists will accept the fact that man is a 'being' surrounded by mysteries.) Is the individual important and should he have rights which the state must recognise ?

Should the state protect the minority, the 'odd-man out', the conscientious objector, and the pacifist?

Books for further reading

Robertson, E. H.   Man's Estimate of Man   S.C.M. *

For some pupils an approach to the assessment of man in his response to the challenge of Christ can be seen in the passage of the Grand Inquisitor, Chapter 12 from 'The Brothers Karamazov' by Dostoevsky F. M.

There is a place for a discussion of Arthur Koestler's 'Darkness at Noon'. The communist interrogator Ivanov is speaking :

'There are only two conceptions of human ethics, and they are at opposite poles. One of them is Christian, and declares the individual to be sacrosanct ; the other starts from the basic principle that a collective aim justifies all means and not only allows, but demands that the individual should in every way be subordinated and sacrificed for the community. . . .

What do you think ?

Books for further study

Cullman, O.	The Earliest Christian Confessions	Lutterworth *
Kelly, J. N. D.	Early Christian Creeds	A. & C. Black
Lewis, C. S.	Mere Christianity	Fontana
Vidler, A. R.	Christian Belief	S.C.M. *
Bull, N. J.	Man and his World	R.E.P. *
Whale, J. S.	Christian Doctrine	Fontana *

How did these ideas and beliefs about God and man reach us ?

Truth reaches men in many ways. Poets, artists, philosophers and scientists speak to us about man and the wonders of the universe and help us to understand more about the creative activity of God. But to the Christian, the supreme revelation comes in the life, works and teaching of Jesus.

'When in former times God spoke to our forefathers, he spoke in fragmentary and varied fashion through the prophets. But in this the final stage He has spoken to us in the Son whom He has made heir to the whole universe, and through whom He created all orders of existence.' (Hebrews 1 v. 1)

Because of His own nature, God does not compel men to respond to Him although He extends His love to all men ; and in the end His will must prevail.

One of the functions of the church is to carry this, the message of Christ, to the world.

1 Through the Church

The Church is not a building: the Church is a body of people learning to live together in love and charity to extend God's Kingdom and help forward His ends and purposes. The story of the development of the church in its religious sense is contained in the Bible; so too, much may be learned about the church, its failures and successes, mistakes and accomplishments, triumphs and disasters in what we call history.

The church is the whole people of God seeking to do God's will. Many criticisms may be made of its failures and these should be faced honestly and dealt with fairly. The point should be made that Christian service and worship calls for full co-operation with others: man does not live in isolation. The continuation of the work of the church in the opinion of Bishop Stephen Neill (The Christian Society) (8) depends on worship. This is the source of the power and achievement because it brings us into a living fellowship with Christ.

Things that could be attempted by the pupils:

Find out what churches and chapels there are in the area where you live. Visits might be made to churches with different traditions (with the agreement of parents) and discussions with clergy and ministers might help. Photographs of and information about local places of worship could be arranged in folio form and could be used side by side with films and film strip on the churches and its worship.

Study the teaching of Jesus about the Church and the Resurrection. What effect did it have on the disciples?   Luke 24 v. 33

The promise of Jesus   Acts 1 v. 8

2 Through the Bible

The work of translation and revision is undertaken by men of varied views and different churches but their scholarship is made available to all. For example, those engaged in the translation of the New English Bible represent the main Protestant churches as stated in the Preface. The delegates of the Church of England, the Church of Scotland, and the Methodist, Baptist, Congregational Churches met in conference in May 1946. By January 1948, at its third meeting, invitations were extended to and accepted by the Presbyterian Church of England, the Society of Friends, the Churches in Wales, the Churches in Ireland, the British and Foreign Bible Society, and the National Bible Society of Scotland.

As an indication of how widespread is the scholarship which contributes to our understanding of the Bible it should be noted that Monsignor Ronald Knox of the Roman Catholic Church made a translation into modern English of the New Testament with a particularly happy rendering of I Cor. 13, and that two of the leaders of the Brethren (Plymouth Brothers) [1] were responsible for one of the best critical editions of the Greek New Testament to appear in the nineteenth century. (See also the section in the syllabus on the English Bible, Stage One, Secondary.)

---

(8) Neill, Stephen   The Christian Society   Fontana

[1] *S. B. Tregelles and B. W. Newton*

3 Through the Hymnology of Christendom

All the main churches have contributed in one way or another to the hymns we use in our churches and a large number have found a place in the hymn books of all denominations.

From very early times the Christian church used hymns in its service. In the New Testament we find that our Lord and His disciples sang a hymn after the institution of the Lord's Supper. In St. Paul's letter to the Corinthians (I Cor. 14 v. 26) he speaks of singing and of 'Everyman's psalms' in a context which shows that hymn singing was the practice in this church.

Here are some examples of hymns used from the earliest times:

Early 2nd century	The Benedicite omnia opera (known as a canticle or song; it appears in the Book of Common Prayer as 'O all ye works of the Lord, bless ye the Lord').
4th century	St. Hilary of Poitiers wrote a book of hymns. St. Ambrose of Milan introduced music of a congregational kind. Although it is not generally accepted that he wrote th~ Te Deum, it almost certainly comes from this century.
5th century	Synesius, Bishop of Ptolemais c. A.D. 400 wrote a well-known hymn 'Lord Jesus think of me' translated by A. Chatfield, 1876. Wrote St. Augustine (of Hippo) : '... hymns and psalms should be sung lest the people grow weary and faint through sorrow, which custom has ever been retained....'
6th century	Pope Gregory introduced the Gregorian chants into the service.
8th century	Theodolph, Bishop of Orleans, A.D. 793–835 gave us another well-known hymn, 'All glory, laud and honour to Thee, Redeemer, King ...' Translated into English by J. M. Neale.
13th century	The Dies Irae ('That day of wrath ...') Thomas of Celano who wrote a life of St. Francis of Assissi. Stabat Mater ('By the cross sad vigil keeping ...') Jacobus de Benedictus.
16th century	With the Reformation came many new hymns. Martin Luther wrote : '... this beautiful ornament might in right manner serve the Great Creator and His Christian people ...'. His followers gave us many, of which the: 'Now thank we all our God ...' (M. Rinkart 1586–1649) is, perhaps, the best known.

From now onwards the churches go their different ways and the hymns they produce are equally varied. During the reign of Mary Tudor, British refugees at Geneva produced a service book with hymns; among the authors were William Whittingham, afterwards Dean of Durham, and William Kethe or Keith, said to have been a Scotsman. On the succession of Elizabeth this collection was brought at once to England and was first used in a London church. Among these hymns was one typical of the Anglican church:

'All people that on earth do dwell' from the 100th Psalm and written by William Kethe.

Hymns typical of other denominations but used in many other churches include :

Baptist	'Lord dismiss us with Thy blessing'	John Fawcett 1740–1817, sometime Minister of Wansgate Baptist Church, Hebden Bridge.
Congregational	'O God our Help...'	Isaac Watts 1674–1784 English theologian and hymn writer. Educated at a non-conformist academy, Stoke Newington. This hymn is one of the many free paraphrases of the Psalms which he made.
Methodist	'Hark the herald angels...'	Chas. Wesley 1708–88, 'The greatest hymn writer of all ages.' The brother of John Wesley and co-worker with him.
Presbyterian	'I heard the voice of Jesus say...'	Horatio Bonar 1808–1889. He was a minister at Kelso and later in Edinburgh.
Presbyterian	'Stand up, stand up for Jesus'	G. Duffield 1818–1888.
Quaker	'Dear Lord and Father of mankind'	J. G. Whittier 1807–92, Poet and writer born at Haverhill, Mass., U.S.A. The Quakers do not as a rule have music or sing hymns ; this hymn was written and used as a poem.
Roman Catholic	'Lead kindly light...'	Cardinal Newman 1801–1890. He worked with Keble and Pusey in forwarding the Oxford Movement and led the High Church party. This brought him into collision with the University authorities. He seceded to the Church of Rome 1845.
Unitarian	'City of God, how broad and far'	S. Johnson. An American Unitarian Minister much beloved of his congregation. It is of interest that this hymn was sung at the consecration of Liverpool (Anglican) Cathedral, 1924.

It would be possible to devise a scheme of church history based on the hymnology of the church down the ages and working with the music and history department of the school. The section on Christianity in Lancashire may help.

The Ecumenical Movement

Although the churches are divided, in recent years there has been a move towards greater understanding between the many denominations. Three things which are shared are a devotion to our Lord, an acceptance of the Bible as the basis for their belief, and the use of many hymns which originated in churches holding different views of the Christian faith.

In seeking to realise the unity which God wills for His Church and the means by which He would have us attain it, the different denominations have agreed to work together in various ways:

The British Council of Churches established, 1942

The World Council of Churches established, 1948.

One great experiment in reunion has been the creation of the Church of South India in which the Anglican, Congregational, Methodist and Presbyterian Churches have come together to make a united church.

Books for further study

Sykes, N.	The English Religious Tradition	S.C.M. *
Latourette, K. S.	The Unquenchable Light	Eyre & Spottiswoode *
	The World Church Changes	Study Outline C.E.M.*
Loosley	Fellowship Then and Now	R.E.P.*
Drewett, J.	The Church's Mission Today	R.E.P. *
	The Church's Mission in the World (On project work in connection with the C.S.E.)	C.E.M. *
Routley, Erik	Hymns and Human Life	J. Murray
Martin, Hugh	They wrote our hymns	S.C.M. *
Bailey, A. E.	The Gospel in Hymns	Scribner

STAGE FIVE

The syllabus which follows is intended for pupils in their fifth year at school but who do not, generally speaking, intend to take the subject in an external examination. The material will overlap with many syllabuses as set for examination purposes but also stands, in its own right, as a continuation of the main syllabus. There are suggestions for topics which may be used in connection with course work or for discussion.

The aim is to show the progress of the Church from the disciples' experience of the risen and ascended Christ to the present day. Such a vast amount of church history is involved that only the most important aspects can be touched upon. The material includes the story of the early church, the people of God in possession of the new covenant and discovering a new way of life. Only topics from a wide field are mentioned and it is not suggested that every one should be fully dealt with but that the material should be used in a way suitable for the children in their fifth year.

From time to time links should be made with other subjects in the curriculum: history, music, literature and art are fairly obvious examples where connections between subjects may be found.

The Church in Action

The witness of the Church in New Testament times

(a) This is a continuation of the work in the previous stage in which the worship of the church has been mentioned.

The impact made by the resurrection on the disciples (the journey to Emmaus)	Luke 24 vv. 13–50
The promise made by Jesus	Acts 1 v. 8
The first Whitsuntide	Acts 2 vv. 1–13
Peter's preaching and its effect on the people	Acts 2 vv. 14–41
The first members of the Church (followers 'in the way')	Acts 4 vv. 32–37 Acts 2 vv. 42–47
The Church grows	Acts 8, 10, 15
One of the ways in which the new spirit showed itself was in the economic sphere. They '. . . had all things in common'. They had a commemoration of the 'breaking of bread' in their houses: a kind of house church	Acts 2 v. 46
Dishonesty creeps in: Annanias and Sapphira (a stroke or heart-attack due to stress of the moment?)	Acts 5 vv. 5 and 10
Persecution begins: Stephen is stoned (the bitter hostility to him among the leaders of the Jews is explained in vv. 48–50 and 54)	Acts 6, 7 vv. 54ff
There is a problem to be solved. On what terms are Gentiles (non-Jews) to be admitted to the Christian Church?	Acts 10

(b) Early Christian teaching and practice : some
principles that emerged :

 Admission was by baptism. From the start the
 Church possessed its distinctive message
 (Kerygma or Gospel) and a confession of this was   Romans 10 v. 9
 made in connection with baptism   I Cor. 12 v. 3

 Even at the time of the Apostles the slogan 'Jesus
 is Lord' was used as a sign of faith.

(c) The Church becomes a missionary force :

 Paul and Barnabas   Acts 13 vv. 1–14
 Paul and Silas   Acts 15 vv. 36–41

 Other references to Paul's work can be made :

 Paul in Asia Minor   Acts 14
 Paul advances into Europe   Acts 16, 17
 Voyage and Shipwreck   Acts 27
 Arrival in Rome   Acts 28

 Books for further reading :

 Dale, A. T.   From Galilee to Rome   O.U.P.
 Dale, A. T.   Paul the Explorer   O.U.P.

Principalities and Powers

(a) The Church and the Roman Empire. Persecution alternated with periods of
tolerance.

 In the persecution of Nero's reign tradition says that SS. Peter and Paul were
 put to death (A.D. 95). This is referred to in a letter written by Clement of Rome
 to the Corinthians. The martyrdom of Polycarp, Bishop of Smyrna, is mentioned
 (A.D. 155).

 ▶ Documents about these events are reproduced in the book :

 Bettenson, H.   Documents of the Christian   O.U.P.
                      Church (pp. 11 and 12)

 It was at this time that the Book of Revelation was in circulation as a kind of
 pamphlet for the 'underground movement' in times of persecution (see also
 Part One of the Main Secondary Syllabus).

 The martyrs of these persecutions were   Revelation 6 vv. 9–11
 remembered.
 Their sufferings would pass away and they would
 find peace in the presence of God.   Revelation 7 vv. 13–17
 The picture of the Holy City.   Revelation 21 vv. 1–7 ;
                                                    vv. 22–27

 When it was dangerous to declare one's faith too openly symbols were used,
 scratched on walls, in the catacombs at Rome for example. One was the sign of
 the 'fish'. The Greek letters of this word stood for :

 'Jesus Christ, Son of God, Saviour.'

 It can often be seen in old churches, sometimes round the font.

 At the beginning of the fourth century the Roman Empire gave toleration to the
 Church, the Christians were free to worship openly.

 The Emperor Galerius made an 'edict of   A.D. 311
 toleration'.
 Constantine issued the edict of Milan.   A.D. 313
 This gave to the Church not only freedom of
 worship but also gave to Christians some
 protection within the law.

 Both these edicts are reproduced in the book :

 Bettenson, H.   Documents of the Christian   O.U.P.
                      Church.

(b)   The Church, however, has met with conflict as well as persecution from time to time even to the present day.

> The conflict with Islam. Although not by any means the worst of the conflicts it is one that continues to the present time, e.g. in Nigeria and other African countries.
>
> Raymond Lully, when about 30 years of age, renounced the world, devoted himself to the conversion of the Moslems in Algeria. He was stoned to death A.D. 1315.
>
> There are many examples of opposition in modern times, in Russia, China and parts of Europe. Some of the background to this anti-Christian movement should be touched on and the reasons, so far as we can understand them, given.
>
> The work of Trevor Huddleston in Africa, and in a different way that of Dr. Martin Luther King in America could be mentioned.

The Church at Work in the World

(a)   *In the New Testament*

The care of the sick and needy	Acts 6 vv. 1–7
The relief of the poor	Acts 11 vv. 27–30

The spirit of Jesus in action e.g.:
Paul's letters —

on behaviour	Romans 12
love is revealed in faith	Galatians 5 and 6
On the need for good works	James's Epistle

(b)   *The Founding of Schools and Hospitals*

There could be a link with the history department over this work. The monasteries and their work:

In the north of England the Benedictines founded monasteries at Wearmouth A.D. 674 and Jarrow A.D. 682 which are described by the Venerable Bede. These two monasteries were equipped with books and had a zest for learning that made them, in their day, the brightest centre for learning in Europe north of the Alps. Bede and his disciples and the artists of Lindisfarne set up a tradition of learning and artistic achievement that, through Alcuin, influenced the whole of north-west Europe. The Cistercians (known as the White Monks as opposed to the Black Monks – the Benedictines – from whom they came as a reformed order under St. Bernard) made great developments in farming in the twelfth century. They made a mark on the economic development of the country. Their centres were at:

Furness Abbey: built A.D. 1127 by Benedictines and later taken over by the Cistercians A.D. 1148. It became one of the richest and largest monasteries in England. It founded an off-shoot at Rushen in the Isle of Man.

Whalley Abbey: a Cistercian centre.

Priory of Cartmel: built A.D. 1188.

St. Chad, who became Bishop of Lichfield, was educated at Lindisfarne in the seventh century. The see of Lichfield extended into what is today most of Lancashire.

From the thirteenth century it was part of the duty of the parish clerk to teach singing, Latin grammar, reading and a little writing. This he did either holding a school for a few boys in the church or in his own poor cottage. Many of these clerks were young men in one of the minor orders of the priesthood. Sir John de Assheton c. 1428 probably sent his son to Whalley Abbey. He made a gift in trust to the Abbot' . . . giving the Abbot 1000 marks for the use of Ralph is son'. After a few years this boy would become a page to a knight and continue his education as a member of the knight's household.

Grammar Schools were founded in the Middle Ages for teaching the rules of Latin and Greek grammar: able pupils made their way to the universities or into the Church and frequently into the service of the state.

Many of the old grammar schools disappeared at the Reformation but they were replaced by new foundations: some of our old Grammar Schools can trace their origin to the time of Henry VIII or one of the Tudor sovereigns. They were church foundations.

The growing need for many more people to be able to read and write and the increase in the numbers of books available made possible through the invention of printing eventually brought about movements and societies for the promotion of schools. Examples:

The Sunday School Movement from 1780.

The Dissenting Academies in the eighteenth century. The one at Warrington was presided over by no less a person than Joseph Priestley, theologian and scientist; made an F.R.S. 1766.

The British and Foreign Schools Society (nineteenth century)

The National Society (nineteenth century)

The monks had their infirmaries mainly for their own members, but they also looked after the sick in the locality. They provided the only means by which people could be cared for in old age.

In England a leper asylum was erected in London A.D. 1118.

St. Bartholomew's Hospital dates from A.D. 1123.

St. Thomas's Hospital A.D. 1200.

All were religious foundations: Rahere the monk founded St. Batholomew's.

(c) *In modern times:* The state has now taken over many of the institutions begun by the churches of all denominations although the churches have a very important part to play in the social activities of the community. Especially is this so wherever personal problems call for that particular form of understanding and compassion which is contained within the Christian view of life.

The Church Army and the Salvation Army do much needed social work.

The churches still have much to contribute to education and in particular in the countries abroad which are endeavouring to establish schools and opportunities for higher education, e.g., universities, colleges and in teacher-training.

Missionary enterprises, although they may change their form of activity, are still needed.

Help is given to refugees and stateless persons through Christian Aid organisations.

The work of the church is concerned in many ways with the new problems of an industrial society.

Industrial missions: helping in establishing good relations between employers and employees. Keeping alive the search for better human relationships at all levels. The Worker Priest movement and the work of Industrial Chaplains.

Helping in developing links between school and work, e.g. conferences for school leavers, etc.

Work in connection with race relationships, e.g., the Notting Hill experiment (Bruce Kenrick).

The rehousing of those in the poor areas of large cities.

The work in connection with racial discrimination. (There are national and local bodies on which eminent men of good will are striving to overcome prejudice and antipathy.)

There is the work of many who undertake difficult tasks in co-operation with people of other views, but who believe in helping others.

The Samaritans (a telephone service for those who are very depressed).

Prison Visitors.

Hospital visiting and voluntary workers: not all these are convinced Christians but Christians, humanists and others work together for the good of others.

There is, too, the important work of helping men and women to come to terms with the new knowledge of all kinds biblical, scientific and social. In the past, the church has often been against the search for truth: today it has an important part to play in helping people to understand the changes in our thinking and our way of life.

Books for further study:

	The World Church Changes	C.E.M. Study Outline
Bainton, R. H.	The Church of Our Fathers	S.C.M.
Kenrick, Bruce	Come Out the Wilderness	Fontana
Barker, Edwin	The Responsible Church	Board for Social Responsibility (Anglican)
Greenslade, S. L.	The Church and Social Order.	S.C.M.

(d) *The Church in Lancashire*

See the section on Christianity in Lancashire. Appendices B and C.

(e) *Some suggestions for the teaching of Church History by means of short biographies (a possible alternative).*

For some pupils the biographical approach may prove more appropriate. The list which follows and from which a selection may be made, is by no means comprehensive and from time to time new information becomes available.

The Church seen in relation to some outstanding personalities:

1 Mediaeval saintliness (the return to nature in art   St. Francis of Assissi
as the basis for inspiration – hence the many
stories of Francis and the animals).
An apostle of the Middle Ages.   St. Francis Xavier

2 The claim of the right to worship in accordance   The Pilgrim Fathers
with conscience (the freedom of the individual).   John Bunyan

3 The evangelists of the nineteenth century.   The Wesleys

4 Pioneers in nineteenth century missions.   David Livingstone
                                                                                Father Damien
                                                                                Mary Slessor
                                                                                William Carey

5 Pioneers in social justice and practical   William Wilberforce
philanthropy.   Lord Shaftesbury
                                                                                John Howard
                                                                                Octavia Hill
                                                                                Elizabeth Fry
                                                                                Kagawa of Japan
                                                                                Dr. Barnardo
                                                                                Dr. Joost de Blank
                                                                                Trevor Huddleston
                                                                                Bruce Kenrick

6 Pioneers in thought and science (Christianity can claim to have created confidence in a rational order which paved the way for scientific thought).

Galileo
Newton
Darwin
Pasteur

7 Christian heroism.

Gladys Aylward
Pope John XXIII
Wilson of Scott's
Antarctic Expedition
Dr. Martin Luther King
Chief Luthuli
Helen Keller
David Sheppard
Dr. Wilson, Bishop of
Birmingham.
Dr. Donald Caskie

Books for reading :

Aylward, G.	Autobiography	Lutterworth
Barne, K.	Elizabeth Fry	Methuen *
Bielby, R. M.	Lady in Prison, Elizabeth Fry	Lutterworth *
Bielby, R. M.	John Bunyan	Lutterworth
Brett, S. R.	John Wesley	Black
Dalton, L. H.	William Carey	Lutterworth *
Davey, C. J.	Kagawa of Japan	Epworth *
Fancourt, M. St. J.	Life of Lord Shaftesbury	Longmans *
Garlick, P.	Hellen Keller	Lutterworth *
Hayes, E. H.	Yarns on Christian Pioneers	R.E.P. *
Latham, R. O.	David Livingstone	Lutterworth *
MacGregor, Hastie	Pope John XXIII	Cassell *
Gaskie, Dr. Donald	The Tartan Pimpernel	Oldbourne*

Personal Relationships and Responsibility

To understand oneself is, in Christian terms, to face the problems that arise in personal relationships in the light of the life and teaching of Jesus Christ. Its purpose is to help young people to come to terms with their personal problems and to learn to accept responsibility, to treat others with respect insofar as all human life is unique.

There are several ways of approaching this : by guided discussion which should be free and open, by drama and role play, and through creative writing in which young people should be encouraged to express their own ideas. In these and other ways, teacher and pupils can gain insights as they consider together many aspects of personal relationships. Other subjects will play their part in developing the themes which are suggested. See also Stages Four and Five in the Alternative Syllabus.

Practical Problems of Teenagers
1 Making Friends

What do we expect of a friend ?
How do we make friends ?
Can we choose friends without being unfriendly ?
What prevents friendship ?

As indicated in 'Teenage Religion' (Harold Loukes, S.C.M.), there is a need at this stage particularly, to give the pupil opportunities for coming to terms with situations which make Christian teaching relevant as the pupils experience them.

(i) **What did Christ say about friendship ?**

On being loyal to ones friends.	John 15 vv. 12–14
On having special friends : there are moments of insight which are gained by talking together.	Mark 9 v. 2
In our darkest moments, we should be responsive to the sufferings and needs of others.	Luke 23 vv. 39–43
The journey to Emmaus.	Luke 24 vv. 13–35

(ii) Where can we find friends?

People are not meant to live alone.
The gang : can a gang be a good thing ?
The Youth Club.
The Church.

It would be dishonest and doing poor service to the Church not to admit that Churches can fail in fostering friendship : nevertheless, it is the Church that should have most to teach us about living in a community.

What is the Church ?
Do I need to go to Church to be a Christian ?
Some passages to study :

The first Christians.	Acts 2 vv. 44–47
Thinking about and praying for others.	Acts 12 vv. 5 and 12
The dwelling place of God	Isaiah 57 v. 15
Meeting together for encouragement.	Hebrews 10 vv. 23–25
Praying together.	Matthew 18 vv. 19–20
Jesus's custom.	Luke 4 v. 16

(iii) What prevents friendship?

What part does snobbery play ? This is a word often used by teenagers. There can be two ways of looking at this situation. It means that a person can have an exaggerated respect for social position or wealth and be ashamed of socially inferior connections : equally harmful is 'inverted snobbery' – a refusal to accept the friendship, sincerely offered, of people with greater ability, more intelligence than oneself and of a higher social standing.

Snobbery comes from having false standards.	James 2 vv. 1–4
Riches can stand in the way.	Mark 10 vv. 17–22
Who is the greatest ?	Mark 10 vv. 35–37, 41–45
The master is the servant.	John 13 vv. 1–7, 12–17
Blessed are the meek.	Matthew 5 v. 5 ; Psalm 37 v. 11
'We love because He first loved us'.	I John 4 v. 19

2 Class distinctions – are they a bad thing?

'Four score years and seven * our fathers brought forth on this continent a new nation conceived in liberty and dedicated to the proposition that all men are created equal.'

Abraham Lincoln's Gettysburg Address July 1863.
*The date of the Declaration of American Independence 1776.

In what sense are people created equal ?

The vision of Cornelius 'God has no favourites'.	Acts 10 vv. 1–35

3 Distinctions between races – what did Jesus teach about racial discrimination?

'For through faith you are all sons of God in union with Christ Jesus. . . . There is no such thing as Jew and Greek, slave and freeman, male and female ; for you all are one person in Christ Jesus.'

If we added 'coloured or white' would this be true to the spirit of the Gospel ? What do you think of 'apartheid' in South Africa in the light of this teaching ?

Philip and the Ethiopian.	Acts 8 vv. 26–40

Should we classify people by their possessions ? Do riches raise a man's status ? What did Jesus say about this ?

Making a god of money.	Matthew 6 vv. 19–21
It's not money but the motive that counts.	James 2 vv. 1–14
The widow's mite – our arithmetic and God's. It is not what is given but what is kept back that counts.	Mark 12 vv. 41–44

4 Sex and Marriage. Is sex enough ?

Choosing the right man or woman for a life partnership. The 'glossy magazine' : some magazines give sound advice, others merely provide excitement or romantic dreams.

How old ought a boy or girl to be when they marry ?
Should the duchess marry her chauffeur ?
Pre-marital sex relationships, or 'How far should I let him go ?'.

The marriage service.

In Church.   Psalm 128 and 67
In a Registry Office.

Marriage is for life and both ceremonies are equally binding.

God's design for the family.   Mark 10 vv. 1–10
The women taken in adultery.   John 7 v. 53 to 8 v. 11
                                                 (R.V. and A.V. only)

The marriage in Cana : Jesus is an honoured
guest.   John 2 vv. 1–10

5 Facing our responsibilities – the challenge of work and a work-a-day world

The philosophy of 'why worry, why work'.   Matthew 6 vv. 25–34
Is work a punishment or a bore ?   Genesis 3 vv. 16–19
Should work be shared or dodged ?   Proverbs 6 vv. 6–11

The hard facts of life have to be faced. Work has to be done ; man has to live, but the trend is today for men to have more leisure ; the five-day week, the forty hour week. Automation in factories increases men's leisure time.

The Christian judgement on this :

'Give the cheerful service of those who serve the
Lord, not men.'   Ephesians 6 v. 7

Books and materials that can be used in developing this section

Various pamphlets and outlines are available for developing discussion. 'Talking about living'. 'The Focus Series' of topics, 'Which and Why Cards', 'Thinking Things Through' (a series) : The Secretary, Christian Education Movement, Annandale, North End Road, London N.W.11.

Hayes, Ernest H.	I Believe.	Religious Education • Press
Hayes, Ernest H.	Begin Here.	Religious Education Press
Cottrell, J. Hills	Let's Discuss	Scripture Union •
Hughes, T.	Life worth living.	Epworth •
Cave	Living with other people.	Ward •
Taylor, D.	Operation Think	Blond
Bruce, V.	Lord of the Dance (an approach to Religious Education through movement).	Pergamon

The B.B.C. Schools' Programmes often deal with 'Personal Relationships'.

Books for further reading

Robinson, J.	Christian Morals Today.	S.C.M. •
Hughes, H. T.	Faith and Life.	Epworth •
Ingleby, Alan St. B.	Learning to love.	Robert Hall •
Barnes, K. C.	He and She	Penguin

139

Some Topics for a Study of Current Problems

There are possibilities of linking these with course work for the Certificate of Secondary Education.

1   The Colour Bar Rational and irrational views on race, prejudice and education.

Books for reading and discussion

Bibby, Cyril	Race, Prejudice and Education.	Heinemann *
Huddleston, Trevor	Naught for Your Comfort.	Fontana
	South Africa.	British Council of Churches Publications *
	Black and White (Thinking things through series).	S.C.M. Press
	White and Black in Britain – Study Outline.	C.E.M. *
	The Colour Problem – Which and Why Card.	C.E.M. *
Paton, Alan	Cry the Beloved Country.	Penguin

Some questions that will arise :

Why are those people of different colour ?
Are differences in intelligence shown as between coloured and white people ?
Is colour only skin deep ?
Christians believe that people regardless of colour are of equal value in the sight of God. Why ?
What did Jesus say about people of different races ?
What causes colour prejudice in Britain ?
Would you like to see mixed marriages in your own family ?

With this might go some study of press references on the position of the negro in the U.S.A. and the work of many Americans to overcome the problem (the Civil Rights Movement). The South African situation could also be discussed. Pupils could make a collection of cuttings from the newspapers about any of these problems.

2   Other Religions The study of comparative religion is a difficult subject calling for knowledge and understanding nearly always beyond the reach of children of this age. Nevertheless, pupils are bound to ask questions about other beliefs. With greater facilities for world travel, the increasing movement of populations, and the impact of a multi-racial Commonwealth bringing with it immigration into this country of peoples with customs and beliefs different from our own, questions about other religions will arise. In recent years, Christians have realised the needs for understanding other beliefs more fully.

Books for reading and discussion:

Hilliard, F. H.	How Men Worship.	Routledge *
	Christianity and Other Religions.	S.C.M *
Parrinder, E. G.	A Book of World Religions	Hulton
Soderblom, Bishop	The Living God.	
Kraemer, H.	Why Christianity of all Religions ?	Lutterworth *
Kraemer, H.	Christianity in a Non-Christian World.	Lutterworth *
	Pupils might begin this topic by finding out what different religions are practised in the locality. How do the followers of other faiths worship ? (This may include Hindus, Sikhs and Buddhists.) What do they believe about God ? Why should we respect other people's ways and customs ? What differences with regard to food do they have ?	

3   About Hunger

This is an urgent problem related to the increase in the world population and the under-developed areas, and it is vital that pupils should have accurate information about it. It should be looked at from all points of view ; not only is there a need for emergency measures to relieve famine conditions but economic development and education are equally important. The Christian concern for people especially when they are in need, should be explored.

The Biblical teaching on the right attitude to those in need : the hungry, the foreigner, orphans and widows.	Deuteronomy 10 vv. 18–19 Deuteronomy 14 vv. 28–29
What Jesus said about this.	Matthew 25 vv. 31–46

What is the Church doing ?

Examples of both kinds of approach can be studied :

British Council of Churches Christian Aid, 10 Eaton Gate, London S.W.1.
The Agricultural Training Programme in Kenya.

The Masai Agriculture and Nutrition Scheme. This is work in agricultural education where the Church (Manchester Diocese) pioneered the setting up of an Agricultural College known as the Masai Rural Training Centre. Here the Masai are being trained in modern ways of farming leading to greater food production. For information write to :

(i) The Manchester and District Council of Churches, 1 Ridgefield, King Street, Manchester 2.

(ii) The Freedom from Hunger Campaign, 17 Northumberland Avenue, London W.C.2.

See also the Appendix on Sources of Information for addresses of organisations which supply information, charts and visual aids.

4 Education

This is often a local as well as a world-wide problem. The presence of immigrants sometimes raises questions of literacy which are a problem for a school. This could lead to a sympathetic enquiry into causes which are world-wide. About half the population of the world are unable to read or write : this is a serious world problem.

Why is it necessary to be able to read and write ? In recent times nations that were backward (in modern terms) have set about the task of mass-education. China under Mao-Tse-Tung is one example : the emergent African nations are another (cf. Britain in the nineteenth century when the first Education Acts were passed).

In many cases, a written language has to be created. The expansion of the Church in Europe, which made necessary the translation of the Bible into the language of the people, led to the making of alphabets.

The Cyrillic alphabet of the Russians ; using Greek symbols, and a few new ones, the Church expanding from Byzantium introduced the written form of the Russian language.

There are many other examples.

The Bible is now translated into more than a thousand languages, and for many of those written alphabets have had to be invented by Christian missionaries. This work continues.

(i) The Wycliffe Bible Translators, 17 Downs Court Road, Purley, Sussex.
An organisation working among South American Indians and elsewhere devising a written language.

(ii) The British and Foreign Bible Society, 146 Queen Victoria Street, London E.C.4.
This organisation works to provide good reading material to the peoples in Asia, Africa and South America.

(iii) Dr. Frank C. Laubach has worked out new ways of teaching illiterates.
Laubach, F. C.   Teaching the World to Read.   U.N.E.S.C.O. literature
Christian Focus Pamphlet –
Illiteracy.

5 Mass Media and Politics

Is advertising necessary ? How much are we influenced by advertisements when we make a purchase ? Are there methods of advertising which should not be used ?

Ought books and plays to be censored? How far are we swayed by the more subtle techniques of television? What are the aims of religious broadcasting? Is brain-washing immoral? Ought the churches to use propaganda methods more than they do?

Make a list of the various ways of advertising. What are slogans? What is their value?

Find out about subliminal advertising. Is it ethical? Collect slogans and compare their effectiveness in various ways.

For reading and discussion:

Packard, Vance   The Hidden Persuaders and other   Penguin
books by the same author.

Examine copies of the magazine 'Which?' and similar magazines. Compare the content and space devoted to matters of public concern in the national press. How do they treat day-to-day events?

Our kind of liberal-democracy can survive only if people are well-informed and concerned about events. How far does the press give us the kind of information we need in order to make up our minds on the big issues of the day? How far are 'gimmicks' permissible? Are 'public opinion' polls fair?

Ought Christian leaders to speak on political issues? Christians should take an active part in politics and be concerned about the decisions made in Parliament and at local government level: how far is the Christian view represented in Parliamentary debates on the moral issues with which we are all concerned? Why do Christians differ quite frequently on moral questions? Should we have political parties based on loyalties to different churches?

Books for reading and discussion

Thomas, G.	The Christian Heritage in Politics.	Epworth
James, W.	The Christian in Politics	O.U.P.

6 Science and Religion

The underlying aim of the syllabus is to give the pupils, among other important matters, a clearer view of the nature of biblical truth. This in itself should help in resolving the tension that, in the minds of many, exists between science (as understood by pupils) and religion. There is a need, nevertheless, to deal with the problem more specifically by reading and discussion.

Books for reading and discussion

Raven, C. E.	Christianity and Science. Science and Religion – Study Outline.	World Christian Books C.E.M. *
Browne, L. E.	Where Science and Religion Meet.	R.E.P. *
Carter, G. S.	Is the theory of evolution consistent with Christian belief? ('Questions at Issue' series).	S.P.C.K.
Coulson, C. A.	Science, Technology and the Christian.	Epworth *
Coulson, C. A.	'Science tells us' – 'How much' ('Questions at Issue' series).	S.P.C.K.
Coulson, C. A.	Some problems of the Atomic Age.	Epworth *
Richardson, A.	The Bible in an Age of Science.	S.C.M.
Richardson, A.	Science, History and Faith.	O.U.P.
Lambert, Jas.	Science and Sanctity.	Faith Press

Some questions that arise and may be the starting point for a discussion would include, does science make religion unnecessary? Can the biologist and psychologist give us a complete answer to the nature of man? Reason alone does not answer the question. Imagination as expressed by the poet, writer, artist and musician play their part in helping us to understand what is expressed in religious insights into the nature of man.

The opening chapters of Genesis should be considered in relation to what has been discussed.

Richardson, A.	Genesis I–XI "	S.C.M.

THE ALTERNATIVE SYLLABUS

These suggestions are intended to follow on from Stage Two of the Main Syllabus

This alternative syllabus is based on the field work carried out in the schools in Lancashire and the north-west by the Student Christian Movement in Schools (now the Christian Education Movement) with the full support of the Lancashire Education Authority. The suggestions which follow are based on practical experience gained in the schools. This is a pioneer experiment as a result of which new insights were obtained into the religious and moral needs of the pupils dealt with in a wider context in the Report of the Central Advisory Council for Education in England: Half our Future (H.M.S.O. 8s. 6d.). In this Report it was recommended that, 'Local Education Authorities should consider a review of their Agreed Syllabuses and determine whether adequate provision is made for the needs of the older boys and girls of average and below average ability and whether they leave sufficient scope for the teachers to develop methods which start with the actual problems which the pupils have to face'. (9). In another section this view is expanded: 'It is unlikely . . . that teachers left to themselves, would choose a literary and historical approach which might suggest to the less intelligent that the Bible belongs to the past and has no contemporary significance. They would be more likely to adopt the kind of case-study methods leading back to the Bible from present problems which the Student Christian Movement in Schools has shown to be successful in secondary modern schools.' (10)

Some consideration of the needs and problems of the less-able pupils (13 to 16 years)

The onset of puberty	'The challenging feature of their lives is now the sexual instinct which is at its most potent in these years.'	'Half Our Future', p. 54 — para. 164
	The less able child is often puzzled and confused by the problems of adolescence with its related social and physical consequences. Puberty is often reached at an earlier age than with his contemporaries, and he feels the pressure of this sexual development all the more because he lacks the intellectual interests of the more able pupils. This may be complicated by the ignorance, superstition and lack of the ability to communicate on the part of his parents and those at home. The sense of isolation, of 'being misunderstood', often becomes acute.	

---

(9) P. 59 Recommendations 'Half Our Future', H.M.S.O.

(10) P. 58 paragraph 173. ibid.

Independence The urge towards independence in financial, social, intellectual and moral matters becomes increasingly strong. These pupils are the more easily a prey to the pressure of commercial advertising and the lure of affluence. Their objectives become firmly fixed upon the world of work and the status which the increased spending powers of employment give. Consequently, talk of rewards to be received later, in return for the immediate sacrifice, win little response from the less able pupils whose main concern becomes a good job at the earliest moment no matter how 'dead-end' the job may be.

The pressure of a secular society The secular non-religious outlook typical of most groups in contemporary society exerts a strong pressure on the less able child for whom religious and moral issues are often intellectual exercises beyond his understanding ; he is essentially pragmatic in his outlook and for him the Bible belongs to another age and is associated with a childhood he has outgrown. Religion will not help him to a better job with higher material rewards ; few adults seem to care and so he comes to accept the apathy of a society which sees little value in religion. He has religious and spiritual needs however to which an answer must be given.

'Most boys and girls want to be what they call "being good" and they want to know what kind of animal man is and ultimately whether each one of them matters, if so, to whom and why.'

'Half Our Future', p. 52 – para. 157

Religious education must meet the needs of the adolescent and be seen to be relevant to the world as he finds it to be. The teaching should, therefore, deal with these problems and situations which press most closely on the pupil in the transition to the work-a-day world, and in the transition from youth to maturity. Teaching must deal with the kind of problems they will meet in the world outside school, the problems they will be expected to face in the same way and on the same terms as adults.

Leaving the sheltered life of school to meet the challenge of the world of work

This will call for adjustments of many kinds in terms of relationships in an unsheltered community; these will be met on the factory floor, in offices, as well as in the freer atmosphere of leisure time pursuits. The problems of mixed communities in terms of race and colour, the question of prejudice as against an imaginative understanding of another's point of view, as well as the basis of a just society in terms of poverty and the lack of cultural amenities, will call for Christian insights.

A mature approach is needed

At this stage, the subject becomes 'difficult and controversial' because any discussion to be worthwhile must be treated openly as mature adults would wish to deal with it; adolescents react strongly to any suggestion that they are being 'got at'. A critical and enquiring attitude should be welcomed but the discussion approach which this demands cannot be without preparation. In particular the leader of the discussion (normally the teacher) should be familiar with the territory to be explored and so able to lead the pupils to wider and better informed views. The ultimate aim in the setting of religious education must be to relate this enquiry to the grand themes of the Bible.

The need for a place in the community

It is almost inevitable that the basic problem facing these children is how to live in a community in which the most challenging and exhilarating jobs go to the better qualified school leavers. This is not only a matter of remuneration in which the less able often gain a short term advantage, but in finding a status in society which is satisfying. The child who, because he finds animals to be an absorbing interest wants to become a veterinary surgeon, or the girl who, finding the care of children a satisfying pastime aspires to be a qualified teacher or nurse but who, nevertheless, lacks the academic basis for such work, has to be guided into new ways of finding a place in society. There are related questions which call for examination in the light of the Biblical teaching on man and the purpose for which we were born into the world.

'Religion is concerned with the relation between man and his Maker, with a personal relationship. Out of the experience of being loved (and of sharing love) springs the motive power of Christian living.'   Ibid p. 56 – para. 168

Relationships are concerned with the whole situation involved in living in the family, in the work-a-day world and in our leisure time.

Making up one's mind – commitment

In an age of multiplicity of choice it is the task of those concerned with religious education to bring adolescents face to face with questions of ultimate significance. The wise use of money, the intelligent choice of friends, the choice of a career, and deeper moral issues depend in the end on the values which we hold.

'It is a major task to steer this new doubting spirit into positive, creative channels avoiding the truculence of "couldn't care less".'

Ibid, para. 159

In an affluent age, uncertain about its moral values as of so much else to do with the aim and purpose of life, the adolescent has to be helped to choose. This calls for the sympathetic guidance of a mature adult so that a choice may be made freely, without being unduly swayed by prejudice, popular fashions in the group, or even family pressures, a superhuman task which calls for more than human aid.

The Outline Scheme (Religion and People)
(13–16 years approx.)

This is intended as an alternative to the Stages Three, Four and Five in the main syllabus. It is intended that all pupils should include the work (based on a realistic scheme of the school's own making) in the Stages One and Two of the main syllabus and then proceed to the Alternative Syllabus where appropriate.

To the mind of the less able child religious education has little utilitarian value largely because it seems isolated and remote from other subjects in the school curriculum. Wherever possible links should be established with other departments notably science, biology, drama, literature, local history, geography and current affairs to show that the subject matter of religious education is related to the whole of the curriculum. It would be of value for a teacher of religious instruction to take some other subject.

STAGES ONE AND TWO

(as in the Main Syllabus – see Part One)

Stage One

For those over 11 years.
The story of the Bible.
The sources of Christianity.
The beginnings of Church History.

Stage Two

For those over 12 years
What the Bible is about.
What the Old Testament has to say.
The life and times of Jesus.
Four portraits of Jesus.

STAGE THREE (children 13 and over)

Outline of topic	Suggestions for the teacher	Reference for teacher
Growing up in the home	The family. Relatives The 'gang'. Group and family pressures. The first boy-friend and girl-friends. Puberty and its problems.	Human Nature and Christian Marriage, Wm. P. Wylie, S.C.M.; * Focus No. 1. 'Your Family', C.E.M.; a link here with biology
Growing up in the neighbour-hood	Who is my neighbour? The Welfare State. Community care. (i) the aged and the lonely; (ii) the handicapped.	A wider meaning to the 'Good Samaritan'. A link with social studies. The point should be taken that the function of organised public support is to strengthen the individual, not weaken it.
Our Responsibilities in the World	Projects on the fight against poverty and hunger. The work of the churches overseas – mission and service. Barrier of class, colour, education and creed.	Focus No. 10 'Our World' (C.E.M.). *

Outline of topics	Suggestions for the teacher	Reference for teacher
Becoming an adult in the community	(i) Independence and its responsibilities. The use of money ; betting and gambling. Saving and giving. The use of leisure. Relationship with adults. Pressures on choice – the necessity for making up one's mind. Good standards.	Thinking Things Through (a series), S.C.M. Press.
	(ii) Personal relationships. What do we look for in friends of the opposite sex ? Conduct on 'dating'. Courtship, petting, promiscuity. Marriage, the family and the home. The community and our own conduct.	Kenneth Barnes, 'He and She'. Some pamphlets issued by the National Marriage Guidance Council are helpful.
	(iii) The transition from school to work. Choosing a job. Why work ? Problems of adjustment – longer hours, living with adults, etc. Standards of behaviour. Trade Unions, new pressures and choice.	

STAGE FIVE (the non-academic child staying on to 16)   'Half our Future'.

The course is meant for the sixteen-year-old leaver not intending to take an external examination.

Contribution to the community

(i) Service to the community

The place of voluntary service in the welfare state. Local survey of the social services.

Opportunities of service by young people the work of C.S.V., and V.S.O., Work Camps, etc. Problems raised by voluntary service, e.g., is it worth it ? Why bother with them ? Aren't they best left alone ?

What is service ? What is love ? The theology of service.

(ii) The Church in the community

The work of the churches in the locality – survey of church life – history of the church in the area.

The impact of the churches on the community.

Youth in the church – challenge and response.

(iii) Responsibilities in the world

The world mission of the church.

The Christian and politics.

Our response.

SYLLABUS IN DETAIL

STAGE THREE (13+)

Outline of topics	Suggestions for the teacher	Reference for teacher
	The aim at this stage (and the subsequent stages) is to show the relevance of Christianity to life and what it has to say about the problems which confront the adolescent. The discussion method can be used to open up the problems in greater depth. Wherever possible other departments of the school could be asked to co-operate; outside contacts can also be employed.	'Talk About Living' (discussion playlets) C.E.M., Annandale, North End Road, London N.W.1.
Growing up in the home 1 The family	What goes to make a Christian home? The importance of the environment. The influence of parents on a child's character. Disagreements in the house; who is at fault? Parental authority; when am I grown up? Honesty with one's parents and with one another. Trust and respect for one another is the basis of all family love.	'God and the Human Family', John G. Williams, S.P.C.K. * Focus No. 1, 'Your Family', C.E.M. * Links should be made with the Home Economics Department.
2 Relatives	Responsibility to older people. Family life in our parents' days and today. The Welfare State and the family. Old People's Homes. The movement of population and the separation of members of the family.	
3 The gang	Choosing our friends. What do we look for in a friend? Can we choose friends without being unfriendly? Falling into line – the group pressure. Making friends with the opposite sex. The Youth Club and similar organisations.	'Getting on with People', Eric Lord, * S.C.M.
4 The break-up of the gang	Boy and girl friendships. Father and mother – what they have to say. What do we look for in our friends of the opposite sex?	'He and She', Kenneth Barnes. 'Broken Date', 'Talk About', C.E.M.
5 Puberty and its problems	Fears and superstitions. Healthy-mindedness about sex.	The teaching in the Biology Department should be linked with this.

Outline of topics	Suggestions for the teacher	Reference for teacher
Growing up in the neighbourhood	This section deals with getting to know about the wider community and the practical work which may be attempted in the form of projects as suggested in the Newsom Report. 'Boys and girls growing up in a Welfare State ought to know how the Social Services are paid for and how they operate locally. They ought to realise the continuing need for sensible self-help and for voluntary assistance to those unable to help themselves.'	'Half Our Future', H.M.S.O., para. 212
	'Community service projects seem to offer particularly satisfying possibilities.'	Ibid., para. 200.
	(a) Who is my neighbour?	A link here with social studies; history teaching.
	(b) How the Social Services have developed and the place Christian people have played in their growth.	
	(c) Community care in the Welfare State.	To support the sense of self-reliance and not to weaken it.
	(d) Problems of the aged and the lonely. Its relation to a changing social pattern — people living longer, and the difficulties of housing and accommodation.	Focus No. 6, 'Christian Giving'.
	What can be done to help old people. Different ways of caring for the aged. Places where old people can be cared for. The fear of loneliness and the loss of independence; old people want to do useful things and not to be forgotten and rejected.	
	Visits to old people's homes. Practical schemes of visiting and helping the aged. Distribution of gifts to old people.	
	(e) The handicapped. Different kinds of handicap (mental, physical, emotional). What can (and is) being done for them. Is sympathy and sentimentality the same as real love?	'Helping the Aged', Christian Education Movement. 'Service to the Handicapped' or the Deprived. 'Practical Service by School Groups', ibid.

STAGE THREE (13+)

Outline of topics	Suggestions for the teacher	Reference for teacher
Our responsibilities in the world	Projects in the fight against poverty and hunger. The under-developed countries of the world.	Links can be made with geography and history teaching.
1 Poverty and hunger	The under-privileged in education. The sick and the hungry. The world population and its increase. What can be done to help? Which is of greater value – gifts of money, or help in technical training? Methods of farming have to be improved. This calls for scientists and technicians in order to overcome local problems of agriculture. Teachers and experts are needed to train people. With all this must go an understanding of the personal needs of others. What individuals and schools can do.	Christian Aid, Oxfam, Feed the Minds. The work of V.S.O.
2 Overseas work of the Churches	The work of the Churches. Overseas Mission and service. Great missionary ventures in education, medical help and in technical assistance.	Livingstone. Albert Schweitzer. Contemporary information may be obtained from the Conference of British Missionary Societies.
3 Barriers between peoples	Barriers in the community. The Colour Bar – racial prejudice. Snobbery – 'looking down on'. Snob appeal – papers read by the 'top people'. Meaning and causes of snobbery. Inverted snobbery.	Focus No. 10 'Our World', C.E.M., Samuel Adjai Crowther – a slave boy in Africa who became a bishop in Nigeria (1864). 'Black and White' John V. Taylor, S.C.M.* 'Race, Prejudice and Education', Cyril Bibby * Heinemann. 'Race Relations', * C.E.M.
4 Christian answers	*The Christian answer is being 'fully human''* Seeing the other persons point of view. Some passages from the Bible related to being 'fully human'. On prudence and wisdom. On man s place in the universe. Making special friendships. Being helpful to all in need. The greatest example of forgiveness. On man's need for imagination. God never makes impossible demands.	'In a conflict between will and imagination, imagination always wins'. Proverbs 8. Psalm 8. John 15 vv. 12–14 Mark 6 vv. 34–42 Luke 23 v. 34; vv. 39–43 Genesis 22 vv. 1–14

151

Outline of topics	Suggestions for the teacher	Reference for teacher
	(e) On being 'fully human'. Riches can be a barrier (more than poverty).	Mark 10 vv. 21–22
	Who is the greatest ? A Christian answer to exclusiveness or snobbery.	Mark 10 vv. 35–37, 41–45
	The Master is servant.	John 13 vv. 1–8, 12–14
	Blessed are the meek (the opposite of 'big headedness').	Matthew 5 v. 5; Psalm 37 v. 11
	There is a common humanity in which we all share. 'You are all one in Christ'.	Galatians 3 v. 28
	You cannot be neutral about good and evil.	Luke 11 v. 23
	Pilate tried to be neutral.	John 18 vv. 37–40
	How far will God's love go ?	Luke 23 vv. 33–35
	We can love others because we have been greatly loved.	I John 4 v. 19

STAGE FOUR (14+)

On Becoming an Adult in the Community

Part one

Independence and its responsibilities	Money, like all sources of power, demands judgement and making of decisions.	Hire purchase and credit facilities. Good and bad reasons for 'borrowing' capital.
1 Money and its uses	Money and snobbery. Grading people according to their income ; 'Keeping up with the Jones's'.	A link with the mathematics department. 'The boy who was loaded'.
	Giving and spending 'Can I afford it ?'	'Getting and Spending' Jack Singleton, S.C.M.
	Stewardship of money involves Christian values. Drinking.	'Alcohol and the Christian Ethic', T. G. Dunning, R.E.P.*
	Betting and gambling : saving for the future.	'Gambling in English Life', E. Benson Perkins, Epworth.* Focus No. 7 'Using Money', Which and Why card, C.E.M. *
2 Leisure time	The use of leisure : what is recreation ? Having a hobby.	Focus No. 5 'Spare Time', C.E.M. *
3 Relationships with older people	The place of authority : respect for other people's opinions.	'Parents in the Way', * Which and Why cards, C.E.M.

152

STAGE FOUR (14+)

Religion and People

Outline of topics	Suggestions for the teacher,	Reference for teacher
4 Making decisions	Pressures on choice : the power of persuasion in advertising and other forms of propaganda. What do the papers say ? A comparison between the appeal of newspapers of different kinds. The space allocated to the sensational. Making up one's mind : being well-informed, 'talking it over' with the more experienced. Our final decisions depend on our standards 'Be ye perfect' – only the best is the yardstick of measurement.	The Temptations Matthew 4 vv. 1–11 Not once but many times : a life time of decision making : each time 'in the wilderness' – 'away from it all'. 'Take Your Choice', Eric Lord, S.C.M. Failure and Recovery – never give up. 'Making Choices', * Which and Why cards, C.E.M.
	A point of departure for this section could be an analysis of the words of one or two 'pop' songs in which the word 'love' is used. As indicated in 'Teenage Religion' * there is a need at this stage, particularly to give the pupil opportunities for coming to terms with situations which make Christian teaching relevant to life as the pupils know it.	
Personal Relationships 1 Friendship	What do we expect of a friend ? How do we make friends ? Can we choose friends without being unfriendly ?	'Getting on with people', Eric Lord, S.C.M. Press. * 'You and Your Friend', Which and Why card, C.E.M. *
2 Christ's attitude to friends	On loyalty. Having special friends. Unfailing friendliness to all. An appeal to God ; the greatest friend.	John 15 vv. 12–14 Mark 5 v. 37 ; 9 v. 2 Luke 23 vv. 34, 39–43 Genesis 22 vv.1–14
3 Practical problems of teenagers	Pre-marital sex relationship or 'How far can I let him go ?'. Love is based on the whole person. How old ought a boy/girl to be when they marry ?	Psalm 8
4 Marriage as a way of life	Should marriage be permanent or for a trial period ? Is an engagement worth while ? What is the difference between marriage in Church or in a registry office ? What goes wrong ? The glossy magazine – is sex appeal enough ?	Mark 10 vv. 1–9 Matthew 19 vv. 10–11 Ephesians 5 vv. 1–5

---

* 'Teenage Religion', Harold Loukes, S.C.M. Press Ltd.

Outline of topics	Suggestions for the teacher	Reference for teacher
	Choosing the right man or the right girl. Should the duchess marry her chauffeur? How much do differences in class, creed, temperament, including intellectual differences, matter? Is colour a barrier? The Christian Judgement.	Mark 7 vv. 9-16 10 vv. 1–12
	God's design for the family. The Marriage at Cana. Evil women. Advice from Paul on right living.	Mark 10 vv. 6–9 John 2 vv. 1–11 Proverbs 6 v. 20, 24–29 Ephesians 6 vv. 10–17 Philippians 4 vv. 6–8 Ephesians 5 vv. 1–12 I Cor. 6 vv. 18–20 'The Human Venture', * Peter A. Bertocci, Longmans Green. 'Human Nature and Christian Marriage', Wm. P. Wylie, S.C.M. Some of the publications of the National Marriage Guidance Council are helpful.
The transition from School to work	The philosophy of 'why worry, why work?'	Focus No .9 'Earning * Your Living', C.E.M. Genesis 3 vv. 16–17
	Is work a punishment? Is work to be dodged or saved?	Proverbs 6 vv. 6–11 Proverbs 26 vv. 14–16
	An honest day's work for an honest day's pay.	'Working for a Living' Jack Singleton, S.C.M.
1 Choosing a job	The hard facts of life : work has to be done. Man has to live in the best sense. Self respect and honest sweat. The Christian judgement 'with a good will', 'as to the Lord'. Some jobs encourage anti-social behaviour. What should the Christian do under such circumstances? Jesus had a purpose in life, but even Jesus found it hard to keep to His purpose. We are here for a partnership with God (the sacrament of the Lord's Supper can be seen in this light too. The wine and the bread are symbolical of the partnership of man with God in caring for man's needs).	Ephesians 6 v. 7

Mark 1 vv. 35–39

Mark 14 vv. 32–36 Genesis 1 vv. 27–28 |

STAGE FOUR (14+)

Outline of topics	Suggestions for the teacher	Reference for teacher
2 Starting in a job	The problems of personal adjustment to the new community. Initiation ceremonies – being teased and made fun of. Asking for help when in a difficulty.	'Talk About', Seeing life at Manders, Nos. 1 to 4.
	Joining a trade union or professional association. Getting used to longer hours and being bored with the monotony of it all.	The Apprentice. Trouble at Wade's Motors. The Second Man. Estate Kid. Late Lunch.
	The first and subsequent pay packet. Helping mother financially, arranging my spending. How much 'fun and games'? Standards of behaviour; loyalties to the firm, to the union, to fellow workers. Social justice calls for many loyalties.	Focus 9, 'Earning your living', 'Choosing a job' – 'Which and Why' (all C.E.M. publications). Garlick, F. V. M., 'Out to Work', Longmans.
	How can these loyalties be viewed in the light of our supreme loyalty to Christ?	Matthew 6 vv. 33–34

STAGE FIVE (15+)

Contributing to the community	This course is intended for the sixteen-year-old leaver who is not concerned with examinations. It is to introduce the non-academic pupil to some three major projects to be carried out in conjunction with other school departments.	A discussion of the use of the word 'love' in many 'pop' songs may be of value. Cf. 1 Cor. 13
Voluntary service to the community	Pupils to use books of reference, school and public libraries and make enquiries about the voluntary services in the area served by the school. This can be attempted as a local survey undertaken in groups, or individually, and brought together as an activity or the whole class – or as many as are interested.	
	(a) (i) The history of the voluntary services.	Link with the social studies department.
	(ii) Their present headquarters and membership. Who is helped by the Society?	The W.V.S. Old People's centres. Meals-on-wheels.
	(iii) The resources of the service. Raising money; help from the state or local authority.	Help with hospitals, etc. Travelling libraries, Help to visitors overseas (meeting
	(iv) How it goes about its work.	lonely boys and girls from overseas), etc.
	(v) The benefits it offers to the individual.	The Y.M.C.A., Y.W.C.A. and other services.

Outline of topics	*Suggestions for the teacher*	*Reference for teacher*
	(b) Opportunities for service by young people.	C.S.V., V.S.O.
	(c) Problems raised by voluntary service, e.g., is it worth it ? Should the State do it all ? Why bother ?	Work camps, etc.
	(d) What is service ? What is love ? The theology of service.	
	The great commandment.	Mark 12 vv. 28–34
	God has no favourites.	Acts 10 vv. 34–43
	Jesus always helped people in need.	Mark 10 vv. 46–48
	He lived out this teaching to the	Luke 23 vv. 32–47
	end. He was willing to die for all men.	John 10 vv. 14–18
The Church in the community	A study of the work of the churches in the Community. What organisations do they have ?	Some links with the history department here.
	What do they offer for young people ? What do they do for older people ? What do people in the congregations do for their church ?	Focus No. 3, 'The Church'.
	(a) How the churches came to the locality. History of local denominations. The Parish Church. The Non-Conformists. The Roman Catholics.	
	(b) The churches come together. The Ecumenical Movement locally. The British Council of Churches. The Free Church Federal Council. Work for Christian Unity.	
	(c) The present impact of the churches on the community. Work for old people. The Samaritans. Work for patients in hospital. Work in industry. Work with ex-prisoners, unmarried mothers.	
	(d) The church in relation to money. The church in education. The church as the 'leaven to leaven the whole.'	
	(e) The place of youth in the Church. The Church Clubs' open' or 'closed' ? Uniformed organisations. Sunday School or Family Church. How do they function ? The Y.M.C.A., Y.W.C.A., Crusaders, Christian Endeavour, Ecumenical Youth Clubs.	

Outline of topics	Suggestions for the teacher	Reference for teacher
The Church in the world	What is the mission of the church? Is there still a place for the church in a modern age? What can young people give to the church? Unity, is it a dream or is there any possibility of Christian unity? Is the church fulfilling its purpose in the community as Jesus would wish?	
1 One world	The world mission of the church. The shrinking world and modern communications. No one, no country can live alone. What happens in Britain is no longer a British concern alone. The Commonwealth. The United Nations. The World Council of Churches. The Conference of British Missionary Societies. The Church's mission in the world. We must look both ways. Immigration is a two-way process. Missionary work now a two-way process. The new role of the missionary. The Young Churches and the Founder Churches. The Christian attitude to other religions. New Churches. The Church of South India. Plans for the reunion of churches abroad and at home.	Information can be obtained from The International Secretary, Christian Education Movement;
2 The Christian and politics	(a) The Mission of the Church is one of reconciliation. The bomb, warfare, peace, colour, capital punishment. Task of the Church in society to improve living conditions.	'In Christ neither bond nor free'.
	(b) Some great Christian reformers and the fight for justice. Christians in political life today.	
	(c) Do Christianity and politics mix? Should the church concern herself with political and international issues? Jesus and His challenge to political and social life. What kind of Messiah? The Young Church and its impact on society – Reformation. Politics concerns people – so does religion.	'Christianity the most materialistic of all religions', Wm. Temple The life of Jesus initiated political and economic change. 'The Church and Social Order', Canon Greenslade (1948), * S.C.M.
3 Our response.	Use of the 'vote' an obligation. The responsibility we have to others. Making up one's mind, commitment to a course of action is a Christian duty.	

Practical help for the teachers

Lancashire County Education Committee has for many years supported the work of the Christian Education Movement and its predecessor, the Student Christian Movement in Schools. The suggestions in the Alternative Syllabus are based on the experience the Movement has had in arranging short and extended courses for pupils of all abilities and backgrounds. The programme of courses provides a valuable additional stimulus to the work of Religious Education Departments and has encouraged the inclusion of religious education in integrated courses.

In addition to the services provided by the Area Secretaries of the Christian Education Movement, a major service to Religious Education teachers is available to Lancashire County schools free on request to the National Office of C.E.M. This service includes publications, reviews, lists of resources, appraisals of films and other AVA, etc.

For full details application should be made to the General Secretary, Christian Education Movement, Annandale, North End Road, London, NW11 7QX.

Part Three

RELIGIOUS EDUCATION IN THE SIXTH FORM

Changes in the Sixth Form

The composition of the sixth form has changed, and is changing in a way that creates a new situation in religious education. Not only do the 'high-flyers' stay on for further studies leading to examinations for university entrance or its equivalent in other forms of higher education, but an increasing number of pupils stay on for perhaps one year or two to take a general course.

It would be very misleading to divide these into 'academic' and 'non-academic' groups purely on the basis of intention and purpose, in utilitarian or practical terms, for two good reasons:

1 The most academic pupil in his own field may be equally uninformed about matters outside his own sphere of interest (witness the problem of 'innumerate' arts students).

2 Others who take a general course in the sixth form may be staying on because of the value the course will have in connection with the profession they have chosen, not because they are incapable of benefiting from the rigours of an academic education.

There are problems of organisation. It would be to the advantage of both groups if they spent some time together. This could lead to the cross-fertilisation of ideas and avoid a mutual exclusiveness. It could also provide opportunities for the examination of problems, ethical, social or theological at greater depth than is possible at the earlier stages in the course. It is unfortunately true that the allocation of one period of forty minutes a week is often regarded as a waste of time which, by the time the pupil reaches the sixth form leads him to believe that the subject is irrelevant to his life and mode of thinking.

Without making unrealistic claims it is clear that religious education must form part of any scheme which deals with the problems of life and it is in the formulation of specific aims and the content of any syllabus that a new approach may be possible. It may well be that the most urgent need in religious education at the fifth and sixth form stage will be a clear linking of the religious insights and information pupils have gained in the previous years to the rest of their studies and to the general experience of living. If this is accepted as true then the object of religious education in the sixth form will not be, primarily, to impart an organised body of knowledge – though clearly a basic minimum of information is necessary and for many this will mean taking some aspect of biblical knowledge to a greater depth – but to show the relevance of the Christian interpretation of life. It will help them to see that the world which is the object of their study in other fields is a world which, from the Christian point of view, is in need of salvation, and one in which the saving acts of God are of urgent importance. To do this it will be necessary to link the work to those movements in theology which are seeking to relate the Gospel to the world as it is, and translate its words and images into terms understandable to modern man.

What might be attempted is an assessment of what is meant by the Christian way of life. This will call for biblical insights to bring about a unifying view of knowledge and experience. These have to be shown to be in need of one another. The relevance of the Bible must be made clear

159

by our understanding of this world. We must work from experience to the Bible; it may be a natural approach for the committed Christian to work from the Bible to an understanding of the world, but, for the majority today, the process has to be reversed.

That this method is the only way likely to create interest and motivation needed for the continuing with religious education in the sixth form is mainly due to the gap which has opened up between what the Church seems to teach and the accepted way of life of the majority. This gap results, not infrequently, in a prejudiced indifference or even hostility to religious education. There are many reasons for this : in an area where the Church (as a whole) is weak, inward-looking, and not involved in the life and problems of ordinary people we are likely to find the assumption that, even if the Gospel is true, it is irrelevant. The Churches are regarded as a relic of the past with no part to play in the world of the future and Christianity an attempt to bolster up an institution which is on the way to complete eclipse. When the spiritual values presented are contrasted with the materialism which is implicit in almost all adult activity the impression of being 'got at' is so strong as to be for the majority overwhelming. For these a new approach is called for on the basis of fresh principles.

**Suggestions for an approach to the subject of
religious education in the sixth form**

A   An outline of the topics which call for enquiry and exploration.

    1   To give the pupil the opportunity to ask questions about life and the relevance of the Christian interpretation of it.
       A starting point might be an enquiry into what is meant by 'knowing'. To what extent is sensory perception the way to the discovery of 'truth' ? Sense perception is at once the most immediate and obvious means of getting to know about and thus regulate, our environment. It is the basis of scientific method by which information is gained and verified. It is essential to our physical survival and it is the path by which communication is made between people and cultures. This approach to knowledge is based on various assumptions many of which are taken for granted. It assumes that the universe is a rational entity capable of interpretation in terms of laws on which we may base valid predictions. In the centuries during which this rational approach has been evolved, Christianity has played an important part in describing a universe which has an aim and purpose which presupposes a coherent system rather than a haphazard and random set of circumstances and forces. In spite of its insistence on a spiritual world over and above the material, this belief in a planned and purposeful universe encouraged the search for meaning which led ultimately to what is known as the scientific approach.

    2   What is meant by morality ? Is it true that, given adequate knowledge, all human actions can be reduced to the laws of stimulus and response ? That the ability to predict behaviour depends on an exhaustive study of human reflexes by scientific means ? Ideas of right and wrong are linked with character or disposition which are more than anything contained by a system of law or code of ethics. We see this in the growth of Israel's ethical monotheism and the reshaping of its outline. Finally, there is the two-fold law of Christ expressed in another way, St. Augustine's maxim, 'Love God, and do what you will.'

B   To examine the issues in relation to other subjects in order to get a wider and if possible a 'world view' of the matters discussed.
    The idea of 'knowing' in a wider context.

    1   Aesthetic experience is one of the most difficult to deal with because it is essentially personal and needs to be cultivated and fed. It is also a means of communication through sense – perception : a language, but a language which defies an attempt to speak in terms which can be closely defined. Its main function is to evoke a different response to the more analytical response as expressed in science (or cf. the place of music, art, drama in religious activities). To others it becomes the creative aspect of life itself.

2   Historical experience calls for the ability to recreate past events and to see their relevance to the present. This also involves making judgements on the way other people have interpreted their own experience – a leap of imagination into the past. Whatever is the nature of revelation it is controlled by the culture of the age into which it comes and which it illuminates (cf. the ideas of magic in the Old Testament and the underlying spiritual truths: the place of myth and legend).

C   To present the Christian answers to these problems, not dogmatically, but in sufficient depth to enable the pupil to make an informed assessment in Christian terms, and to choose freely and intelligently as between one point of view and another.

1   Questions about 'man' and his place in the universe have been asked in previous ages. How did the Greeks and Romans see him? In what ways did the Hebrew view differ from these? What were the influences which resulted in a transformation of this earlier view of man? In modern times, can the biologist or the psychologist answer the question 'What is man –' (e.g. just an intelligent animal). What has literature to say about man? (a study of some of literature dealing with a human situation might be made, e.g. 'Lord of the Flies' by Wm. Golding).

2   What has Christianity to say about man? That he is a child of God: a fallen creature but redeemed: made in the image of God. Some modern interpretations of man's ethical and moral behaviour such as, What has the Church taught about man's experience and his concept of God? What is the Church saying today?

3   Questions about 'man' in terms of his relationship with the community: the idea of nationhood and the 'people of God'. Universalism as opposed to particularism and the brotherhood of man. Race and colour, and the divisions of the world and in the world.

D   The task that faced the early Church was similar to that which faces us today. The work of St. Paul had this in common with our own dilemma: to interpret for his generation what the Gospel meant in terms which they could accept and understand.

1   After the crucifixion of Our Lord for what in the eyes of the Romans and the Jews amounted to sedition and blasphemy, the Church existed for a few years as a small group of Jewish Christians, frowned upon by other Jews and in bad odour because of their association with the Crucified. Then it began its phase of readjustment. Its members in Jerusalem continued to live as Jews. They kept the Law and hoped for their Lord's return to complete His work. Jerusalem was gradually overshadowed by the missions. In that field the most vocal figure was Paul, formerly called Saul. After his conversion Paul threw himself into missions in Asia Minor. He applied himself to two main problems :—
(a) The meaning of Christ's death and resurrection.
(b) The method of teaching and appealing to pagan minds.

2   These he resolved by developing the doctrine of Divine salvation through Jesus the Christ and the reconciling of God and man. His experience among the Gentiles helped him to see that the Jewish Law was transcended by a higher law and that the old law was not binding on the converts.

3   The new teaching as Paul saw it, did not say that earthly life was irredeemably evil and that salvation lay in escaping from it. It did, however, put the inward transformation first stressing 'Seek ye first the Kingdom of God and all these things shall be added unto you'. The stress on individual salvation and the Hereafter seemed to offer nothing in political terms to the social order in all its struggles and agonies. So the estrangement between the Jews and the Christian grew. Paul lived long enough to see this happening. His chief pronouncement on this is in the letter which he wrote to the Romans (i.e. Christians in Rome) in the eleventh chapter. How far is this view prevalent today not among the Jews but among Christians and others? In his letters to the young Churches he deals with many problems which, although not identical have similarities with our problems? How far ought Christians to put political and social problems in the forefront of their mission to men?

161

E   A study of parts of the Fourth Gospel. This is in many ways the most important book
of the New Testament. It contains history and interpretation, biography and
theology by which we come to see the Jesus of history with a deeper insight in the
light of Christian experience.

The author's purpose in writing the Gospel is given in St. John 20 v. 31. It continues
the work of interpretation and in particular develops the theme proclaimed in the
opening verses 1–5 which call for a special study in the light of modern problems.

1   If God is love, why the Cross ? A perplexing question which goes to the heart of
the modern dilemma. The Gospel of John shows clearly that the cross was
chosen deliberately by Our Lord as essential to the completion of His purpose.

It is accomplished'.	John 19 v. 30
The bread of life.	John 6 v. 51
The cross is the basis of faith.	John 3 v. 14
Christ sees the cross as inevitable.	John 12 vv. 32–33
The principle which lies at the heart of the Gospel.	John 12 v. 24 ; John 10 v. 11 ; vv. 17–18

2   The Resurrection.

John 20–21
(see I Cor. 15
vv. 13–14)

3   One of the most striking features of the Gospel of St. John is the detail that is
given of the way Jesus dealt with the personal needs of the people He met.

Nicodemus.	John 3 vv. 10–21
The woman of Samaria	John 4 vv. 1–41
The woman taken in adultery.	John 8 vv. 1–11
(There are doubts as to whether this was originally part of John's Gospel ; it is nevertheless quite in keeping.)	(A.V. and R.V. only)
The blind beggar.	John 9
The doubts of Thomas.	John 11 v. 16 ; 14 vv. 5–7
Peter.	John 21

SOME ALTERNATIVE SUGGESTIONS
The Book of Job

This may be suitable for some sixth forms as a pre-Christian treatment of the problem of
evil and particularly of innocent suffering. It is better studied through a modern
translation helped by a good commentary. Another approach to this subject is through
listening to the rendering of passages from the Book of Job in the series :

The Living Bible :   No. 8   A Chariot of Fire   Sir Laurence Olivier
                                                                (Job).

A good reading can bring out the splendour of the theme and help towards a better
understanding of the problems involved.

The Apocalyptic Literature

Writings or tracts handed down from troubled times of persecution and meant to sustain
a belief that, whatever may be the circumstances, God is in control of history ; they use
a form of symbolism which is foreign to the modern mind. Two such books are to be
found in the Bible :

The Book of Daniel.
The Book of Revelation.

If studied within the framework of the history of the period for which they were
written, many unfortunate and inaccurate conceptions can be avoided ; but it is not

wise to attempt such studies unless they can be done thoroughly and with an understanding of the purpose behind the books. It may be necessary to deal with some ways in which the Jews used numbers.

Other religions and philosophies

In view of the families arriving from the Commonwealth and the need for a more sympathetic understanding of their problems, there is a need to introduce pupils to the main faiths held by many Afro-Asian peoples. It is worth mentioning that the colour of ones skin has nothing to do with the beliefs held by different peoples. For example, the majority of families arriving from the West Indies are fellow Christians, many of whom are far more concerned about their faith than is the case with a large number of the population among whom they settle. Others, too, from Africa and India, belong to the same group of churches as are found here; there is a link with the many missionary activities that have worked for and founded Christian churches overseas.

Nevertheless, there is no room for the patronising attitude of superiority to the ancient customs and beliefs of other peoples.

The historic faiths of Judaism, Christianity and Islam

From Judaism there is a link with Christianity and Mohammedism. Christianity as an historic religion springs from the Hebrew teaching on the nature and purposes of God; Jesus the fulfilment of Old Testament prophecy, the expected Messiah, leads to the foundation of the Christian church.

Islam is the name given in Christian countries to the followers of Mohammed. Their belief embraces (1) a belief in God, who is eternal, the sole creator and lord of the universe having absolute power, knowledge, glory and perfection, (2) a belief in God's angels who are perfect beings, (3) a belief in good and evil spirits which are subject to death as human beings are, (4) a belief in the Holy Scriptures which are the spoken word of God. These include the Pentateuch, Psalms, and the Gospels though in a greatly corrupted form: but the Koran, the book containing the religious and moral code of the Mohammedans, is the real foundation of Islam. To Moslems this is their most sacred book and is believed to have been communicated to Mohammed by the angel Gabriel. As a merchant travelling in the Middle East, Mohammed was much influenced by his contacts with Hebrew religion.

Hinduism

It is difficult to give a precise definition of Hinduism as the beliefs and practices of the Hindus vary widely as between regions and classes. The origin of the beliefs is extremely ancient. The earliest phase is rooted in the religion of the Vedas which consist of hymns, sacrificial formulas, and incantations going back to the first millenium B.C. It would seem that from about 600 B.C. a new doctrine appeared based on the law of cause and effect whereby there is a reincarnation by which the evil-doer is reborn into unhappy conditions in another body. The idea spread rapidly and was accepted almost universally in India at the time of the Buddha (sixth century B.C.). These new ideas of reincarnation were accompanied by a desire to escape from the round of birth and death and were given written form in the Upanishads. New sects emerged, the best known of which is Buddhism.

From now on Hinduism, in its higher form, was concerned mainly with obtaining release from the frustrations and limitations of life. Morality and religious observance were thought to be conducive to favourable rebirths into a better state. One effect has been the development of a system of classes known as 'castes'. These keep rigidly apart from one another and intermarriage is forbidden. Second only to the preservation of the social order is the preservation of the family and the utmost respect is given to the head of the family whose authority may extend to a whole family group including distant relatives.

Animism plays a part and many animals, plants, and natural objects are sacred. The most noteworthy animal is the cow which is regarded as sacred and represents Mother Earth. All rivers and hills are more or less sacred and the river Ganges is regarded as especially holy.

In recent times, the system of belief and conduct in Hinduism has altered considerably. There have been reformers, notably Mahatma Gandhi, whose bringing together of religion and politics gave rise to the movement for the independence of India. India is now a republic within the Commonwealth.

One of the differences between east and west has been the influence of religion. The Hindu has absorbed many ideas from other religions notably Zorastrianism, Islam and Christianity as well as many local tribal notions. Hinduism absorbs these ideas easily. In its practical way of life it has remained linked in every aspect with its 'caste' system. On the other hand the western attitude has been expressed in the words of Yahweh on Mount Sinai, 'You shall have no other gods before me' (Exodus 20 v. 3). This stands for exclusiveness in belief and by contrast it has developed a belief in a social system (not by any means always lived up to) based on the idea of the brotherhood of man and the equality of all men before God.

Buddhism and Buddha

The Buddha was born probably 560 B.C. near Benares, India. He was filled with deep compassion for the human race, ran away from his father's court and lived for years in solitude in order to penetrate the mysteries of life and become the Buddha. In his mildness and his readiness to overlook insults, his zeal and simplicity, he was not unlike St. Francis of Assissi.

One of the most prominent doctrines of the religious system founded by Buddha is a belief in Nirvana or an absolute release from existence as its chief good. The faith came into conflict with the prevailing religious system of the Brahmins of India and its followers fled to Ceylon, Burma and the Chinese mainland (including what is now known as Vietnam).

The comparative study of religion

A very difficult subject which has a wide appeal. Hinduism, Buddhism (especially Zen-Buddhism), Shinto, Judaism, Islam and Christianity as beliefs whose influence in the modern world are of the greatest importance.

Parrinder, G.	Books of the World's Religions.	Hulton
Hilliard, F. H.	How Men Worship.	Clarke *
Bouquet, A. C.	Should Christianity be Exclusive ?	S.P.C.K.
Kraemer, H.	Why Christianity of all Religions ?	Lutterworth *
Kellett, A.	1 Isms and Ologies.	Epworth *
	Christianity and Other Religions.	Study Outline C.E.M. *

Discussion of philosophic topics

Greek thought.
Humanism.
Dialectical materialism.

Much of the work could be done by means of private reading followed by discussion. For a line of study such a framework as the following could be used.
History of the movement.
The ethical factor :

The effects on the social situation.
The encouragement of sympathy for others.
The main motives for action.
How is the insight into reality gained ?
Freedom to choose and make decisions.

---

1 Mainly for teacher's use.

164

Some further suggestions for discussions, and group or individual work in connection with themes in religious education

This material may prove useful in the development of fifth or sixth year courses. The need for probing more deeply into many of the issues raised previously can lead to an individual enquiry based on guided reading. A good many of the topics will call for a free and frank discussion.

Suggested reading on selected topics – Christian doctrine

This can be a development of the work in Stage Four, which began a study of the Apostles' Creed.

Caird, G. B.	The Truth of the Gospel.	O.U.P.
Walton, R. C.	God and You.	S.C.M.
Sellers, R. V.	Are Creeds Out of Date ?	S.P.C.K.
Wilson, J.	Is there a God ?	S.P.C.K.
	Be Honest about God.	Study Outlines C.E.M. *
Whale, J. S.	Christian Doctrine.	C.U.P.
Lewis, C. S.	Mere Christianity.	Fontana

Christian morality

A development of the section on 'the Law and the Prophets'.

Bull, N. J.	Man and his Society.	R.E.P. *
Counsell, M. J.	Are we free to act as we will ?	S.P.C.K.
Hughes, H. T.	Faith and Life.	Epworth *
Robinson, J.	Christian Morals Today.	S.C.M. *
Williams, J.	God and the Human Family.	S.P.C.K. *
Purcell, W.	The Plain Man looks at the Commandments.	Collins (1966)

Some practical issues of morality

The Christian attitude to recreation and amusement has varied down the ages. Both extremes, Puritanism and the excesses of the Restoration, have been dominant at certain periods in our history. They still call for a wise and balanced judgement.

Perkins, E. Benson	Gambling in English Life.	Epworth *
Dunning, T. G.	Alcohol and the Christian Ethic.	R.E.P. *

Faith and reason

An interpretation of Biblical theology.

Burnaby, I.	In What Sense is the Bible Inspired ?	S.P.C.K.
Richardson, A.	Science, History and Faith.	O.U.P. *
Whitfield, G.	Philosophy and Religion.	R.E.P. *
Rhine, J. B.	The Reach of Mind.	Penguin

Alternatives to the Christian faith

The challenge of the modern age has to be met : communism and the various shades of communism.

	What is Communism ?	Study Outline C.E.M. *
Foster, M. B.	Marxism	S.P.C.K.
Rogers, Ed.	A Christian Commentary on Communism.	Wyvern Books *
Mitchell, B.	Humanism.	S.P.C.K. *

Christian deviations

There are many groups offering their distinctive views on life which are a departure from the traditional pattern of Christianity. Some knowledge of their origin or history may be called for. The most common deviations to be found in this country are: Christian Science, Jehovah's Witnesses, the Seventh Day Adventists, Latter Day Saints (Mormons), while Spiritualism and Theosophy are attractive to some.

Davies, H.	Christian Dev ations.	S.C.M. *
Kellett, A.	Isms and Ologies.	Epworth *
Robinson, W.	The Shattered Cross.	Berean Press
Kraemer, H.	Why Christianity of All Religions ?	Lutterworth *

For general information about these groups see the following. Further and more specific information can be obtained from the Headquarters of the groups concerned.

The Ecumenical movement

Christian unity and co-operation between the Churches: a modern movement towards reconciliation.

Bide, P.	The Necessity of the Church.	S.P.C.K. *
	The World Church Changes.	Study Outline C.E.M. *
	Christian Unity.	Study Outline C.E.M. *
Oyen, H. V.	Affluence and the Christian.	S.P.C.K. *

Another movement which shows a development in Christian worship in the forms of service.

| Shands, A. R. | The Liturgical Movement. | S.C.M. * |
| | Approach to Worship. | Study Outline C.E.M. * |

S.P.C.K. – Society for the Propagation of Christian Knowledge (bookshops in most large towns).

C.E.M. – Christian Education Movement.

S.C.M. – Student Christian Movement Press Ltd.

Crime and punishment

This will call for yet more consideration from the Christian point of view:

Is there a criminal class ?
Are criminals born ?
Should punishment be remedial or retributory ?

Hoyles, J. Arthur	The Church and the Criminal.	Epworth *
Carpenter, J. E.	The Life and Works of Mary Carpenter.	Macmillan * (in most libraries)
Elliott, Mabel	Crime in Modern Society.	Harper *
Hamel, I.	A Christian in East Germany.	S.C.M. 1960 *
Mays, J. B.	Crime and the Social Structure.	Faber & Faber 1963

War and peace

These are important issues. Young people need help in facing up to the causes of conflict and considering the ways of averting wars.

Is there any aspect of war which can be justified ?
Is there such a thing as a 'just' war – as defined by the Church in the past ?
What do you consider are the causes of war ?
What more could be done to ensure peace ?
Is pacifism and non-violent resistance (Gandhi) an alternative to war ?
How does modern warfare differ from wars in the past ?

| Schweitzer, Albert | The Problems of Peace in the World Today. | A. & C. Black * |
| Roberts, J. E. | **Nuclear War and Peace.** | National Peace Council * |

Further information can be obtained from the publications issued by the United Nations Organisations and U.N.E.S.C.O.

There are links with history and literature :

| | The War Poets. | Penguin |
| Fry, Christopher | Sleep of Prisoners. | O.U.P. |

An allied problem is that of displaced persons and refugees. One of the evil consequences of war is the persecution of minorities and the movement of populations to escape tyrannies of various kinds. The application of Christian principles to these issues is needed. Films on these problems :

Over the Hill.
The Long March.

Christianity and the arts

Information on the works of great masters are to be found under the heading Sources of Information in connection with Religious Information, Art and Visual Aids.

There are many links with art in all its forms in music, drama, poetry, novels, as well as in the more visual forms.

Some books for further reading :—

Baxter, K. M.	Speak what we feel. (A Christian looks at the contemporary drama.)	S.P.C.K. *
Merchant, E. M.	Creed and the Drama.	S.P.C.K.*
Morgan, S. K.	Christian Themes in Contemporary Poets.	S.C.M.*
Stewart, D.	The Ark of God. (A study of five novelists of today.)	Carey Kingsgate

The connection between the works of old masters and aspects of Christianity is to be found in the section on Sources of Information.

APPENDIX 'A'

AN OUTLINE OF JEWISH HISTORY

About 2000 B.C.

A The 'Sons of Israel' came from Ur of the Chaldees probably the ancient city of Uru in Babylonia. At this stage Israel was a band of nomads whose leader (sheikh) bore the name of Abram. Genesis 11 v. 31, 15 v. 7. The clan wandered : settlement began at :

Shechem	Genesis 12 v. 6, 33 v. 18
Bethel	Genesis 12 v. 8, 13 v. 3, 28 v. 19
Hebron	Genesis 13 v. 18, 23 v. 2
Beersheba	Genesis 21 v. 31, 26 v. 23

Other settlements of Semitic tribes (sons of Shem) moved away from north Arabia to settle in what became :

Babylonia at the southern end of the Euphrates.
Assyria further north on the river Tigris.
Aram (Syria) in between these two rivers (Mesopotamia).

B The settled population of Canaan into which the Abram clan moved consisted of :

1 Phoenicians, chief seafarers of the ancient world, living on the coast.

2 Amorites and other small tribes living between the Jordan valley and the coast.

3 Moabites and Ammonites east of the Jordan valley.

4 Midianites, Amalekites, Ishmaelites living in the south of Judah.

C The relations of Israel with some of the surrounding peoples are to be read about in the stories of the Patriarchs where :

Isaac stands for Israel (the father figure of the tribe) ;
Ishmael is his 'brother' son of Hagar, banished in the desert ;
Jacob stands for Israel as a whole ;
Esau, his brother, stands for the Edomite tribe akin to Jacob as a blood relation but Jacob's bitterest enemy.

D Possibly due to the friendship of the Hyskos Pharaohs, who introduced the horse into Egypt and who were descendants of the Semites, the Israel clans were allowed to settle in the delta area of the river Nile known as the Land of Goshen. This may be the origin of the Joseph stories. The change when a new Pharaoh became ruler may indicate that the Semitic dynasty was driven out of Egypt. Rameses II who succeeded was a great builder and employed foreign slaves including Israelites. His son Meneptah was probably the Pharaoh of the Exodus.

About 1250 B.C.

E The success of the Exodus was due to the inspiring leadership of Moses, and the religion of the Hebrews was rooted in an historical fact, the deliverance from Egypt. From the point of view of their religion these events were of the greatest importance illustrating as they did the loving care shown by Yahweh for the people – 'his people' – Israel. Yahweh led his people out of bondage in Egypt with a '. . . strong hand' or a 'strong right arm'. The Passover ceremony celebrated each year signifies this turning point (some would say their setting-out point) in the history expressed in religious terms.

F The consolidation of these loosely-knit tribes during their sojourn in the wilderness – the peninsula of Sinai – followed. It is at this stage that the giving of the Law happened. Moses caused the tribes to enter into a solemn covenant (a two-fold promise) to serve and worship Yahweh. The earliest tradition that has reached us as to the laws to which they promised obedience is found in:

Exodus 31 vv. 12–18
Exodus 20 v 23, 23 vv. 32, 33
Exodus 20 vv. 1–17

(Deuteronomy 5 vv. 6–21 is a later development of the Law, and accepted as the covenant code.)
It was by this that Israel was drawn into a sense of unity and ever afterwards the laws and customs, religious, social and ethical, which grew up during the whole history of the nation until the close of the Old Testament canon, were ascribed to Moses.

G About 1235 to 1200 B.C.:
  1 A southern group Judah, Simeon, Levi, three of the first four sons of Leah (Genesis 29 vv. 31–35) settled in Canaan.
  Reuben is found east of Jordan and finally joined up with non-Israel clans.
  2 The central group Ephraim and Manasseh 'the house of Joseph' who was the elder son of Rachel. Benjamin, a warlike tribe joined up with Judah.
  3 The northern group Isachar, Zebulon, Napthali, Asher and Dan settled in the north of the plain of Jezreel.

H These several communities, each under a separate sheikh, or elder, now began to enlarge their borders; this often meant conflicts with the local people and in the course of events an outstanding man would become a leader and set himself up as a petty king or ruler (in opposition to the elders), such a man being referred to as a Judge. The accounts of their doings are to be found in the book of Judges. Deborah about 1150 B.C. Gideon comes after 1150 B.C.

I As the tribes became more settled the local 'Judges' paved the way for the idea of a monarchy. It was Samuel who made this possible but in this he was acting against God's will (I Samuel 8). Saul, a member of the most warlike tribe, a young Benjamite, was chosen. The threat to the Israelites was now mainly from settlers on the coast, the Philistines. They were sea-raiders, possibly from Crete and known as the Pelestu. They gave the name Palestine to the part of the Middle East we are concerned with. Saul disobeyed Samuel and fell into disfavour and was replaced by David. Samuel lived about 1050 B.C. Saul reigned from about 1036 to 1016 B.C.

J David began the consolidation of the kingdom by capturing the hill fortress called Zion, known later as Jerusalem, from the Jebusites. He undertook successful campaigns against the Philistines but ended as a typical oriental monarch. This period marks the zenith of Hebrew power and even today the re-establishment of the kingdom with the boundaries as David left them is often given as the aspiration of the modern state of Israel; not all Jews would accept this as their ambition. The overlordship of David was effective from Dan to Beersheba (north to south). David reigned from about 1016 to 976 B.C.

K   After a palace revolt Solomon (the son of Bathsheba) was established as king; he was a man of iron and a tyrant. North and south were held together in a precarious unity; there was little foreign opposition and he was able to achieve his oriental ideal of barbaric magnificence. His reign from 976 to 936 B.C. had three permanent results.

1   His tyranny caused seething discontent. Jeroboam attempted a revolt but failed and fled to Egypt.

2   The heavy taxation due to Solomon's extravagance created class hatred and undermined unity.

3   But the building of the Temple in Jerusalem provided a nucleus for all that was best in national worship.

L   After Solomon's death Jeroboam returned from Egypt. Rehoboam, Solomon's son declared his intention of adding to the people's burdens. This brought disruption, Jeroboam becoming king of the northern kingdom henceforth called Israel as distinct from the southern highland part, Judah. The breech between north and south was never healed. 'There was war between Jeroboam and Rehoboam continually.' I Kings 14 v. 30. As a counter attraction to the Temple at Jerusalem, Jeroboam set up a golden bull as a symbol of Jahweh in the royal sanctuary at Bethel. As all·images were idolatory he was denounced as 'he who made Israel to sin'.

M   From 937 to 722 B.C. the divided kingdom was in a state of unrest, civil war, or under foreign attack. The two external threats came from Syria (Aram in the Hebrew Bible – Syria in the LXX and Vulgate and is adopted in the English versions) and later from Assyria who eventually overthrew Israel and carried off the population into captivity (722 B.C.). Hosea gives a despairing impression of the situation (Hosea 7 v. 11, 12 v. 1).

N   Judah in the south survived for another century and a half. Judah was under pressure from Assyria and Isaiah did his best to persuade the king and the people (Isaiah 7 vv. 1–16, 8 vv. 1–15) that the danger would pass '. . . in quietness and confidence shall be your strength'. A period of unrest, revolts and general tension followed until the time of Hezekiah. Isaiah encouraged Hezekiah to hold out against Sennacherib (Isaiah 37 vv. 33–38 gives an account of the Assyrian soldiers smitten by 'an angel of Yahweh' – pestilence). After a resurgence of power at which time Assyria attacked Egypt and captured Thebes (now Amman) 660 B.C. but 53 years later Assyria fell never to rise again. Isaiah had felt sure that pride would be her downfall (Isaiah 10 vv. 5–34). As Assyria's power waned, Egypt took advantage to attack her; Josiah, king of Judah who had taken over part of Israel when Assyria fell, dared to stand in Pharaoh Necho's way when the Egyptians advanced. Josiah was slain and his forces destroyed at Megiddo. Josiah's successor, Jeboaz was made king but captured and sent in chains to Egypt. Jeremiah lamented this (Jeremiah 22 vv. 10–12). The Pharaoh was in turn overwhelmed at Carchemish 604 B.C. (Jeremiah 46 vv. 2–26) by the Babylonians (Chaldeans). Judah now became a vassal to Babylon instead of Egypt.

O Judah was again badly ruled; the prophecies of Jeremiah were rejected (Jeremiah 36 vv. 9–32) and the Babylonians attacked. Jerusalem surrendered and the king Jehoiachin, the queen-mother and the most influential members of the court, including 700 soldiers and 1000 artisans were carried off into captivity. But intrigue continued in spite of Jeremiah's warnings; the prophet Ezekiel too added his warnings. In 588 B.C. Judah revolted again and asked Egypt for help against Babylon; no help came. Jerusalem was besieged and Zedekiah was carried off to Babylon with the rest of the population, the walls of Jerusalem were destroyed and the Temple sacked 586 B.C.

P With the fall of Jerusalem 586 B.C. the national life of the Hebrews was ended. The very roots of their way of life were torn up and they found themselves living on foreign soil and surrounded by a people busy with commercial activities in which they soon began to play an active part. That the exiles rallied from the shock so well was due to the moral courage and spiritual insight of their leaders who taught them to see in this disaster a purpose of Yahweh for his people and eventually for the whole human race. Morally, intellectually and spiritually the Jews in Babylon were the best of the nation. Many of them became leaders not only of the Jewish community but of the nation as a whole. A number rose to positions of importance at the court of Babylon and later of the Persian monarchy. The story of Nehemiah shows this to be true and, '. . . in every matter of wisdom and understanding concerning which the king enquired of them he found them ten times better than all the magicians and enchanters that were in the kingdom'. (Daniel 1 v. 20)

Q The two outstanding teachers of the exile period are Ezekiel who was a young priest deported to Babylon with king Jehoiachin 597 B.C. and the anonymous author of Isaiah 40–55 who, for convenience we know as the Second Isaiah. Ezekiel died before the Jews received permission to return to Judah but his work was carried on by his followers and by the second Isaiah who lived when Cyrus the Persian king had begun his career of conquest. Cyrus was regarded as the divinely appointed deliverer of the Hebrews and the prophet's message is one of consolation. He opens with the words 'Comfort ye, comfort ye my people'. Included in the work of this prophet we find passages of wonderful tenderness and beauty which are generally known as the 'Songs of the Sufferent Servant'. (Isaiah 42 vv. 1–4, 49 vv. 1–6, 50 vv. 4–9, 52 v. 13, 53 v. 12)

R In 539 B.C. Cyrus, king of Persia, became master of all of what we now call Asia Minor. He overwhelmed Babylon and in the following year he issued an edict giving all foreigners permission to go home to their native lands. The history of this period is obscure. The writers of the books known as Chronicles selected such incidents as they found interesting and in so doing left out much that was of value. They also modified statements and facts in accordance with what they themselves believed to be true. Three great men stand out as leaders and were responsible for stirring their fellow-countrymen into action on behalf of their religion and their way of life, Zerubbabel, Nehemiah and Ezra.

S The Jews who returned to Judah whether in 536 or 520 B.C. had to contend with many difficulties. The cities of the land were in ruins and the earth had remained untilled for many years.

T   Two prophets, Haggai and Zechariah declared that the poverty of the Jews would cease and the harvests become plentiful if the people would put Yahweh's service before their own needs and at once begin to rebuild the ruined Temple. So stirring was their appeal that by the autumn of 516 B.C. the Temple was completely restored. While this was happening the Samaritans, regarded as unfaithful by the Jews because they had not shared in their exile, asked to be allowed to help in the work. Haggai opposed this on the grounds that the true faith would be corrupted if the Jews mingled with the Samaritans. This gave offence to the Samaritans so when the Jews began to rebuild the city walls as well – against the orders of the Persian king – the Samaritans sent word to the Persians (as we should say 'out of pique'). The Persians who were sensitive to any signs of insurrection on their borders gave word that the work should be stopped and this the Samaritans lost no time in carrying out. The enmity between Samaritan and Jew was intensified and this dislike and hostility continued into New Testament times (cf. The Woman at the Well, John 4).

U   During the centuries of the exile and immediately after there was great literary activity among the Jews in Babylon. This continued through-out the fifth century. The followers of Ezekiel embodied the leading ideas of their master's teaching in 'The Law of Holiness'. The injunc-tions found in the books of Exodus and Numbers together with many fresh regulations in regard to fasts and feasts were combined with some old traditions making what is known as the Priestly Code. Many parts of the Old Testament show insertions by these compilers as for instance the first account of the Creation story in Genesis 1 vv. 1–31, 2 v. 1.

V   The Jews were subjected to Persian rule from 538 to 331 B.C. when the conquests of Alexander the Great brought them a change of masters. The Jews were treated well by the Persians and provided the Jews paid their taxes regularly and remained passive, a great measure of freedom in civil and religious matters was given them. Some insubordination at a later date when the power of the Persian was declining, caused the Persians to transplant some of the Jews to the shores of the Caspian Sea. During this period Aramaic, a sister language of Hebrew, which had been long used as the language of commerce and diplomacy in Syria, became the language of the common people (II Kings 18 v. 26).

W   Little is known of Jewish history during the last years of Persian rule but when Alexander the Great moved southwards into Egypt, tradition asserts that Jadduah, the High Priest at Jerusalem, who had sworn allegiance to the Persians, refused to break his word. So impressed was Alexander by the integrity of the man that he treated the Jews in Palestine extremely well. He encouraged them to settle in his new capital Alexandria and soon this city contained the largest Jewish population outside Palestine. After a while these Jews so lost touch with their homeland that they no longer understood their Hebrew language; they had become Greek speaking. So about 250 B.C. a Greek translation from the Hebrew of the first five books of the Old Testament (the Pentateuch) was made in Greek and this is known as the Septuagint (written LXX). During the centuries preceding the birth of Our Lord, the scriptures were read in Greek in every synagogue outside Palestine with the result that many Gentiles (for the most part Greek speaking peoples who were not Jews) became adherents of the synagogue and observed the rules with regard to prayers, fasting, and almsgiving; they were known as God-fearers. This situation had much to do with the later spread of Christianity throughout the Greek speaking peoples of Asia Minor and of the Roman world.

X On the death of Alexander a fierce struggle began for his possessions. One of his generals seized Egypt and another Syria, while Palestine, lying between them, became the prey first of one then the other. At first the Jews were well treated but when, in 176 B.C. Antiochus Epiphanes became king, he despised the stern religion of the Jews and determined to abolish practices which seemed to him to be uncouth. He gave orders for the destruction of the Jewish sacred books and placed an altar to Zeus in the Temple, which to the Jews was 'the abomination that makes desolate' (Daniel 11 v. 31). The Jews revolted. Judas, who was a fine soldier and leader of the Jewish forces won a battle against Antiochus and recaptured Jerusalem 165 B.C. and a great feast was celebrated for eight days and this is still remembered as the Feast of Lights. The Jews won back their freedom for a short while but unfortunately they were divided. Some tolerated or even entered into the pagan way of life; some we are told would hurry away from the Temple to take part in throwing the 'discus'. There was an open breach between the Chasidim, the strict Jews and those who wanted to enter into the Greek way of life. The Chasidim, or strict Jews separated themselves from the others and became known as 'the separated ones' or Pharisees.

Y The Jews established a rather insecure independence for a short while under what are known as the Hasmonean princes during which time the Pharisees were cruelly treated. Those who supported the Hellenizing faction became known as Sadducees. The quarrels so weakened the remains of the Greek empire that a new power, the Roman, became the dominant influence. Quarrels and civil war in Palestine at last resulted in the intervention of the Romans. In 63 B.C. Pompey captured Jerusalem and massacred thousands of Jews and from this time Palestine was subject to Rome and fell into the hands of the Herods, an Edomite family, who first intrigued on behalf of the Hasmoneans and then overthrew them. To give colour to his claim to rule Judea, Herod, after murdering all the remaining Hasmonean princes, married Mariamne grand-daughter of Aristobulus II. Known in history as Herod the Great he reigned from 37 to 4 B.C. His reign was marked by great material prosperity; new and beautiful cities were built the most important of which was Caesarea. Greatest of his works was the new and magnificent Temple at Jerusalem which replaced the one built after the exile by Zerubbabel.

It was towards the end of this capable, but cruel tyrant's reign that we come to New Testament times. Most authorities accept the date 6 B.C. as the time when Jesus of Nazareth was born. (Johann Kepler, born 1571, the mathematician and astronomer, whose calculations on the appearance of the 'star' would suggest this correction in the date.) If so, Jesus was born some two years before Herod the Great died. It was into this Roman occupied area of Palestine, with all its intrigues and cruelty, the divisions among the Jews themselves, that Jesus came.

BRANCHES OF THE CHRISTIAN CHURCH TO BE
FOUND IN LANCASHIRE

The following are not in all cases authoritative statements about the
churches they describe, although they are acceptable to the local
denominations about which statements are made. They are not meant to
emphasise denominational differences but it is hoped that they will help
teachers to answer questions raised by their pupils.

The Anglican Communion

The Anglican Communion consists of those churches which are in
communion and recognise the leadership of the See of Canterbury. It
includes in our own islands the Church of England – which alone is
established, that is, has close links with the State – the Church of Wales,
the Episcopal Church of Scotland, the Church of Ireland, and many other
churches throughout the world in Africa, Asia, Australasia, and not least
the Protestant Episcopal Church of America.

The Church of England, with its inheritance of ancient Cathedrals and
Parish Churches, claims continuity with the first Christian Church
founded in Great Britain by the Celtic missionaries and by St. Augustine in
Southern England. Anglican Churches, like the Church of England itself,
claim to be Catholic, retaining the historic creeds, sacraments and
traditional orders of the ministry – bishops, priests and deacons; but is
also reformed, rejecting the jurisdiction of the Pope, and some beliefs and
practices current in the mediaeval Church. The formularies and forms of
worship of the Church of England were mainly crystallised during the
reign of Elizabeth I.

Because of its history, the Anglican Communion is very comprehensive
and allows within certain limits considerable freedom to its members.
One tradition stresses its Catholic heritage; another looks more for its
inspiration to the Reformation and Scripture as the one ultimate authority;
but this Church has also sought to establish its authority on an appeal to
reason.

The Baptist Churches

The first English Baptist Church was founded in Holland in 1609 by a
group of people who had fled abroad. They were part of a large body of
'Dissenters' – men and women who could not agree with the religious
settlement of that period.

In 1611 some of the members of the Amsterdam church returned to
England to set up their first Baptist Church on English soil at Spitalfields
in London. But Lancashire, indeed the whole of the North of England,
had to wait nearly forty years for its first Baptist chapel which was
established in Manchester in 1650.

The Baptist churches, now a world fellowship of over twenty-seven million members, are co-ordinated through the work of the Baptist World Alliance: in this country, most are members of the Baptist Union of Great Britain and Ireland, which was founded in 1812.

The three principles which may be said to characterise Baptist witness are first, a belief in the supreme importance of Scripture; second, baptism of 'believers' only; and third, 'congregational' government in which Baptist and Congregational practice are almost identical.

The Brethren

The movement originated in about 1825. The founders were young men, mostly associated with Trinity College, Dublin, who wanted to find a way in which they might come together for worship and communion as fellow-Christians. From Dublin the movement spread to England where the first Brethren assembly was established at Plymouth in 1831; hence arose the popular term 'Plymouth Brethren'. Two of their leaders were responsible for one of the best critical editions of the Greek New Testament to appear in the nineteenth century.[1] The Brethren hold the historic Christian faith. Their worship consists in the 'breaking of bread' in a weekly meeting without any officiating minister. They are evangelical and support missionary enterprises in many parts of the world. A cleavage between what have come to be known as the Exclusive Brethren who followed the lead given by John N. Darby (1800–1882) took place in 1848. Their policy is not shared by the Open Brethren.

The Congregational Church

Congregationalism began in the last third of the sixteenth century in a new conception of the Church, differing from that of the national Church of Elizabeth I in that it consisted of voluntary associations of committed Christians, joined in a 'covenant' with each other and with God, and calling themselves 'gathered churches' (as distinct from churches which embraced everybody in the nation or in a parish). Each local church is self-governing, free to choose its own minister and to order its own life, but not in isolation. They recognise a common faith and order and an obligation to help each other. Recently a 'Union' of churches in England and Wales has become the Congregational Church, thus signifying this unity. Congregationalists had a great influence in the seventeenth, eighteenth and nineteenth centuries through their Academies, their preachers, their scholars and their overseas missionaries.

The Lutheran Church

Members of this church are followers of the forthright teaching of Martin Luther at the time of the Reformation. It is the dominant church in Germany and is the national church of the Scandinavian countries. Lutheran belief was summed up in the Augsberg Confession 1530. The purpose of this was to defend the Lutherans against misrepresentations and to show to what degree they accepted the basic Christian doctrines and rejected what they regarded as abuses that had crept in, in the years preceding the Reformation.

---

[1] S. B. Tregelles and B. W. Newton.

The Methodist Church

This sprang from a movement that began in the Church of England under the leadership of John and Charles Wesley in the eighteenth century. This was at a time when a vast number of men and women, affected by the early stages of the industrial revolution, had lost touch with any form of organised religion. John Wesley showed great courage and endurance in travelling up and down the country, preaching mainly in the open air to great numbers of people, many of whom were hostile, uneducated and ill-informed. He possessed a great power of eloquence and many were converted to Christianity from which they had lapsed or become estranged. His followers broke away from the Church of England mainly because of the lack of sympathy of many of the parish priests and others who disliked the lay-preachers on whom Wesley had come to rely. The word Methodist was applied to the new group because of the systematic way in which their work and the worship they encouraged were conducted. Wesley himself, while at Oxford University made it a rule to attend communion regularly. The members of this movement made a point of having a genuine concern for one another: fellowship is still one of the main features of the Methodist Church. In England the organisation of the church is much like that of the Presbyterians but in America bishops are in charge. The Methodists are the largest single group in the United States. They are also strongly represented in the Commonwealth, in various parts of Africa, where missionary work has been carried on. It is estimated that there are some forty million Methodists in the world.

The Moravian Church, Fairfield, Manchester

The Moravian Church is one of the smaller religious bodies in this country; but it has a long and honourable history. It is an episcopal church, being a reformed church sixty years before the Reformation. It was founded in 1457, arising out of the work of John Huss, the martyr of Bohemia who was himself inspired by the Englishman, John Wycliffe. After flourishing in Moravia and Bohemia as the 'United Brethren', it was practically wiped out during the Thirty Years War. A small section survived, however, and fled into Saxony, where they found refuge with the generous and pious Count Zinzendorf, under whose leadership the church began a new lease of life in 1722.

The Moravians took an active part in the evangelical revival in England during the eighteenth century and were closely associated for a time with John Wesley. It was the calm confidence of the Moravian fellow-passengers on his voyage to Georgia 1735 that convinced Wesley that he did not possess the faith which casts out fear. On his return to England he attended a society meeting of the Moravians in Aldersgate Street, London, and it was here that, 'About a quarter before nine, while (the preacher) was describing the change which God works in the heart through faith in Christ, I felt my heart strangely warmed'. So wrote Wesley in his Journal and it was this conviction that flashed into the mind of one of the most powerful intellects in the England of that period that is 'the true source of English Methodism'. (Lecky, History of England in the 18th century).

In the eighteenth century settlements were established in various parts and Fairfield, Manchester, was one of these. Opened in 1785 it was planned and built by its own people. The village was self-contained and self-governed, with its inn, shop, bakery, laundry and farm; its fire-engine, night-watchman, inspector of weights and measures, an overseer of roads and a physician.

'. . . The place was a hive of industry and of religious activity. . . . The "single brethren" had a bakery, and every week-day a "single brother" rode out on horseback delivering bread. The "single sisters" had a farm and a laundry, did beautiful needlework, sent some to Queen Adelaide, and it pleased her so much that she ordered more. . . . In all this there was two-fold ambition. On the one hand they were money-making concerns; on the other hand they had a definite religious mission; and even the inn was considered a place where Gospel tracts might fitly be left. . . . The little village was the home of law and order, peace and quiet. No trades-man was allowed to create a monopoly; no dogs were allowed to roam the streets, and no children played therein after eight p.m. Nor was the spiritual side of life neglected. Each week-night there was a service in the church. . . .'

The Moravians were educational pioneers. Comenius, whose views did much to further education, was a Moravian bishop.

Five congregations were established in Lancashire:

Dukinfield established	1755	Westwood (Oldham)	1874
Fairfield (Manchester)	1785	Wheler Street (Openshaw)	1899
Salem (Oldham)	1836		

The Orthodox Church

More often known as the Greek Orthodox Church, it claims to be the original Catholic Church but, because it believes the centralisation of authority (in Rome) to be wrong, it calls itself the Orthodox Catholic Church. Its main principle is 'unity in diversity' and while accepting much that is common to all the historic churches of Christendom it allows for a degree of independence as between its branches. The organisation of the Orthodox Church is administered by Patriarchs: the Patriarchs were originally the bishops of the three cities venerated for their Christian associations: Rome, Alexandria and Jerusalem. During the fourth century Constantinople became the imperial capital of the eastern half of the Roman Empire and the Patriarch of this city gained considerable authority from the prestige this brought to his office. From the eleventh century encouragement was given to missionary enterprise into what is now known as the Balkans and Russia, and through its educational enterprise it gave to Russia its alphabet. The Russian alphabet is based on letters from the Greek with the addition of some symbols needed to express sounds not covered in the Greek alphabet.

The Pentecostal Movement

The Pentecostal Movement as it is represented in the major denomina-tions originated in the early part of the twentieth century. It is very numerous in the United States of America and has its branches in Britain. They are known by various names, the Elim Church, the Apostolic Church and the Assemblies of God. The Movement believes that the Bible is the inspired Word of God and that 'none may add thereto or take away there-from except at their peril'. This does not mean that no allowance is made for figurative language as found in the Scriptures. The Movement is evangelical in outlook and practises baptism by total immersion.

The Presbyterian Church

This is the distinguishing name given to a group of churches which took form during the time of the Reformation in England. It is the specific name of a form of church constitution or policy which claims for itself an origin in the Christian church in apostolic times, reformulated later on (in the sixteenth and seventeenth centuries) in Geneva and Switzerland. It took deep roots in Scotland but is represented in most parts of the world: Presbyterian missions are to be found in Africa and congregations are to be found wherever Scotsmen have made their home. In government it is a church in which laymen, set apart to serve as elders, with pastoral functions in local congregations, share, with ministers, at every level in the work of the Church. All ministers are of equal rank. Although there is no fixed liturgy there are normal forms of the orders of the services.

The Roman Catholic Church

The Roman Catholic Church forms the largest Christian Community in the world. It is called Catholic because the word 'Catholic' means universal and the Catholic Church is spread all over the world serving people of every race, culture and nationality.

The 575 million catholics in the world are spiritually looked after by 500,000 priests working in parishes that make up the two thousand diocese of the Church. Each diocese is ruled by a bishop who, together with the Pope, constitute the teaching authority of the Church.

The Catholic Church is also the most ancient of all Christian communities. It is sometimes called the Roman Catholic Church because the Pope, the chief bishop, is always the Bishop of Rome where St. Peter, the leader of the Apostles, was the first bishop. The Catholic Church has many links with Apostolic times.

The Catholic Church forms a united community, living a definite way of life and sharing the same ideals and values. Every Catholic parish is one with the rest of the Church in Faith and Worship. At the heart of the Catholic faith is the belief that the risen Christ teaches and makes men holy, now, through his church and that He becomes truly present in sacramental form at the sacrifice of the Mass. The Mass is the central act of Catholic worship.

Over a million and a half Catholics totally dedicate their lives to God in the different religious orders within the Church. They express their love of God through service to their fellow-men in such works as teaching, looking after the sick, the aged and the dying, caring for orphans, meeting whatever is the human need.

Pope John and the Bishops which he called together in the second Vatican Council have stressed the great need for the Church today to be open to all that is best in the modern world and to be eager to co-operate with men of good will from all faiths in the great work of establishing truth and justice, peace and human dignity among the world family.

The Salvation Army

Founded by William Booth in 1863. He was a Methodist minister with a passion for evangelism and who held revival meetings. He directed his work towards the great and pressing evils of the times in which he lived. Today the movement is world-wide and has a well-established organisation based on army lines (but is not a military movement) which emphasises the value of mutual help and work for the common good based on Christian principles.

The Society of Friends

A movement launched by George Fox (1624–1691) a Christian having a remarkable insight into spiritual matters and social evils. He was frequently imprisoned for his beliefs and bore his sufferings and misfortunes with great courage. He won a wide response to his appeal especially in the north of England. In 1650 he was committed to Derby gaol for his views and it was on this occasion that the presiding judge used the term 'Quaker' as a term of abuse for his followers; they were known first as 'seekers'. The centre of the movement was for some years at Swarthmore Hall, near Ulverston, the home of Judge Fell, Oliver Cromwell's Chancellor of the Duchy of Lancaster, whose wife Margaret became a Quaker. The movement continues to take a leading part in many social activities especially in promoting efforts for international peace. It has world-wide connections and is particularly concerned in international relief work. Quaker worship is a silent waiting on God without the mediation of minister or priest. Anyone may make a contribution if he or she feels 'moved' to do so. To the Friend, all life is a sacrament.

The Unitarian Church

Unitarianism first came to birth in Hungary in the sixteenth century and spread to various parts of Europe. The first publicly avowed church in England was opened in London in 1774 by Theophilus Lindsaye. In America it has been established since the early part of the eighteenth century due, in the first place, to Joseph Priestley who emigrated there from England.

The movement grew out of the disputes, not to say confusions in theological circles of the eighteenth century. This was a time when men disagreed on many issues: political, philosophical as well as theological. Unitarianism is characterised by its stress upon the exercise of reason, upon freedom of conscience and thinking in all matters of religious faith and belief. Toleration for all religious convictions if sincerely held was not then, as now, so easily conceded.

The basic and unifying belief is the unity and oneness of God, their churches exist for the worship of God alone and the promotion of the religious faith of Jesus. Unrestricted by specific creeds in their search for and practice of religious truth they believe that, while men may not all think alike or be of one opinion, they can all love alike and be one in heart.

The Swedenborgian Church

Emmanuel Swedenborg, a Swedish scientist, philosopher and theologian, one of the most learned men of his country was born in Stockholm in 1688. He died in London in 1772. His body was taken later to Upsala Cathedral in Sweden. Adherents to his theological thinking and writings founded the New Jerusalem Church in 1784. There are branches in Lancashire, one of which is at Radcliffe.

In his writings Swedenborg draws from the Scriptures to illustrate the nature of the Trinity in the One God, the Lord Jesus Christ, and stresses the view that all creation originates from the divine love and wisdom. Among other doctrines, he presents the internal meaning of passages of the Bible and underlines the importance of man's life in this world as a preparation for eternal life.

There are other sects and denominations, not associated with the Council of Churches, but holding meetings in various parts of the County. Useful books containing information about them are:

Davies, H.	Christian Deviations.	S.C.M.*
Kellett, A.	Isms and Ologies.	Epworth*
Eddy, Mary Baker	Science and Health with Key to the Scriptures.	Available Christian Science Reading Rooms.
De Witt, John	The Christian Science Way of Life.	Prentice Hall Inc.

See also page 166.

APPENDIX 'C'

PLACES OF INTEREST IN THE HISTORY OF CHRISTIANITY IN THE COUNTY OF LANCASHIRE

Some Ancient Dissenting Meeting-houses in Lancashire

Information connected with the development of the Methodist Movement was supplied by Mr. E. A. Rose, Secretary of the Lancashire and Cheshire branch of the Wesley Historical Society.

Introduction

by Dr. W. Gordon Robinson, Principal, Northern Congregational College.

Lancashire is rich in reminders of the long story of the Christian Church in the county and in the north; it provides interesting examples which can add considerably to the study of church history. There are many local histories of towns, districts and individual churches which can be drawn upon; the county history in the Victoria County History series is useful; there are several popular histories such as Henry Fishwick's *History of Lancashire* and Arthur Mee's *Lancashire* in the King's England series; the Record Office at Preston can be helpful; and the many volumes of the *Dictionary of National Biography* are invaluable for biographies of individual men and women.

There are some few remains which go back to Roman and Saxon times and these include doorways, windows, fragments of crosses and even traces of Mithraism, Christianity's contemporary rival in the earliest centuries. With the coming of the Normans came also the beginnings of church building most notably at Furness Abbey. The Reformation brought its own memorials though Roman Catholicism remained still strong in various parts of the county. The long drawn-out 'settlement of the Church' from Henry VIII to Elizabeth I and the succeeding changes of the seventeenth century have their memorials as have the centuries which followed.

If we look first at the buildings, the cathedrals of Lancashire are important though not of very great date since Lancashire was part of the Diocese of Chester until last century. Manchester and Blackburn have Anglican Cathedrals; Salford and Preston Roman Catholic ones. Liverpool has both, each an outstanding monument of modern architecture. Local parish churches are always of great interest and a starting point for extensive study. Begin then with one's own parish church. If it is of some historic interest, so much the better. If not, there are historic parish churches at, for example, Ashton-under-Lyne, Bury, Deane, Huyton, Middleton, Ormskirk, Rochdale and Winwick near Warrington. In these churches look for windows, pulpits, fonts, statues, brasses, bells and memorials. Look also for new churches in the modern architectural idiom.

Lancashire is rich in monastic remains – some reasonably well-preserved though in ruins, some still in use as parish churches, and some of which there are only the merest traces. Furness, Cartmell and Whalley are the best known and most worth seeing but the whole history of monasticism in England can be traced in Penwortham, Lytham and Up Holland (Benedictine priories), Kersal (a Cluniac cell), Furness, Wyresdale and Whalley (Cistercian), Cockersand (Praemonstratensian), and the

Dominican, Franciscan and Austin friaries at Lancaster, Preston and Warrington, and there are remains of a chantry near St. Helens called Windleshaw 'Abbey'.

When the Dissenters broke away from the Church of England from the end of the sixteenth century onwards, they left their remains and these are seen in many places in the original buildings (or traces of them) from the end of the seventeenth century. There are reminders of the famous Warrington Academy at Warrington, and 'ancient chapels' (or as they should be more rightly called 'meeting houses') at Toxteth and Gateacre in Liverpool, at Chowbent, Elswick, Rivington, Tunley, Wymondhouses and Cross Street, Manchester (now rebuilt), and Quaker meeting houses in Lancaster, Ulverston and Manchester.

Look next for people because there are many such associated with the story of the Church in Lancashire. Here are a few examples. First, take a conspectus of heroes and heroines as seen, for example, in the Lady Chapel windows in Liverpool Cathedral, or in the windows and statues of the Rylands Library, Manchester, or the monument in Dalton Square, Lancaster, or the Ford Madox Brown frescoes in Manchester Town Hall. Next, look for outstanding figures who mirror the history of their own times: John Paslew, Abbot at Whalley; George Marsh at Deane, and John Bradford, in Manchester Cathedral, martyrs of Marian times; Edmund Arrowsmith, at Ashton-in-Makerfield and Haydock and Cardinal William Allen, at Fleetwood, heroes of the attempt to win back England to Roman Catholicism in Elizabeth's reign; Archbishop Bancroft of the reign of James I, at Farnworth; Miles Standish, of the Pilgrim Fathers at Duxbury; Laurence Chadderton, who helped to translate the Authorised Version at Chadderton; George Fox, founder of the Quakers at Pendleton and Ulverston; Joseph Priestley, the minister-scientist at Warrington; John Byrom, author of 'Christians Awake', St. Ann's, Manchester; Mrs. Gaskell at Cross Street Chapel, Manchester.

There are many examples to be seen of Bibles and books of great historic interest. Among the many books at Stonyhurst is a Book of Hours which belonged to Mary Queen of Scots; in the Rylands Library, Manchester, a Wycliffe Bible which belonged to Elizabeth I (and here too are countless treasures which include the earliest fragment on papyrus of the Gospel according to St. John); Manchester Central Library and Chetham's Library, Manchester, have their treasures, as has the Picton Library in Liverpool. In the Congregational Church at Elswick there are surviving chained books, and in the library at Bolton School and at Turton there are collections of chained books given by Humphrey Chetham who founded the school and library in Manchester.

From the times when, according to tradition, or legend, St. Patrick came to Heysham and St. Cuthbert to Kirkby Ireleth, until today with its still unfinished great cathedrals at Liverpool, the whole panorama of the Church in Britain unfolds before us with endless possibilities of evoking the past and linking it to the present in the people who can be remembered and the places that can be seen and visited.

The Celtic Church

After the Roman withdrawal in the fifth century, a British chieftain named Rhydderch Hael of Strathclyde, a friend and contemporary of St. Columba and St. Kentigern (the patron saint of Glasgow or Gleschu), gained a great victory over the other British princes: his domains included the southern counties of Scotland as well as Cumberland and Westmorland. As a result of this victory and the influence of Rhydderch, who supported Columba, the Celtic Church sent its missionaries all over the territory. The impact of this missionary enterprise can be seen today in several ruins and remains.

Heysham

The parish church of Heysham was consecrated in 967 but there is a well authenticated tradition that the church is built on the site of the spot where St. Patrick landed after being shipwrecked in Morecambe Bay when he was returning from Ireland to Strathclyde. There was certainly a Christian settlement here in the fifth century and the nearby remains of a stone circle (possibly Druidic) gives further proof of the ancient practice of Celtic missionaries in building their Christian settlements at the heart of the ancient pagan worship.

There are interesting grave-coffins cut in the natural rock which are unique as well as being good examples of this type of burial. There is, too, a good example of a Viking hog-back grave stone.

These remains mean that Heysham is one of the oldest places of Christian worship in the county.

Buildings in connection with the Christian Church in Norman times

The Norman period marks the real beginning of church building in this country. In the north we have several examples of this.

Monastic Remains

It is important to remember that these places were houses where people lived. They occupied a place in mediaeval life of great importance: they also were concerned not only with the spiritual life but with the social and economic life of the period. They were founded to pursue a particular vision of the Christian way of life but as their vision faded their discipline slackened, their numbers and influence declined, and they fell victims to the changing spirit of the age in which they lived. In the Tudor period the communities were dissolved, their property taken away and in many cases the buildings fell into decay. The dissolution of the monasteries was met with varying degree of opposition by the orders. Most were complaisant, a few resisted. The dispossessed monks were given either benifices (a parish to administer) or were pensioned: in most cases they were adequately provided with the means of 'survival'. The few who resisted were brutally killed.

To many of the people, the poor in particular, the loss was great. The monasteries often provided the only means of care in days of near-famine or in illness. The monks who maintained a worthy sense of their calling were respected and regarded with affection. It is possible that this was one of the reasons for the Pilgrimage of Grace, which was a stirring protest against the closure of places where people had looked for some protection, guidance and education. In another sense the revolt was a protest against the 'new ways' and the 'new men' of the Tudor government; an expression of the frustration of the last days of feudalism (see Knowles, 'Religious Orders in the Sixteenth Century').

The remains of monasteries vary in interest. Those of Furness Abbey are remarkably complete; the church alone survives at Cartmel and that in excellent order though much restored; of Penwortham, Cockersand, and Cockerham virtually nothing remains.

Furness Abbey

In a remarkably beautiful situation on the road from Dalton to Barrow-in-Furness. The sandstone ruins are evocative, well kept, and guarded by the Ministry of Public Buildings and Works.

The main features of its history are as follows:

1127 Norman monks of Savigny, of the Benedictine order, settled on the site. It was given by Stephen, Count of Boulogne, King of England 1135–54.

1147 The brotherhood joined the Cistercian order, a very strict order originating at Citeaux in Burgundy, and then at the height of its influence. Their houses were to be in remote situations, their churches to be plain, their lives secluded and devoted to prayer, study and manual labour. It was this order which did much to develop agriculture at this time.

1250 Furness suffered from Scottish raids and border warfare, but nevertheless grew rich and powerful through benefactions, sheep-farming, and exploitation of the local iron-ore. The community produced only one literary monk, Jocelyn of Furness, whose lives of St. Patrick, St. Kentigern and others became famous.

1500 In the sixteenth century the few monks remaining, seem to have been on good terms with their neighbours and tenants for whose children they provided a 'School for Grammar and Singing' with dinner or supper every day.

1537 The Abbot surrendered the Abbey to the Royal Commissioners. He became Vicar of Dalton-in-Furness; the monks were pensioned.

Subsequently the lands passed to the Preston family and thence to the Dukes of Devonshire.

The original abbey buildings of 1123 were rough and temporary. Permanent buildings were added and they were adapted as necessity arose and opportunity offered. This Abbey became the second richest Cistercian Abbey after Fountains in Yorkshire. The ruins are sufficiently complete to give a fair idea of the daily life of the community at its most flourishing period.

There are all the necessities of a Christian community, be it monastery, college, or school, and few sites show them as plainly:

Eating. The kitchen can be traced, the dining rooms, and the stores.

Sleeping. The dormitories with the night stairs are still standing.

Hygiene. Latrines, washing facilities, heating are all marked out.

Worship. The chapel, or church of the Community, is the most prominent feature of the ruins; some very fine architectural and decorative work remains.

Administration. The Chapter House for meetings and the conduct of official business is in good condition.

Study. The Cloisters were used for study and the 'cells' used for the library are well preserved.

Recreation. The parlour (for talking and general conversation), the warming room (the only fire) and a games-board scratched on a stone threshold.

Sickness. There is a very fine infirmary with its own chapel (now a museum with figures of crusaders, abbots, bishops and a deacon).

Social life. Indicated by the Guest House with its stables, and the Abbot's lodging.

The 'lay brothers' were largely the servants of the Community living under a simple rule but it is difficult to avoid the conclusion that the worldly success of Furness Abbey was the cause of its decay and subsequent destruction.

Cartmel Priory

The church is virtually all that remains of the House of the Canons of St. Augustine which flourished in this beautiful place for some three hundred years. Their Rule was made primarily for parish clergy and others living an 'active' life in the world: it originated in North Africa in the fifth century though not much in evidence in Western Europe until the middle of the eleventh century. The canons settled in Cartmel in 1188 and the same order served the cathedral at Carlisle. They prospered and were able to build their fine church and other necessary buildings. The nave of the church was finished in 1400 and the choir stalls were put in about 1450. A part of the Priory Church had always been used as the parish church of the village and the surrounding countryside. When the ten remaining Canons with their servants surrendered to the Royal Commissioners in 1537, the parishioners claimed the church as their own. All but the 'Town Choir' fell in to disrepair until about 1620; George Preston of Holker Hall began the work of restoration (largely at his own expense). The examples of Jacobean oak screens were added to the original choir-stalls. The church continues to be the Parish Church of Cartmel.

Cockerham Priory

A small house of three or four Augustinian Canons some five miles south of Lancaster. There is little to see.

Cockersand Abbey

The Abbey of Saint Mary of the Marsh is in a bleak situation on the marsh-land between the estuaries of the rivers Lune and Cocker, some six miles south of Lancaster. It was founded in 1190 by an order of Canons living under a rule similar to that of St. Augustine. (The 'Praemonstratensians' originated at the Abbey of Premontre, near Laon in France.) This became one of the great Abbeys of Lancashire in spite of its precarious situation. Few remains are visible and many of the conventual buildings have been washed away by the sea. The Chapter House has been restored as a family mausoleum. There are visible outlines of the transept walls of the church, of the warming house (under the dormitory), the cellars, and the fresh water system. Some stalls of fine workmanship in Lancaster Parish Church, are said to have come from Cockersand.

Whalley Abbey

Whalley is one of the ancient 'holy places' in the north and has been a place of pilgrimage from very early times. Although it is fairly certain that Paulinus of York visited here in the seventh century, preached and baptised here in the river Calder, there has been a church on this site since the ninth century. The Abbey was not founded until the end of the thirteenth century. After the Dissolution of the Monasteries in 1537 the property passed into private hands and for the next four hundred years it was a private house. It is now a place of retreat and conference for the Diocese of Blackburn.

Enquiries to the Warden, Whalley Abbey, Blackburn.

IMPORTANT CHURCHES, SOME OF THEM MODERN, IN USE TODAY

CATHEDRALS

Blackburn

An Abbot of Whalley, writing in the fourteenth century said that the date of the foundation of this church at Blackburn was 595, two years before Augustine landed in Kent and Columba died in Iona. The Saxon church mentioned in the Domesday Book was replaced by a mediaeval one from which there still remain eight misericord stalls, a fifteenth century chalice and a 'pax' (a piece of ritual furniture which the celebrant kissed at mass and which was handed round to the clergy and lay people to convey the kiss of peace).

In 1826 a new church was consecrated in which can be demonstrated the evolution of nineteenth century Gothic from eighteenth century classicism. As the new church was built on a slope, a platform had first to be built which gives the building a deep crypt. When in 1926 the Diocese of Blackburn was formed the old parish church became the Cathedral. See 'Blackburn Cathedral' Canon G. A. Williams, Pitkin Pictorials Ltd.

Liverpool

The Anglican Cathedral was designed by Sir Giles Gilbert Scott and was the first cathedral to be built on virgin soil in England since the Reformation. The foundation stone was laid by King Edward VII on 14th July, 1904, and the Lady Chapel was completed in 1910. Building was continued with short interruptions due to two world wars. In the great Vestey Tower (331 feet) completed in 1951 hangs the highest and heaviest ringing peal in the world (thirteen bells weighing $16\frac{1}{2}$ tons in a circle with the addition of the great Bourdon in the centre). The two transverse arches are believed to be the highest Gothic arches ever built. There is some fine stained glass of modern design and manufacture.

Manchester

The present building was begun in 1422. It is in the Gothic perpendicular style as seen in King's College, Cambridge and All Souls, Oxford. Originally a parish church for the whole of Manchester and served by a community of priests and lay-clerks, it was raised to the status of the Cathedral in 1847 when the Diocese of Manchester was formed out of Chester which in turn had once belonged to Lichfield.

The 'angel stone' so called, a relic of Saxon workmanship, suggests that there was once a Saxon church on the same site. Monuments of interest are to be found within including one to Humphrey Chetham, a Manchester citizen and benefactor (1580 to 1653). The school he founded and which adjoins the Cathedral, has close links with the church: in 1653, a John Wigan who was Colonel of Cromwell's Guards at Westminster came to Manchester to act as chief mourner at the funeral of Humphrey Chetham and at the request of Chetham's executors, who wanted to found a school and library, agreed to sell his property, known as Chetham's Hospital. The present school and library are the result. In those troubled times, divisions about doctrine and on grounds of politics created new situations; John Wigan, a Baptist, founded a Baptist church in a barn in the precincts of the College. The buildings known as Chetham's Hospital had once belonged to the Earl of Derby who espoused the Royalist cause. His property was confiscated by the Parliamentarians and then bought by John Wigan.

See the 'Pictorial History of Manchester Cathedral', Canon H. Hodkin, Pitkin Pictorials Ltd.

PARISH CHURCHES

One of the best ways of studying an ancient church is to begin with the exterior. There may be some signs of old entrances, now closed, which give a clue to its age and the nature of its early days. Next look at the inside where windows, brasses and memorials of many kinds may give a clue to its history. Very revealing too, are the pulpit, font and the bells. Permission should always be obtained beforehand and those in authority may be able to offer more information; frequently a guidebook is obtainable. Those wishing to make 'brass rubbings' are not always welcome unless the incumbent has been approached beforehand. Many old churches have had to protect their historic furnishings from damage and this is true of old brasses in particular. Obtain permission first.

The following are only a few of the more interesting churches.

Ashton-under-Lyne

The 'Old Church', as it is still referred to, is closely linked with the earliest education given to the people of the town; the care of the sick and the relief of the poor was also the concern of the authorities of the church. It seems likely that there was a church on this site before Norman times; the earlier dedication was to St. Helen. The ancient glass window (now in the south aisle) was once above the altar. It illustrates the story of the daughter, Helen by name, of a king named Coel or Coyle (commemorated in the nursery rhyme 'Old King Cole').'His capital was at Colchester and his daughter, Helen, married Constantius the Roman Emperor whose son became the Constantine whose edict gave to Christianity its freedom. Helen devoted her life to good works and the stained glass depicts some of the outstanding events associated with her name. When in the reign of Henry V a new church was built, John Huntington the Rector wished that it should be known as St. Michaels. The full title St. Michaels and All Angels was probably added later.

See 'England in Ashton-under-Lyne', Winifred M. Bowman; J. Sherratt and Son.

Bury

The parish of Bury is one of the great ancient parishes of Lancashire. The church is not mentioned in Domesday Book; indeed there are many omissions in the north due to the fact that the area was sparsely inhabited, fairly unproductive and, therefore, not likely to produce much taxable income. A church existed at the end of the eleventh century on this site; it was rebuilt in the sixteenth century, in the second half of the eighteenth and again between 1871 and 1876. The living of Bury has remained in he patronage of the Earls of Derby since 1485. It was given to Sir Thomas Stanley after the battle of Bosworth Field, by Henry Tudor.

See 'Bury Parish Church', Rev. R. S. Wingfield Digby; British Publishing Co. Ltd.

Deane

The parish church of St. Mary the Virgin is built on the site of an earlier church. The church was rebuilt about 1452 and fifty years later the present nave with its Gothic arches and panelled ceiling was added. Alterations and repairs have gone on ever since, the latest in the quincentenary year 1952. The pulpit is Elizabethan and, it is claimed, is unique in point of age in the County of Lancashire.

Halsall

It has a fourteenth century chancel of great beauty, with fifteenth century carved stalls with original misericords : the tower was built in the fifteenth century (the top stage is octagonal as at Aughton) with a modern spire. In the sanctuary, there is an elaborate altar tomb of Sir Henry Halsall and his wife Margaret. There is a pulpit 'hour glass'. The ancient grammar school (1593) founded by Edward Halsall serves as a vestry today.

'A Guide to Halsall and its Church', Rev. W. H. Bullough.

Huyton

The parish church of St. Michael has a fourteenth century nave. It has a magnificent chancel screen of the early Tudor period while the chancel itself was built in the fifteenth century. Some fine old furniture and ancient stone carvings are to be seen.

Middleton

The parish church of Middleton is one of the most ancient in Lancashire. The present church retains evidence of three buildings which have stood on this site for eight hundred years. The second fifteenth century church was the gift of Thomas Langley, Bishop of Durham (1406–1437) created Cardinal and made Lord Chancellor of England in the reign of Henry IV, and who was born at Langley Hall in the Parish of Middleton. The next rebuilding took place between 1515 and 1524 and is regarded as a thank-offering for the victory at Flodden where Sir Richard Assheton and his archers distinguished themselves.

'A Brief History of the Parish Church of St. Leonard, Middleton', W. T. Smith, A.T.D. ; British Publishing Co. Ltd.

Ormskirk

The name Ormskirk has been traced to a Saxon landowner by the name of Orm. It is said that he was the founder of Ormskirk Parish Church. It was certainly in existence at the time of Richard I. The church is closely associated with the Stanley family and to the south of the 'High Chancel' is the Derby Chapel. It has a seventeenth century parclose screen and is separated from the 'High Chancel' by a thirteenth century arcade. In the fourteenth century Lathom, Knowsley, and other large estates were brought into the family of the Stanleys. Isabella, daughter and heiress of Sir Thomas de Lathom who claimed descent from Orm, married Sir John Stanley. Jas. Stanley, 7th Earl of Derby, was buried here after his execution in Bolton market (1651). Buried near him is his brave French wife Charlotte who made history by her defence of Lathom House against the Parliamentarians. She features in Sir Walter Scott's Peveril of the Peak. The church stands on a hill and is remarkable for both a spire and a massive square tower (c. 1540) built to house the bells from Burscough Priory at its dissolution in 1536.

Sefton

The tower, spire and north chapel date from the fourteenth century. There is a fine chancel screen, some brasses and carved 'poppy head' pews. It has a seventeenth century pulpit.

Warrington

A town which has been the gateway between Lancashire and Cheshire since Roman times. It has a fine church with a central tower and spire (modern) rising to 300 feet. Inside is a fifteenth century alabaster tomb where Sir John Boteler is buried.

Wigan

A town loyal to the Royalist cause and so won for itself the motto 'Ancient and Loyal'. The Parish Church is on the site of a Saxon church but only the tower is mediaeval. The rest is largely restored and comparatively recent. The remains of a Roman altar are to be found, built into the splay of one of the windows. One of its Rectors was Thomas Linacre who founded the Royal College of Physicians 1518 and of which he remained President until 1524. He was a teacher of Greek at Oxford and Erasmus and Sir Thomas More were among his pupils.

Winwick

The church is very ancient in origin and the foundation is pre-conquest. Mostly fourteenth century as it stands today. In the chapel of the Legh family is a brass of Sir Peter Legh (1527), a Tudor knight who became a priest after his wife's death. There are too, associations with Saxon battles, the Wars of the Roses and the Civil War.

SOME ANCIENT DISSENTING MEETING-HOUSES IN LANCASHIRE

Information connected with the development of the Methodist Movement was supplied by Mr. E. A. Rose, Secretary of the Lancashire and Cheshire branch of the Wesley Historical Society.

By the Act of Uniformity in 1662, episcopal ordination was made essential for all ministers of the established church, and all clergy had to take an oath of 'unfeigned assent and consent to all and everything contained and prescribed in' the revised Prayer Book. The result: about 1760 incumbents were ejected from their livings. From this date, the parting of the ways brought about the separation of what are known as 'free churches' from the Church of England as established by law. The present trend towards unity and understanding between the churches is an attempt to restore as much unity as possible. It should be noted that as no less a leader of non-conformity than Nathaniel Micklem has said, 'There is not, and there never has been, any controversy between the Church of England and orthodox dissent in respect of the articles of the Christian faith'. The differences were mostly about the relation between the church and the state and on matters of church government. The effects upon the social and political as well as religious history of England were to be profound and far-reaching. Protestant dissenters had to accept a position of civic and social inferiority which lasted until the middle of the nineteenth century.

Ashton-under-Lyne

The Congregational Church goes back to the 1780's and was firmly established by 1816. There is now a strikingly fine church completed in 1894 which contains many windows by Burne-Jones.

A religious society was formed in Ashton in 1741 by a travelling evangelist, David Taylor, but this later became Moravian. The earliest Methodist centre was Staley Hall (still standing) on the Cheshire side of the river Tame. A society met here from 1743–1752 and was visited by John Bennet, a Methodist preacher, once a fortnight as a rule. John Wesley preached at Staley Hall on 7th November, 1745. Later the society moved to Higham Fold, near the present Stamford Park. A chapel was built in Ashton in 1781 : this was the first non-conformist chapel in the town. Ashton became a stronghold of the Methodist New Connexion, a group which broke away from the main body in 1797. A stone from the first chapel can still be seen in Warrington Street, outside Stamford Street chapel.

Primitive Methodists first visited Ashton in June 1821. One of them, Samuel Waller, was imprisoned for preaching at Ashton Cross.

Ainsworth

Presbyterian services were held at Cockey Chapel-of-ease for at least ten years after the Act of Uniformity 1662. In 1672 a licence was obtained for a meeting house, and the Presbyterians became a separate congregation. The present chapel was built in 1715, and enlarged in 1773. In 1718 out of 69 families in the chapelry of Cockey, 56 were Presbyterians. From 1813 the chapel has been Unitarian.

Audenshaw

The old hamlet of Audenshaw now lies under the reservoirs, but a Methodist society was established here in 1777. Red Hall chapel was built in 1782 and became a centre for Methodists between Manchester and Ashton. It was the only place of worship in the village for sixty years. Like its Ashton counterpart it joined the Methodist New Connexion in 1797.

Bacup

A chapel was built in Lane Head Lane in 1751, the first in Rossendale. It was followed by a second in 1786 and a third in 1840. Baptists were strong in this town.

Blackburn

An Academy for the training of Congregational ministers was established in Blackburn in 1816. It was transferred to Manchester in 1843 and became Lancashire Independent College (now the Northern Congregational College).

A Methodist class of twelve members was formed in 1758 and Wesley paid his first visit in 1759. Other visits are recorded in 1780, 1784, 1785 and 1790. The 'Old Calendar House' in Chapel Street was secured as a preaching house in 1780. A new chapel was built in 1785 in Clayton Street.

Bolton

On the spot where George Whitefield had preached and prayed about 1750, Duke's Alley Chapel was erected and from it grew the present St. George's Road Congregational Church. At Walmsley, near Bolton, non-conformity flourished in the mid-seventeenth century and there was a chapel which was almost continuously used by dissenting worshippers: this ultimately became a Unitarian centre.

John Bennet (see Ashton-under-Lyne) began a society of Methodists here on 5th November, 1747 and twenty-nine persons entered their names. John Wesley preached at Bolton Cross in August 1748, the first of many visits. The first Methodist chapel was opened in Acresfield in 1751. Methodism flourished, and in 1776 a new chapel was opened in Ridgeway Gates. Bolton became one of the strongest centres in the county.

Burnley

A Methodist society was established in 1763 but it appears to have died out. Wesley preached for the first time on 13th July, 1784, and following this visit, Methodism took permanent root. They met in a joiner's workshop until the erection of Keighley Green chapel.

Congregationalism was not established here until the beginning of the nineteenth century.

Chipping

First visited by John Wesley 4th April, 1751, in company with the Vicar, John Milner (1710 to 1777) who was a friend of Wesley. Wesley preached in the Parish Church 6th June, 1752. He visited again 8th April, 1753. On the last occasion there was opposition and Wesley was not allowed to preach in the church, so they adjourned to the Vicarage.

Chowbent (Atherton)

An early centre of Puritanism. A chapel was erected in 1645 and it was used for Puritan worship until 1662 and from 1672 to about 1720 when it was consecrated for Anglican use. The congregation then built the present chapel in 1721. A vestibule was added in 1901 but the building remains substantially unaltered including the three-decker pulpit.

Colne

The first evangelical preaching was by Wesley's former friend, Benjamin Ingham, in 1743 and one or two 'Inghamite' societies were established. John Wesley arrived in August 1748, when he encountered the Colne mob at Roughlee. The mob was organised by the Rev. George White, 'Commander in Chief' of His Majesty's Forces for the Defence of the Church of England. The preachers were roughly handled 'whilst Mr. White looked well-pleased . . . and attempted not to hinder them'. This was the fiercest opposition Wesley met in Lancashire. White was perpetual curate of Colne. In July 1759 Wesley preached in the town. After many difficulties, a chapel was built in 1776–7 in Colne Lane and in the same year Colne became the centre of an extensive circuit.

Davyhulme

An important Methodist centre for many years. A society existed in 1747, when John Bennet the preacher, was attacked by a violent mob. 'The bells were set ringing at Flixton and Eccles for joy that a Methodist had been taken, but it proved not according to expectation'. The Wesley Chapel was opened in 1779.

Droylsden

The Dukinfield Moravians (see below) migrated here in 1783 to found a settlement. This was completed here in 1785 and named Fairfield. It was one of three in England, and the pleasant old buildings still survive. The Moravian chapel was the first place of worship in Droylsden.

Mary Smith, wife of Robert Moffat and mother of David Livingstone's wife, was educated at the Moravian school in Fairfield.

Dukinfield

An early centre of 'dissent'. An independent congregation is said to have met in the chapel of Dukinfield Hall in the 1640's one of the earliest in England. Dukinfield Dissenters supported the Puritans who were ejected from their parishes; John Angier at Denton chapel was one of those ejected after 1662. A dissenting chapel was built in 1707 which afterwards became Unitarian. David Taylor (see Ashton) established a society in 1741 which joined the Moravians at the end of 1743. Dukinfield became the centre of Moravian work in Lancashire, Cheshire and Derbyshire and a chapel was built in 1751. The work in outlying areas gradually faded away and in 1783 the bulk of the congregation moved to Fairfield to found a settlement. A remnant continued to meet at Dukinfield, however, and the church was rebuilt in the 1850's. Charles Hindley, first M.P. for Ashton, was a prominent member of the congregation in the first half of the nineteenth century.

Elswick

A village in the Fylde which has a dissenting church which claims to trace its history to about 1650. An anniversary service is held in a great marquee each year at Whitsuntide. The church has always been associated with the family of Cuthbert Harrison, an ejected minister of 1662.

Goodshaw

The old Baptist chapel was built about 1760 and remains substantially unaltered. Although a new chapel was erected in Victorian times, the old chapel is still used for occasional services.

Haslingden

A Methodist society was founded in 1775 and the first chapel was built in 1786 by John Holden. Visited by Wesley in 1788 when he complained of the state of the road from Padiham to Haslingden: a new chapel was opened in 1798.

Hindley

The Hindley non-conformists continued to worship in the Episcopal Chapel, built in 1641, up to 1698 when it was consecrated. A new chapel was built for the non-conformists by Richard Crook of Abram, in 1700. This building is still used by the congregation.

Lancaster

This town is associated with George Fox and the early days of the Quaker movement. Fox was imprisoned in Lancaster Castle. A Presbyterian meeting-house is known to have existed in the seventeenth century. The Congregational Church is an interesting example of a fairly typical non-conformist meeting house.

Leigh (Shackerley)

Often visited by Methodist preachers on their way from Davyhulme to Bolton. The first Methodist society was formed in January 1748.

Liverpool (Toxteth)

The ancient chapel (near the Dingle) is one of the oldest dissenting chapels in the county. It was rebuilt in 1774. It has a tiny churchyard behind the chapel and, within, old box pews, galleries, and an eighteenth century pulpit.

Manchester

Methodism was established in the villages around Manchester before it took root in the city. Benjamin Ingham preached in 1742 in Long Millgate, and in 1743 John Nelson, the Methodist stone-mason, preached at Manchester cross. Charles Wesley came in January 1747 and as a result a society was formed by 'some young men'. John Wesley paid his first visit after 1738 and on 7th May, 1747, when he preached at Salford Cross. The society had several homes before taking the top floor of a house overlooking the Irwell. (The site is now occupied by W. H. Smith's in Blackfriars Street.) One preacher found '. . . the coals in one corner, the looms in another and I was in danger of breaking my neck in getting up to it'.

In 1750 a chapel was started in Birchin Lane, off Church Street. With Liverpool, this was the first Methodist chapel in Lancashire. A plaque in Church Street marks the spot today. In 1781 Birchin Lane chapel was replaced by a much larger chapel in Oldham Street on the site of the present Central Hall. Later chapels were built at Gravel Lane, Salford, in 1791, great Bridgewater Street 1801, Chancery Lane 1818 and in many other localities of Manchester.

Middleton

The first society was formed in 1760. Wesley preached here in April 1766 and the first chapel was built in Wood Street in 1805. The Sunday School is described in Samuel Bamford's 'Early Days'.

Oldham

This town was visited by Methodist lay preachers from about 1763 but a society was not established until 1774. Manchester Street chapel was opened 1790.

Greenacre Chapel is claimed to be a 'Five-Mile Act' meeting house set up for Robert Constantine who was ejected from Oldham Parish church in 1662.

Preston

The first Methodist centre was Brimicroft, six miles from Preston. Preaching had been established here before 1751. Societies were started at Ollerton in 1762 and at Walton-le-Dale in 1763, but not until about 1776 was a Methodist centre established in Preston. Wesley came in 1780 and again in 1781, 1784 and 1790. A room was hired in St. John Street for some years before a chapel was opened in Back Lane in 1787. Lune Street chapel was opened in 1817. A chapel was built at Leyland in 1814 at Golden Hill.

Poulton-le-Fylde

Methodism was late in reaching the Fylde. Although lay preachers toured the villages in the 1780's, Poulton was the only society in the area in 1810 with only ten members. The work revived in 1811 and chapels were built at Thornton in 1812 and at Poulton in 1819.

Ramsbottom (Dundee Lane)

The first congregation was formed in 1651 at Holcombe under the leadership of the Rev. Henry Pendlebury and they moved to Ramsbottom in 1712 when the present chapel was built. The congregation did not change to Unitarianism as many other dissenting bodies did and it is one of the oldest Presbyterian congregations in England.

Rivington

One of the most unspoiled places of worship in Lancashire. The founding dates from 1662 but the chapel was built in 1703. One of the chief supporters when it was built was Lord Willoughby of Parham and his special pew can be seen today: both exterior and interior remain unchanged.

Rochdale

A Methodist society was formed by John Bennet in 1746. Wesley paid his first visit 18th October, 1749. An early preaching place was Bank House, near Bagslate two miles north of the town. A room was taken in 1760 on the site of the present Town Hall, then a room in Blackwall Lane until a room was opened in Toad Lane in 1770. Wesley preached here in April 1770. A Sunday School was begun in 1784. Union Street chapel was opened in 1793 but in 1806 came the secession of the 'Cookites' which led to the formation of Providence Chapel, High Street, which afterwards became independent. At Newchurch, the Cookites became Unitarian. In 1834 there was another division at Union Street when the greater part of the congregation left to form Baillie Street Free Methodist Chapel.

St. Helens

Ormskirk Street Congregational Church is an example of what happened in some parts of Lancashire at the ejectment of 1662. The minister at St. Helen's Chapel of Ease was in reality a dissenter but remained undisturbed and was not ejected. When he died in 1710 the new incumbent was a member of the established church and the dissenters left to start a new chapel.

Tockholes (near Blackburn)

This chapel has a continuous history reaching back to the days of the Civil War. Its earlier ministers were all trained at various Dissenting Academies.

Ulverston

This place has associations with George Fox and some of his relics are preserved (a Bible and a chair). There was no non-conformist place of worship until the mid-eighteenth century. At Tottlebank, a few miles away, is a Baptist Church founded in 1669 which is a very good example of a dissenting Meeting House. Wesley and Whitefield both preached at Ulverston and nearby is Swarthmore Hall where Judge Fell, Oliver Cromwell's Chancellor of the Duchy of Lancaster, lived. His wife became a Quaker.

Warrington

Wesley preached here for the first time 14th April, 1755, and the second time 2nd May, 1757, '. . . to a wild staring people, who seemed just ripe for mischief'. The town lay on his route from Chester to Liverpool and so received many visits. Later it became a stronghold of Independent Methodism. The town is also noteworthy for housing one of the foremost Dissenting Academies under Joseph Priestley, who is remembered, among other things, for his discovery of oxygen.

Wheatley (Burnley)

This town has one of the few 'Inghamite' churches still surviving. Such churches were founded by Benjamin Ingham, a travelling preacher about the year 1742. The chapel at Wheatley was built in 1750. It has since been rebuilt but in the same style as before. There is an extensive 'Inghamite' burial ground.

Wigan (Park Lane)

The chapel was built in 1697 for the followers of James Wood who was ejected from Ashton-in-Makerfield Episcopal Chapel in 1662.

At Tunley, Mossy Lea, Wrighton, is the oldest Presbyterian chapel in England.

NOTES ON THE DISSENTING MEETING HOUSES

The 'Inghamites' were the followers of the Rev. Benjamin Ingham, who was a colleague of Wesley at Oxford and in Georgia, and who began evangelical preaching in the West Riding in 1737. He was greatly influenced by the Moravians and handed over his converts to them in 1742 – the origin of Moravian work in Yorkshire today. However, he later left the Moravians and founded a 'connexion' of societies on both sides of the Pennines. These called themselves Inghamites, and a few remain, notably at Wheatley and Kendal. For more information about Ingham see:

Tyerman, L.   The Oxford Methodists.
(There are also the Inghamite MSS at the Ryland's Library, Manchester.)

The 'Cookites' were followers of Joseph Cooke of Rochdale, who left Methodism in 1806. His followers built him a chapel in Rochdale, but they soon dwindled in numbers. A full account is given in:

McLachlan, H.   The Methodist Unitarians.

Samuel Bamford was an early Radical and Chartist, who describes his childhood in Middleton in the 1790's in a book:

Bamford, Samuel. Early Days.

Bamford, Samuel. Passages in the life of a Radical (1841).
(In this book he describes the events at 'Peterloo'.)

NOTE ON THE MORE HISTORIC SCHOOLS OF LANCASHIRE

Many of the more historic schools in Lancashire were church foundations, the deeds of which go back to Elizabethan times or beyond. An account of these schools is given in the publication:

Jordan, W. K.   The Social Institutions of Lancashire.
(Printed for the Chetham Society at Manchester 1962.)

APPENDIX 'D'

THE COMPARATIVE STUDY OF RELIGIONS
by the late
Rev. Professor F. H. Smith, D.D.

(1) Religion and Religions

Religion is a universal experience of which actual religions are concrete expressions. The basic fact of religion is the same everywhere, namely, 'reverence for the supernatural order enriching the natural order, and expressed in acts of devotion, as the source of spiritual, moral and material betterment'. Actual concrete religions, however, are not the same everywhere. They are differing interpretations on this universal experience which find expression in the natural order as institutions or systems.

The untutored soul bears witness to natural religion. Tertullian, the Church Father, was even prepared to call the 'soul naturally Christian', but this religion became something different as it 'had been shaped in the schools, trained in libraries, fed in Attic Academies and Porches' (de testimonio animae, chap. 1). Religion as a primary fundamental fact makes the whole world akin, but as interpreted in systems, religions divide the world.

It is essential first to be clear as to this distinction between 'religion' and 'religions'. The Christian exponent need have no fear in regarding religion, in a true sense, as a fundamental fact underlying all religions, and as a real point of contact between them and Christianity. There could be no comparison of religions, if there were no basic universal underlying them all. The universal fact of religion is testimony to the Christian conviction that there is one God and Father of all who has not left Himself without witness in the human soul.

(2) Degrees of Truth

Why not then, it might be urged, aim at one universal religion in terms of this basic fact by eliminating all the differences in the actual religions? This would only court failure because (a) as a universal concept religion is an abstraction from the actual concrete religions and does not exist apart from them, (b) this universal, shorn of all its particular characteristics, only represents religion in its lowest terms and is too vague to stand for a living religion, and (c) religion is known best in its richest expressions as concrete systems. Our task as students of 'the comparative study of religions' is to show that Christianity, as a concrete religion, is the richest expression, satisfying in the highest degree all that is potentially involved in the universal fact of religion. Christianity claims indeed to be unique in its conviction that God became man in Christ to reconcile the world unto Himself. The Christian student might indicate, for example, that the Christian Incarnation is the only satisfactory answer to the universal spiritual quest. If other religions point to Christ, we need not deny to them degrees of truth in so far as they more or less adequately or inadequately express in concrete teaching and life the meaning and significance of the underlying universal. The ethical monotheism of Amos, for example, bears a higher imprint of truth than the omnipotent monotheism of Islam, and both of these a higher degree of truth than the polytheism of the Homeric Epics. But in so far as Homer expurgated the ancient Hellenic myths of immoral rites, and presented the Olympian gods as 'personal and reasoning rulers, like men but unspeakably higher' (Gilbert Murray) in this fact we can still recognise a certain measure of truth.

In view then of the universal fact of religion we shall not summarily dismiss non-Christian religions as entirely false, nor can we, in view of the varying interpretations, maintain the superficial judgement that they are all equally true.

(3) The Lower Cultures

If the universal in all faiths fails to satisfy the highest reaches of the spiritual life, much less can we expect the religion of the lower races to satisfy us. Nevertheless, there has been a tendency for scholars to judge religion by its elementary expressions. Reinach's definition of religion as 'a sum of scruples which impede the free exercise of the faculties' (Orpheus) takes primitive tabu as characteristic of religion. Or Father W. Schmidt, with a blind eye to lower elements, interprets primitive 'high gods', such as Daramulum of S.E. Australia, as monotheistic deities. There is, of course, no reason why the primitive should not be as near to God as the modern city worker, but his interpretation may express less. We shall not, however, idealise him as in a golden age of perfection, nor depreciate him as without any visio dei at all.

Strictly the term 'primitive' means a member of the lower races surviving into historical times, but it is often applied by a tour de force to prehistoric man at the dawn of human development, who being prehistoric, can only by the nature of the case, be hypothetically reconstructed. Arrow heads and other artifacts tell us only a little (though they tell us something of his hopes and fears). The logical student will keep his picture of 'primitive' man quite distinct from his ideal reconstruction of 'primaeval' man, only using carefully chosen analogies from the former to illustrate tentatively the latter. Professor John Murphy's 'Lamps of Anthropology' is a useful introduction to the study of primaeval man, through the metaphor of horizons, as primitive, tribal, civilised and later prophetic.

Three main theories have been put forward on the nature of primitive religion as possibly throwing light on archaic or primaeval religion: (a) mana, supernatural impersonal power manifesting itself in strange and marvellous objects or in remarkable individuals (Codrington, Marett), (b) animism, spirits or separable souls animating natural objects (Tylor, Karsten), and (c) primitive monotheism, and belief in one God (Lang, Schmidt). Briefly, we might say that mana or any of its higher correlates (holy, sacred, numinous) actually underlies all religion and is not in itself peculiarly primitive; animism is very widespread, but the dualism of spirit and matter is not primaeval; many primitives find it difficult to distinguish soul from matter; monotheism, as a clearly thought-out belief in one God, to the exclusion of all other deities or spirits, can hardly be true of the elementary mind, which relies mainly on the manifold of sense experience and can only with difficulty affirm a unity behind the manifold. But inasmuch as man by his very nature is a 'thinking' creature, as testified even by lower palaeolithic remains, there is every reason to affirm his capacity from the earliest times, to transcend sense-experience in a vague way at least, by a belief in the supernatural whether as a manifold or undefined unity; 'a beyond that is akin'. The line of progress would not be a series of clear ideas but a progress from vague to distinct. In any event origins do not tell us so much as the whole process does, later stages bringing to clearer light what in the beginning was only implicit. At the same time we cannot regard progress as inevitable, in the course of later interpretation and practice much error has also occurred.

(4) The Higher Religions

The more developed religions include the ancient civilisations; Sumeria, Egypt, Greece, Rome and also the living religions, of which the chief are Shinto, Confucianism, Taoism, Hinduism, Parsiism (Zoroastrianism), Judaism, Buddhism, Islam. The first six of the living religions are primarily national or racial, the last two, with Christianity, claim, at the outset, universality.

With regard to these great surviving religions (on which we shall now concentrate) we shall need to remind ourselves that specific doctrines can only be understood on the background of the particular religion as a whole in which the doctrine occurs. Also that religions as concrete wholes can only, if at all, adequately be understood through a study of their historical development. For example, the Hindu worship of bhakti (loving trust and faith in deity) must be interpreted in the light of Hinduism as a whole which (a) is polytheistic and (b) moves far more in the direction of an impersonal idea of God than to the belief in a Heavenly Father and (c) lays more stress on ecstatic union or identity with God rather than moral likeness to God. Further, the religion as a whole must be studied historically through the Vedic and Epic literature, on to the sectarian movements, if the idea of bhakti is to be at all adequately understood. It is important, therefore, that as much of the history of religion as possible should be attempted before making comparisons of particular doctrines, to avoid unfair play in argument on the one hand, and superficial comparisons with Christianity on the other.

(5) National Religions

(a) *Shinto*

Of the national religions Shinto of Japan is primarily a form of religious patriotism, which since the restoration of the Meiji dynasty (1868) has held, in an exaggerated form, the divine status of the Emperor. The sacred literature maintains that the Mikado has descended from the sun-goddess Amaterasu. The religion is also humanitarian in character. Man is not clearly conscious of the need of God, but affirms the sufficiency of his own innate capacities and of his natural conscience. There is little sense of sin and practically no moral code. Shinto has depended on Confucianism and Buddhism from China for its ethical development. Bushido, 'the soul of Japan', its warrior code is a development of three strands, Shinto loyalty, Confucian Ethic and Zen Buddhist discipline.

(b) *Confucianism*

Confucianism is also humanitarian in character, and today is little more than an ethical system. Confucius (c. 551–479 B.C.) introduced a deeper sense of moral responsibility, by emphasising the power of example on the part of the ruler, and the spirit of reverence towards those in authority. He held that God (T'ien) was the author of the moral sense in man, but, as an ethical teacher, he actually started from jen or fellow-feeling as natural to man. His refusal to speculate on or discuss the nature of God turned men's thoughts to the natural ethic of human endeavour rather than to the conscious need of divine grace.

(c) *Taoism*

The Chinese sister-religion of Taoism was in origin a philosophic mysticism. Lao-tze, an elder contemporary of Confucius, deprecated the Confucian effort to attain goodness as unnatural moralising, and urged on his disciples that no effort was needed if a man allowed the Tao (the first principle of all things) to work in the heart. Effort of will led to artificial virtue, spontaneity produced natural goodness. As time went on his Tao-mysticism absorbed a vast number of the crudest magical practices, which converted a not unattractive mysticism into a degenerate system of magic, relieved only slightly by an attempt to moralise religion.

(d) *Hinduism*

This religion in its normal expression holds that Spirit (Brahman) is alone real, but all methods of representing the divine from the simplest idolatry upwards are justified as relative truth or steps on the way to ultimate identity with Brahman. Hinduism can therefore hold in solution the most diverse systems of thought as concessions to human limitations. Brahman, the only strict Reality, is impersonal, but men have nevertheless sought a personal God as the only real satisfaction of spiritual needs. Consequently the history of the sectarian movement is largely an account of the attempts to conceive deity as personal. Thus men thought of Rama as the divine in human form.

As a father to his children to his loving men he came,
Blessed our homes and maids and matrons till our infants lisped his name.
For our humble woes and troubles Rama hath the ready tear,
To our humble tales of suffering Rama lends his willing ear.

But there is always present, in view of the religion as a whole, an uncertain note; is God ultimately personal? Can the passive self-existent Brahman really care for man?

(e) *Zoroastrianism*

The Parsi community in India as heirs to the teaching of Zarathushtra (date uncertain; between 1000 and 600 B.C.) worship one God symbolised by the fire. This God (Ahura Mazda) is good in the ethical sense, but the use of prayers in a dead language, and of a formal ritual, with only a minimum of religious instruction, holds the religion back, while its unmissionary exclusiveness prevents Parsiism from being a spiritual force in the world.

(f) *Judaism*

The religion of the Jews creates a serious problem for the Christian, because its unique past made it the herald and cradle of Christianity. But since the parting of the ways after Our Lord's crucifixion and the fall of Jerusalem (A.D. 70) Judaism has dug itself in as a book religion, the religion of the Torah or the Law, as against the Christian creed that God has spoken to man in His Son. Judaism is primarily a way of conduct as revealed by God. It is 'loyalty to God and His Law'. Our aim as students will be to show as sympathetically as possible that Christ has fulfilled the highest hopes of the Old Testament prophets and the Messianic ideals of Israel.

(6) The Universal Religions

(a) *Buddhism*

The universal religions make an appeal to men, independently of nation or race on the ground that they supply the answer to universal spiritual needs. Even national religions do not necessarily limit their appeal to the nation. Radhakrishnan, for example, puts forward today a philosophical Hinduism as a world-view for universal acceptance as religion behind all religions. But Hinduism as a system, with its caste rules and polytheism, is essentially a national religion. Gotama Buddha, however, broke with Hinduism and proclaimed a message for all. Life, he affirmed, is fundamentally bound up with suffering, because it is a thirst for individual expression which can never be satisfied. The only way to end suffering is to end the thirst for life. Buddhism is the negative way of annihilation of all desire except the aspiration for the peace of nirvana. It means the destruction of the natural gifts of life, rather than an attempt to regulate and discipline them. The method (mental training) is a purely human one, for no deity or priest can help man to achieve this end, beyond preaching dharma or spiritual law (religion). Dharma indeed took the place of God. What Buddha himself taught is not crystal clear, but this brief account is substantially what the earliest Pali canon teaches. (See book at end of bibliography for Mrs. Rhys David's reinterpretation of Buddha's teaching.)

Developed or Mahayana Buddhism, as taught in China and Japan, holds that supreme Buddhas, for there are now thought to be many others in addition to Gotama, are manifestations of the eternal Buddha principle or Absolute, an impersonal Reality underlying all things. These Buddhas, or more correctly bodhisattvas (especially Amida of Japan) because of their great purity can save men who put their faith in them. But, as with the Indian Brahman, there is no certainty that this Eternal Buddha Principle is personal, and although in the Pure Land Sects countless Buddhists pay homage to a personal Buddha, the real thinkers of Mahayana Buddhism maintain that personality is only an appearance of the Absolute and is not characteristic of its ultimate nature.

(b) *Islam*

This religion contrasts strikingly with Buddhism. Buddhism is a philosophical religion of redemption from suffering, Islam is a practical religion of definite concrete acts. The first is the religion of the introvert, the second of the extrovert. The pre-eminent message of Islam is the unity of God (Allah), its way of life is absolute submission to Him, testified by recital of creed, ritual prayer, giving of alms, fast and pilgrimage to Mecca. God's ways are inscrutable, His doings are not explicable to the human intellect, His commands must be obeyed, even if they violate the intellect or moral sense of man, because Allah's will is paramount. Consequently, though the Qur'an contains ethical commands, it cannot be said that God's nature is primarily ethical. Whatever Allah commands is good because He wills it, He does not will it because His nature is good. 'God misleadeth whom He will, and whom He will doth He guide aright', (Sura 74). God's chief attribute is Power – the unity of omnipotence – which overrides all His other attributes. Power may often be tempered by mercy, but mercy is subordinate to it. Muhammad could not say 'God is love' nor could he pray 'Our Father'.

(c) *Christianity*

Christianity claims to be universal as the supreme revelation of God in a Son (Hebrews 1 v. 2) reconciling the world unto Himself. "God loved the world so much that he gave his only Son, that everyone who has faith in him may not die but have external life". (John 3 v. 16). His Spirit, mediated normally through the Fellowship of the Church, His Body, convicts man of sin and witnesses to the power of a new life of grace by communion with the living Christ, dying and rising with Him in the power of His Resurrection. Christianity is not primarily a system of thought but a Gospel of redemption from sin. God seeks man, redeems him and calls him to life in His Kingdom, where obedience to His will demands sacrifice in a world-wide mission of service to all men as potential children of God.

This new life in Christ involves at the outset certain doctrines. Our first duty is to mediate Christ to others by our life, our second might be to show that this new life depends on certain beliefs, viz., the personality of God, His ethical nature, His rule in the heart, and the redemptive power of suffering, all of which meet in the doctrine of the Incarnation and Atonement, and are conserved by the doctrine of the Holy Trinity: One God in three Persons, Father, Son and Holy Spirit.

(7) Doctrines

(a) *Revelation*

After a careful study of the history of religions as systems we can apply ourselves to the comparison of particular doctrines, such as Revelation, God, Human Nature and Salvation. These four are chosen here as leading examples for study.

The naturalistic religions of Shinto and Confucianism are hardly aware of the need of revelation. Man is naturally in touch with God and does not stand in need of grace. In primitive (Hinayana) Buddhism and Taoism revelation means intuitive insight by mystic sympathy with the universe, e.g., insight into the fact of suffering and its cure, or in Taoism and spontaneity of Tao. These are not revelations from a personal deity. Hindu revelation is that of the written text of the Vedic documents as inherently divine; which led later either to the repetition of magical mantras, or to the arbitrary deduction of 'orthodox' philosophies from the text. In Zoroastrianism and Judaism God speaks through his messengers the prophets. Islam is also a prophetic religion, but much is made by the orthodox of the exact verbal sacredness of the text, as the source of authority in religion.

The Hindu and Mahayana Buddhist Jodo sects hint at the idea of incarnation. But neither is clearly an historical incarnation. The Hindu avatars of Rama and Krishna are almost entirely poetic idealisations and the manifestation of Amida, as compassionate Father, is a picture of the imagination. Each has indeed a message; Rama on the discipline of suffering, Krishna as to caste duty, and Amida as to the all-sufficiency of grace. All teach loving trust (bhakti) on deity. But in no case is there an essential revelation of the fulness of the Godhead bodily, for the highest is normally conceived of as impersonal.

The Christian Gospels present Christ, as the revealer of the Father, and giving His life a ransom for many, the historical authenticity of which is beyond doubt. The revelation is that of a personal God in a personal life. 'He that hath seen Me hath seen the Father.'

(b) *God*

The chief religions can be classified into those which maintain the personality of God — Shinto, Confucianism, Zoroastrianism, Judaism and Islam, and those which normally interpret the Highest as impersonal — Taoism, Hinduism and Buddhism.

As regards the first class, Shinto gives an elementary mythological account of many Gods. Confucianism presents God as a Supreme Spirit (Shang-ti) above many spiritual beings. Parsi Zoroastrianism is a somewhat cold theism not entirely freed from a magical ritual, the God of Islam is a capricious numinous being hardly amenable to reason or morality.

Judaism is the only example of an ethical monotheism formative of future religion. The monotheism of Akhnatron of Egypt faded away after his reign, the potential monotheism of Zarathushtra became dim in post-Gothic dualism and magic, Islam learnt her monotheism from Judaism and Christianity, Sikh monotheism in its turn was inspired by Indian Islam.

As regards Taoism, Hinduism and Buddhism, the question arises, can abstract principles such as Tao, Brahman and Dharma adequately account for the riches of personal life and personal values (truth, goodness, etc.) ? God normally stands for the highest we can conceive, and more — He is the guarantee that our highest values are not illusions but standards of life. Can He be such a guarantee if He is not at least personal, even if He is immeasurably more ? Christianity stands for the conviction that the idea of Fatherhood is a true analogy for understanding the divine nature.

(c) *Human Nature*

Shinto and Confucianism regard man as ethically good by nature and so self-sufficient. If these two religions are humanistic, the three religions of Taoism, Hinduism and Buddhism are dehumanistic; for Taoism would eliminate will-effort, Hinduism the individual self and Buddhism natural desires. Theocentric religions, such as Zoroastrianism, Judaism, and Islam aim at the salvation of the whole man by recognising the need for God. But emphasis on this need varies. Zoroastrianism falls back mainly on man's power to choose the right, Judaism maintains that man still has a good imagination (yetzer) to balance his evil imagination, and Islam regards man as weak rather than a fallen creature.

Christianity stands alone in the conviction that 'original sin' in man demands for him a Redeemer. Man 'is very far gone from original righteousness, so that the flesh lusteth always contrary to the spirit' and redemption means the healing of the whole man; body, soul and spirit, there is no dehumanisation.

(d) *Salvation*

Legalistic religions regard obedience, or human effort, whether ritual or ethical, as the ruling condition of salvation. Redemptive religions provide the means of salvation; man responds to this gift of grace.

The legalistic religions are Shinto, Confucianism, Zoroastrianism, Judaism and Islam. Shinto involves obedience to certain ritual at the Purification Ceremony (Ohoharahi), Confucianism demands uprightness in the sacrificer as the condition of a successful sacrifice. Zoroastrianism makes the condition of salvation a preponderance of good thoughts, words and deeds, Judaism stresses obedience to the Mosaic Law, Islam obedience to Allah's commands.

The redemptive religions are Taoism, Hinduism and Buddhism. In pure Taoism the supernatural Tao does everything, man remains inactive. In Hinduism man gains enlightenment in a kind of trance (samadhi), so in primitive Buddhism. When deliverance really comes man is in a passive mental state. Later Jodo and Shin Buddhism insist on a passive faith apart from works ; Amida's grace is all-sufficient, man is passive recipient.

Some of the conditions from which salvation rescues a man are : Shinto from ceremonial defilement, Confucian State worship (now defunct) from material distress, Zoroastrianism (in the main) from demonic impurity, Judaism from exile or other punishment for sin, Islam from hell, Taoism (as it developed) from malevolent evil spirits, Hinduism from rebirth and mundane limitations, Buddhism from rebirth, desire and suffering, Christianity from bondage to sin.

Christianity is par excellence a redemptive religion. God has provided for man in the Atonement of the Cross the means of salvation. Man is 'justified freely by grace, through the redemption that is in Christ Jesus' (Romans 3 v. 24). But man is not passive as in Taoism, or in a mystic trance as in Hinduism or Buddhism, nor does he exhibit a mere passive faith. It is active appropriation, suffering with Christ and rising with Him to newness of life. Christianity recognises that sin is rebellion against God, an outrage on His holiness, breaking of fellowship with Him. Salvation is from sin and restoration to divine fellowship. Justification means that God pardons and accepts the sinner, in that His faith is a token of what he can become through the active appropriation of grace. The disciple does not as in Buddhism merely seek relief from suffering. He learns that God suffers, and knows enough, at least, to realise that suffering has a meaning in the nature of things.

(8) Conclusion

The inevitable brevity of this essay has only allowed, of course, for reference to salient points and has also given the appearance of super-ficial generalisation. The writer has, however, endeavoured to make no judgement without careful thought and urges the reader to do the same. In any event, the above is only intended to supply sign-posts in what might be a bewildering forest, the provisional character of which is subject to revision in the light of fresh facts and further study.

APPENDIX 'E'

GENERAL INFORMATION ON RELIGIOUS EDUCATION

A BIBLIOGRAPHY

SOURCES OF INFORMATION ON ART AND VISUAL AIDS ADDRESSES OF SOCIETIES AND ORGANISATIONS

Books about religious education

Acland, R.	We Teach Them Wrong	Gollancz
Acland, R.	Curriculum or Life A sequel to the above book.	Gollancz
Cully, Iris V.	The Dynamics of Christian Education A stimulating book by an American educationalist.	Westminster Press *
Clarke, F.	Freedom in the Educative Society A comparison of theories of education.	U.L.P.*
Cox, E.	Sixth Form Religion.	S.C.M. Press
Goldman, R. J.	Religious Thinking from Childhood to Adolescence.	Routledge, Kegan * Paul
Goldman, R. J.	Readiness for Religion	Routledge, Kegan * Paul
Havighurst, R.	Human Development and Education A clearly written account of the tasks to be faced by teachers at each stage of a child's development.	Longmans Green *
Hilliard, F. H.	The Teacher and Religion A discussion of religious education from an educational point of view.	Jas. Clarke
Hubery, S. D.	The Experiential Approach to Christian Education.	N.C.E.C.
Hyde, K. E.	Religious Learning in Adolescence An account of research into the communication of religious ideas and attitudes among children of secondary age.	Oliver and Boyd * (Published for the Birmingham Institute of Education.)
Jeffreys, M. V. C.	Glaucon	Pitman
Jeffreys, M. V. C.	Personal Values in the Modern World.	Pelican Original *
Loukes, H.	Teenage Religion An enquiry into the attitudes of mainly secondary modern pupils towards religion.	S.C.M. Press 1961
Loukes, H.	New Ground in Christian Education A sequel to 'Teenage Religion': an outline of a practical approach to religious education in schools.	S.C.M. Press 1965
Madge, Violet	Children in Search of Meaning	S.C.M. Press 1965
Ross, J.	Groundwork of Educational Psychology	Harrap

204

Sheffield Institute of Education	Religious Education in Secondary Schools. An enquiry and a survey of attainment in religious knowledge.	Nelson *
Tillich, Paul	Theology of Culture	O.U.P.
Wickham, E. R.	Encounter with Modern Society	Lutterworth

The Bible – versions and abridgements

Bibles	The Bible, Authorised Version, edited by John Stirling.	British and Foreign Bible Society
	Holy Bible (A.V.)	Epworth
	Holy Bible (A.V.)	Lutterworth
	Holy Bible, Revised Standard Version.	Nelson
	Collin's Revised Standard Bible	Collins
	The Bible in Basic English	C.U.P.
	The Holy Bible translated by Ronald Knox.	Burns and Oates
	The Shorter Knox Bible (An abridgement of the Old Testament translated by Ronald Knox.)	Burns and Oates
	The Beginner's Bible (A shortened Bible in modern English by Margherita Fanchiotti. This edition has an all round value for use in secondary schools. It is well illustrated with good engravings, is arranged chronologically and has notes giving basic information with a commentary.)	O.U.P.
	The Shorter Bible, Heaton, E. W. & Lawson, W. S. (A selection of passages from the Bible.)	Nelson
	The Nelson Authorised Version (Selected passages from the A.V. for use in school and home.)	Nelson
	The Children's Bible	O.U.P.
	A First Bible ; an abridgement by James Reeves.	Heinemann
	The Little Bible	O.U.P.
	The Moffatt Translation of the Bible, 2nd edition.	Hodder and Stoughton
	The New Cambridge Picture Bible	Epworth
	A Short Bible, arranged by Austin Farrer from the A.V.	Collins
	The Story in Scripture, a shorter version of the Revised Standard Version.	Nelson
The Bible Apocrypha	The Apocrypha A.V.	O.U.P.
	The Apocrypha R.S.V.	Nelson
New Testament	The New Testament in Modern English. Translated by Jas. Moffatt.	E.U.P.
	New English Bible, New Testament	O.U.P.
	New English Bible, Library edition	O.U.P.
	New English Bible, New Testament (A smaller popular edition without full notes.)	O.U.P.
	Clarendon Bible, New Testament – 8 vols.	O.U.P.
	The New Testament in Modern English. Translated by J. B. Phillips.	Bles

Acts	The Holy Spirit in the Acts of the Apostles by J. H. E. Hull.	Lutterworth
	The Acts of the Apostles by St. Luke, translated by C. H. Rieu.	Penguin
Epistle	The Young Church in Action, translated by J. B. Phillips.	Collins
Gospels	The Gospel in Many Tongues	British and Foreign Bible Society
	The Four Gospels, by E. V. Rieu	Penguin
	New World, by Alan Dale. There are five books in the series which have a special value in terms of their translation and quite outstanding illustrations.	O.U.P.
	Gospel Parallels, 2nd revised edition	Nelson
	Jesus Christ : an illustrated life of Christ with text from the New English Bible.	Prentice Hall *
	The Gospels translated into modern English by J. B. Phillips.	Collins
	Gospel according to St. Matthew — volume F (an A.V. with introduction and notes by F. C. Grant — Annotated Bible Series).	Eyre & Spottiswoode *
	St. Luke's Life of Christ, translated into modern English by J. B. Phillips.	Collins
	The Synoptic Gospels — arranged by J. M. Thompson.	O.U.P.
Bible Old Testament	Clarendon Bible, Old Testament, volumes 1–6.	O.U.P.
Psalms	Make His Praise Glorious. A selection from the Psalms.	Blandford *
	The Revised Psalter	S.P.C.K.

Books of reference

Black, M. & Rowley, H. H.	Peake's Commentary on the Bible Revised edition.	Nelson
Clarke, W. K. L.	Concise Bible Commentary	S.P.C.K.
Cruden, A.	Cruden's Concordance	Epworth *
Davies, G. H. & Richardson, Alan	The Teacher's Commentary — 9th edition.	S.C.M. *
Neil, Wm.	A One Volume Bible Commentary	Hodder & Stoughton
	The Cambridge New English Bible Commentaries.	C.U.P.
	The Layman's Bible Commentaries	S.C.M. *
	The Torch Bible Commentaries	S.C.M. *
	The Penguin Gospel Commentaries	Penguin
	Black's Bible Dictionary.	A. & C. Black

Books about the Bible

It is only possible to give a very short list out of a wide selection of books. Books for use in connection with the syllabus are given with each phase or section.

Abba, R.	The Nature and Authority of the Bible. (A scholarly book which relates the authority of the Bible to present day issues.)	J Clarke
Barclay, W.	The Making of the Bible	Lutterworth
Bouquet, A. C.	Everyday Life in New Testament Times.	Batsford

Bruce, F. F.	The English Bible	Lutterworth
Dodd, C. H.	The Bible Today (A short but authoritative account of what the Bible means in terms of Christianity.)	C.U.P.
Deursen, A. Van	Illustrated Dictionary of Bible Manners and Customs. (A useful reference book both for teachers and pupils.)	Marshall Morgan
Heaton, A.	Everyday Life in Old Testament Times.	Batsford *
Herklots, H. G. G.	How the Bible Came to Us (A scholarly account of the sources on which the books of the Bible are based up to and including the Dead Sea Scrolls.)	Pelican *
Kenyon, Sir F.	The Story of the Bible	Murray
Murray, A. V.	How to know your Bible	Allen & Unwin *
Neil, W.	The Rediscovery of the Bible	Hodder & Stoughton

Geography and Atlases

Gröllenberg	The Shorter Atlas of the Bible (A good introduction to the history, geography, and archaeology of Palestine mainly for teachers.)	Nelson
Hilliard, F. H.	Behold the Land ; a Pictorial Atlas of the Bible.	G. Philip
Sanders, E. M.	The Holy Land. Books 1 and 2 Simple and useful for class use.	G. Philip *
	Westminster Smaller Bible Atlas Suitable for class use.	S.C.M. Press

Archaeology

Woolley, L.	Digging Up The Past	Penguin
Wright, G. E.	Biblical Archaeology	Duckworth
	Studies in Biblical Archaeology (Five books covering the periods from the Flood to the Temple at Jerusalem.)	S.C.M. Press *

Christian Belief – New Testament

Barclay, W.	The Master's Men	S.C.M.
Bruce, F. F.	The Spreading Flame	Patern Press *
Caird, G. B.	The Apostolic Age	Duckworth
Dodd, C. H.	The Apostolic Preaching and its Development.	Hodder & Stoughton
Fuller, R. H.	The New Testament in Current Study	S.C.M. 1963 *
Fuller, R. H.	Interpreting the Miracles	S.C.M. Press
Grant, R. M.	An Historical Introduction to the New Testament.	Collins
Grant, R. M.	The Formation of the New Testament.	Hutchinson
Hunter, A. M.	Introducing the New Testament, 2nd edition.	S.C.M. Press *

Hunter, A. M.	Interpreting the New Testament (1900–50).	S.C.M. Press *
Hunter, A. M.	Interpreting the Parables	S.C.M. Press
Hunter, A. M.	The Work and Words of Jesus	S.C.M. Press
Hunter, A. M.	Design for Life	S.C.M. Press
Hunter, A. M.	Introducing New Testament Theology.	S.C.M. Press
Jeremias, J.	The Parables of Jesus	S.C.M. Press *
Kelly, J. N. D.	Early Christian Creeds	A. & C. Black
Lewis, C. S.	Mere Christianity	Fontana
Lewis, G. P.	An Approach to Christian Doctrine	Epworth
Manson, T. W.	Studies in the Gospels and Epistles, edited by M. Black.	Manchester University Press
Manson, T. W.	The Servant Messiah	C.U.P. *
Manson, T. W.	The Teaching of Jesus, 2nd edition 1935.	C.U.P. *
Manson, T. W.	The Sayings of Jesus, 1949	C.U.P.
McNeile, A. H.	An Introduction to the Study of the New Testament, 2nd edition revised by C. S. C. Williams, 1953.	O.U.P.
Ramsey, A. M.	The Resurrection of Christ	Geoffrey Bles
Richardson, A.	An Introduction to the Theology of the New Testament.	S.C.M.
Richardson, A.	The Miracle Stories of the Gospels	S.C.M.
Scott, C. A.	Christianity According to St. Paul (reprint 1961).	C.U.P. *
Stauffer, E.	New Testament Theology	S.C.M. *
Stauffer, E.	Jesus and His Story	S.C.M. *
Taylor, V.	The Gospels ; a Short Introduction	Epworth*
Taylor, V.	The Person of Christ in New Testament Teaching.	MacMillan
Taylor, V.	Jesus and His Sacrifice	Epworth *

Christian Belief – Old Testament

Anderson, S. W.	History and Religion of Israel	O.U.P.
Anderson, S. W.	A Critical Introduction to the Old Testament.	Duckworth
Anderson, B. W.	The Living World of the Old Testament.	Longmans
Bright, J.	The History of Israel	S.C.M.
Jones, E.	The Cross in the Psalms	Ind. Press
Jones, E.	The Triumph of Job	S.C.M. *
Knight, S. A. F.	A Christian Theology of the Old Testament.	S.C.M. *
Kapel, A. S.	Israel	Blackwell
Martin-Acland, R.	A Light to the Nations	Oliver & Boyd *
Robinson, H. W.	The Cross in the Old Testament	S.C.M. *
Robinson, H. W.	The Religious Ideas of the Old Testament.	S.C.M. *
Robinson, T. H.	Peoples and Prophecy in Ancient Israel.	Duckworth

Robinson, T. H.	Poetry of the Old Testament	Duckworth
Rowley, H. H.	The Fall of Israel	S.C.M. *
Rowley, H. H.	The Old Testament and Modern Study.	O.U.P.
Russell, D. S.	Between the Testaments	S.C.M.
Skinner, J.	Prophecy and Religion	C.U.P.
Thomas, D. Winton	Documents from Old Testament Times.	Nelson

Some general books on Christian Belief

Bailey, A. E.	The Gospel in Hymns	Scribner
Leeuwen, Arend	Christianity in World History	Lutterworth
Robinson, J. A. T.	Honest to God	S.C.M.
Robinson, J. A. T.	The New Reformation	S.C.M.
Robinson, J. A. T.	This I Can't Believe	S.C.M.*
Vidler, Alec	Christian Belief	S.C.M.*
Whale, J. S.	Christian Doctrine	Fontana*

THE COMPARATIVE STUDY OF WORLD RELIGIONS

The book referred to in the text of the Appendix on Comparative Religions ('The Comparative Study of Religions' by F. H. Smith, D.D., Appendix 'D') is :

Rhys Davids, C.A.F.	Outlines of Buddhism	Methuen*

Some recent publications

Bouquet, A. C.	Christian Faith and Non-Christian Religions.	Nisbet
Dewick, E. C.	The Christian Attitude to Other Religions.	C.U.P.*
Hilliard, F. H.	Teaching Children about World Religions.	Harrap
Micklem, N.	Religion (An introduction to the vital element in religious experience.)	O.U.P.*
Luce, H. K.	The Religions of Mankind	Christophers
Neill, S.	Christian Faith and Other Faiths	O.U.P.
Phillips, G. E.	The Religions of the World (A brief outline of the non-Christian religions.)	R.E.P.*
Robinson, T. H.	A Short Comparative History of Religions. (A review of primitive religions, animism, polytheism, monotheism, Islam and Christianity.)	Duckworth

Books on individual religions

Bouquet, A. C.	Sacred Books of the World	Pelican*
Epstein, I.	Judaism	Pelican
Guillaume, A.	Islam	Pelican
Humphries, C.	Buddhism	Pelican
Hilliard, F. H.	How Men Worship	Routledge & Kegan* Paul
Jones, E. O.	The Beginnings of Religion	Arrow Books *
Mayhem, C.	Men Seeking God	Allen & Unwin*
Sen, K. M.	Hinduism	Pelican

A few standard works

James, E. O.	Comparative Religion	Methuen
Karsten, R.	The Origins of Religion	Kegan Paul *
Marett, R. R.	The Threshold of Religion	Methuen *
Murphy, J.	Lamps of Anthropology	Manchester University *
Hume, R. E.	The World's Living Religions	T. & T. Clark
Leeuwen, Arend	Christianity in World History	Lutterworth *
	(An imaginative assessment of the the impact of Christianity on the cultures of the world.)	

Films, Film-strips and Transparencies

There is a wide range of films and film-strips available, the quality of which varies a great deal. For further information the Advisory Service of the Christian Education Movement is available:

> The Secretary for Advisory Service,
> Christian Education Movement,
> 'Annandale',
> North End Road,
> London N.W.11   Telephone 01–458 4366

Films which can be used in connection with sections in the syllabus; there are many others.

Examples of 16 mm. recommended films

	Source of supply
'Food or Famine', 45 minutes, colour. Free. Made with the help of the Food and Agriculture Division of the United Nations.	Petroleum Films Bureau, 4 Brook Street, London W.1
'Four Religions', 60 minutes. Free. Arnold Toynbee discusses Hinduism, Buddhism, Islam and Christianity.	Canada House, Trafalgar Square, London S.W.1
'Great Endeavours', 22 minutes. Free. A documentary on a home for handicapped children.	Dr. Barnardo's Homes, Film Library, 18–26 Stepney Causeway, London E.1
'Let My People Go', 23 minutes. A powerful documentary on apartheid in South Africa; good as an aid to study and discussion with sixth forms.	Contemporary Films Ltd., 14 Soho Square, London W.1
'Colour of Man', 10 minutes, colour. A cartoon examining the scientific nature of race and showing that there is no foundation for race prejudice.	Contemporary Films Ltd., 14 Soho Square, London W.1
'Overture', 9 minutes. A documentary illustrating the futility of war.	Contemporary Films Ltd., 14 Soho Square, London W.1
'The Shadow of Hiroshima', 22 minutes. A realistic picture of the handful of survivors and sufferings.	Contemporary Films Ltd., 14 Soho Square, London W.1
'Bible Background', 50 minutes. The use of the Bible from the early reading of Hebrew scrolls in the synagogue until the present day.	British & Foreign Bible Society, 146 Queen Victoria Street, London E.C.4
'The Dead Sea Scrolls', 15 minutes, colour. The story of the discovery of the scrolls.	Concordia Films Ltd., Golden Lane, London E.C.
'Journey of a Lifetime', each 15 minutes, colour. Each 30s. 0d. Thirteen films showing a journey through Bible lands.	Warner Pathe Ltd., Wardour Street, London W.1

210

Examples of film-strips

Only a small selection of a large number which are now available.

On Church history:

'The Spread of the Church'	27 frames	Educational Productions Ltd., East Ardsley, Wakefield, Yorks.
'New Testament Times'	20 frames	Educational Productions Ltd., East Ardsley, Wakefield, Yorks.

Bible background:

'When Jesus was born'	25 frames Coloured	Concordia Films Ltd., Golden Lane, London E.C.
'Where Jesus worked'	18 frames Coloured	Concordia Films Ltd., Golden Lane, London E.C.
'At home and at work in Bible lands'	28 frames Coloured	Concordia Films Ltd., Golden Lane, London E.C.
'Shepherds in Bible Lands'	31 frames Coloured	Concordia Films Ltd., Golden Lane, London E.C.
'Everyday life in Palestine'	53 frames Coloured	Concordia Films Ltd., Golden Lane, London E.C.
'Palestine past and future'	31 frames Coloured	Concordia Films Ltd., Golden Lane, London E.C.

SOURCES OF PICTORIAL MATERIAL SUITABLE FOR PRIMARY AND SECONDARY SCHOOLS

Observing Bible Lands

A set of 8 photographic reproductions of places of interest connected with the New Testament. Full colour 30 in. by 40 in.

Purnell Educational Ltd.,
1–5 Portpool Lane,
London E.C.1

Christian Year Pictures

In full colour and in monochrome : some of the best examples of classical and contemporary religious art. 21 in. by 15 in. pictures, singly or in book form.

S.P.C.K.,
69 Great Peter Street,
London S.W.1

Wall Pictures

Abbaye de la Rochette – modern French illustrations of Old Testament and New Testament scenes in vivid colours. A series of 5 pictures in 14 series.

The Catechetical Centre,
13–15 Denbigh Street,
London W.11

Groger Wall Pictures – a series of 26 illustrations of New Testament events in the life of Christ ; a series on Old Testament are also available. Painted in vivid style.

The Fortress Bookshop,
71 Edgware Road,
London W.2

Swedish New Testament Pictures — a series of high quality colour paintings of incidents in the life of Christ.

S.P.C.K.
69 Great Peter Street,
London S.W.1

Wall Charts

A wide range of wall charts are available about biblical and sociological topics at various prices ; from the Pictorial Charts Educational Trust.

P.C.E.T.,
132 Uxbridge Road,
West Ealing, London W.13

Focus Wall Charts — a series of 10, three-colour charts dealing with teenage discussion topics.

C.E.M.,
Annandale,
North End Road,
London N.W.11

World Problems. Materials which can help to provide a better understanding of some of the difficult problems can be obtained from a number of organisations.

*Christian Aid,
Schools Department,
P.O. Box 1
London S.W.1

*Youth Against Hunger,
17 Northumberland Avenue,
London W.C.2

*Oxfam,
Schools Department,
Oxford.

*World Health Organisation,
c/o British School of Hygiene
& Tropical Medicine,
Keppel Street,
London W.C.1

* All organisations whose addresses are given at the side will supply diagrams and charts to illustrate the problem of world population, famine, malnutrition and disease.

Charts and pictures for use with themes

Caring for sick or unfortunate people ; there is a wealth of suitable material.

1 The Spastics Society,
   12 Park Crescent,
   London W.1

2 The Children's Society,
   Old Town Hall,
   Kennington, London S.E.11

3 War on Want,
   9 Madeley Road,
   London W.5

On blindness and disablement

4 Helen Keller House,
   Jerusalem

Orphan children.

5 Dr. Barnardo's,
   553B Stepney Causeway,
   London E.1

The needs of the world.

6 United Nations Information
   Centre,
   14–15 Stratford Place,
   London W.1

Kindness to birds and animals.

7 The Council for Nature,
   41 Queen's Gate,
   London S.W.7

8 Royal Society for the
   Protection of Birds,
   The Lodge,
   Sandy, Herts.

9 Royal Society for the
   Protection of Birds and
   Animals,
   105 Jermyn Street,
   London S.W.1

Books and Exhibitions

Models and charts on work in the mission fields can be had from :—

British and Foreign Bible Society, 146 Queen Victoria Street, London E.C.4.
The Methodist Missionary Society, 25 Marylebone Road, London, N.W.1
National Christian Education Council, Robert Denholm House, Nutfield, Redhill, Surrey.
Religious Education Press, Film Bureau,Wallington, Surrey.
Society for Promoting Christian Knowledge, Holy Trinity Church, Marylebone Road, London N.W.1.

Programmes of Religious Broadcasting

The Department of School Broadcasting, Broadcasting House, Portland House, London W.1.

Drama

The Religious Drama Society, S.P.C.K. House, Northumberland Avenue, London W.C.2.

Hiring of Costumes

Miss W. Hoyle, Arden House, Page Street, Mill Hill, London N.W.7.

THE CONNECTION BETWEEN ART IN ITS BROADEST SENSE AND RELIGIOUS EDUCATION

For many reasons the portrayal of most of the great themes of the Bible can best be seen in the work of great masters; such works have a special appeal in so far as they are good art in its own right.

Subjects and Stories for which illustrations can be found from the Great Masters

The Annunciation	Fillippo Lippi Duccio – N.G. Simone Martini – N.G. Verrocchio and Leonardo de Vinci and many others.
The Nativity	Piero della Francesca – N.G. Botticelli – N.G. Geerten Tot Sint Jans – N.G. Georges de la Tour
The 'Holy Family' and 'Virgin and Child'	Titian – N.G. Botticelli – N.G. Leonardo 'Madonna of the Rocks' – N.G. Giovanni Bellini 'Madonna of the Meadow' Michael Angelo – N.G.
The Adoration	Mabuse – N.G. Rembrandt – N.G. Brueghel – N.G. Gerard David – N.G. Rubens and many others

Incidents in the Life of Christ

Christ in the home of His parents	Millais
Christ disputing with the Doctors	Holman Hunt
Baptism of Christ	Piero della Francesco – N.G.
Miraculous Draught of Fishes	Raphael – V. & A.
Christ driving the Traders from the Temple	El Greco – N.G.
The Tribute Money	Massaccio – Florence
Jesus healing the Blind Man	Duccio – N.G.
Christ at the Pool of Bethseda	Murillo – N.G.
Christ in the House of Martha and Mary	Vermeer – Edinburgh
Christ washes the feet of His disciples	Ford Madox Brown – N.G.
Marriage at Cana	Veronese – Venice
Marriage at Cana	Gerard David – Louvre
Christ blessing Little Children	School of Rembrandt – N.G.
The Raising of Lazarus	Geertgen Tot Sint Jans – Louvre
The Last Supper	Leonardo – Milan
	Stanley Spencer
The Agony in the Garden	El Greco – N.G.
	Bellini – N.G.
	Mantegna – N.G.
The Betrayal	Ugolino – N.G.
	Dirk Bouts – Munich
Christ before Caiaphas	Honthorst – N.G.
Christ before Pilate	Rembrandt – N.G.
Christ bearing the Cross	Raphael – Madrid
	Stanley Spencer – N.G.
The Crucifixion	Rubens
	Perugino – N.G.
	Gaugin (Le Christ Jaune)
The Deposition	Rubens (The Wallace Collection)
	Ugolino – N.G.
	Roger van der Weyden
	Rembrandt
Mourning over the Dead Christ	The Piete of Avignon – Louvre
The Entombment	Dirk Bouts – N.G.
	Michael Angelo – N.G.
The Three Marys of the Tomb	Duccio
Noli me Tangere	Fra Angelico (S. Marco)
Christ's charge to Peter	Rubens (Wallace Collection)
	Raphael Cartoon – V. & A.
The Supper at Emmaus	Rembrandt – Louvre
	Vermeer – Rotterdam
The Resurrection	El Greco
	Raphael and others.

Old Testament subjects have been painted by Michael Angelo (Sistine Chapel), Titian, Giorgione and many others.

Lives of Saints have also been the subject for many paintings.

Saint Francis	Giotto – Assissi
	Sassetta – N.G.
	El Greco
Saint Ursula	Carpuccio – Venice
Saint Cecilia	Raphael – Rome
Saint Sebastian	Pollaiuolo – N.G.
Saint Christopher	Tintoretto – Venice

Mediaeval manuscripts are a fruitful source of illustration for Old and New Testament stories. They can be found in the British Museum, The Victoria and Albert Museum and in the Bodleian Library, Oxford, to name only a few places. Visits to cathedrals and churches will open up a rich store of works of art, including stained glass and stone and wood carvings, which might provide an inspiring accompaniment to lessons in religious knowledge.

214

Reproductions can be obtained from:

The National Gallery. — Publications Department, Trafalgar Square, London W.C.2

The Wallace Collection. — Manchester Square, London W.1

The Victoria and Albert Museum publishes books and postcards of its own exhibits. — South Kensington, London S.W.7

The Medici Society Ltd. — Educational Department, 36 Pentonville Road, London N.1

(Probably the main source of supply of small inexpensive reproductions of pictures which do not belong to collections in this country, but the quality of the reproductions varies greatly.)

N.G. – National Gallery.

V. & A. – Victoria and Albert Museum and Art Gallery.

School Prints Ltd. — 13 Motcomb Street, Belgrave Square, London W.1

The Zwemmer Gallery — Lisle Street, London W.C.

Ganymede Press — 10–11 Great Turnstile, London W.C.1

(Ganymede Prints are probably the best coloured prints now obtainable and the list includes several pictures with a religious theme. They are rather expensive but are well worth the money.)

Phoenix Picture Gallery — 36A St. Martin's Lane, London W.C.2

SOME USEFUL ADDRESSES

Contemporary Church History

Baptist Missionary Society — 93 Gloucester Place, London W.1

Church Missionary Society — 137 Waterloo Road, London S.E.1

Congregational Council for World Missions — Livingstone House, 11 Cartaret Street, London W.1

Methodist Missionary Society — 25 Marylebone Road, London N.W.1

The Methodist Youth Department, — 2 Chester House, Pages Lane, Muswell Hill, London N.10

Presbyterian C. of E. Mission — 26 Tavistock Place, London N.W.1

Society for the Propagation of the Gospel — 15 Tufton Street, P.O. Box 1

Christian Aid — 10 Eaton Gate, London S.W.1

British and Foreign Bible Society * — 146 Queen Victoria Street, London E.C.4

Mission to Lepers * — 7 Bloomsbury Square, London W.C.1
   (*Both the above are inter-denominational.)

British Council of Churches — 10 Eaton Gate, London S.W.1

The Iona Community. — Candlemakers' Hall, Candlemaker Row, Edinburgh 1

The Conference of British Missionary Societies — Edinburgh House, Eaton Gate, London S.W.1

215

On Social Service and Community Values

National Old People's Welfare Association and National Council of Social Service	26 Bedford Square, London W.C.1
The Invalid Children's Aid Association	14 Palace Gate, London W.8
The Shaftesbury Society	112 Regency Street, London S.W.1
Dr. Barnardo's Homes	Stepney Causeway, London E.1
National Children's Home	85 Highbury Park, London E.C.3
Church of England Children's Society	Old Town Hall, Kennington, London S.E. Kennington, London S.E.11
The Civic Trust	79 Buckingham Palace Road, London S.W.1
The National Trust	42 Queen's Gate, London S.W.1
The National Federation of Housing Societies	12 Suffolk Street, London S.W.1
Keep Britain Tidy Group	39 Eccleston Street, London S.W.1
Scottish Council of Social Service	10 Alva Street, Edinburgh 2
Toc H & Community Service Volunteers	15 Trinity Square, London E.C.3
Voluntary Service Overseas	18 Northumberland Ave., London W.C.2
National Association for Mental Health	39 Queen Anne Street, London W.1
National Association of Workshops for the Blind Inc.	105 Salisbury Road, London N.W.6
U.N.E.S.C.O.	9 Place de Fontenoy, Paris, 7 EME

On Christian Education

The Christian Education Movement, Annandale, North End Road, London N.W.11	This incorporates the Student Christian Movement in schools and the Institute of Christian Education.

Other Sources of Information

John Rylands Library, Deansgate, Manchester	Reproductions of a fragment of St. John's Gospel and of Deuteronomy. These are from a very early date. Other manuscripts are available too.
The County Archivist, Sessions House, Lancaster Road, Preston	A source of much valuable information in connection with local surveys.
Assistant Librarian, Department of Western Manuscripts, Bodleian Library, Oxford	The Library has a wide selection of transparencies on religious topics including manuscripts. A list of subjects can be obtained on request to the Assistant Librarian.